Barbara Morson

I Talk to the Animals

I talk to the Animals

Barbara Morrison

2001

I talk to the Animals

Copyright © 2001 Barbara Morrison
All rights reserved.

No part of this book may be reproduced
or transmitted in any form or by any means
without written permission from the author,
except for the inclusion of brief quotations in a review.

FIRST PRINTING

Front cover photograph of my Xoloitzcuintlis,
Weissleader's Aliska and *Weissleader's Tigger,*
and back cover photograph of my Anatolian Shepherd,
Mountain Bear's Spirit of Lakota
by Cordova Photography.

Designed and Produced by Joseph Cowles
at Event Horizon Press
Palm Springs, California.

ISBN 0-9706449-0-6.
Library of Congress Control Number 00-093544.

Printed and Bound in the United States of America.
Text paper recycled.

*In loving memory of Darby,
my extraordinary English-born whippet,
who with his grace and dignity
taught me so much of unconditional love
and unwavering understanding.*

Contents

Acknowledgments ... 9

Introduction ... 10

Foreword ... 14

1: How It Works ... 17

2: Zoning In ... 43

3: Animal Illness ... 66

4: Animal Attitudes And Behavior ... 97

5: Animals That Are Ready to Die ... 142

6: Reincarnation ... 171

7: Metaphysical Issues ... 182

8: Pigs And Fishes ... 233

Epilogue ... 264

Acknowledgments

MANY PEOPLE HAVE ASSISTED ME in the creation of this book. At the beginning, during my quest for who I was to be in this lifetime, I want to thank my many spiritual teachers such as Ophelia, Lazaris, and Robert Petro. For it was with their encouragement and guidance that I have found who I am and the path that I am on.

I am indebted to my closet and dearest friends, Haruko Fuchs and Elizabeth Medearis, for their inspiration and advice—for without their many years of faith in me, and encouragement to go on to search my path, I might not be here sharing this material with you at this time.

I am grateful to Pat Weissleader, for it is her talents and skills that brought together this book and have given it it life and energy, and who so successfully edited this text and offered advice with exceptional insight and sensitivity.

I am extremely grateful to Joseph Cowles for his knowledge and talent to make this book a finished product.

And the ultimate thanks to my clients for sharing their experiences, which has created the sharing of Universal knowledge that animals have more depth and insight then most humans care to acknowledge.

I acknowledge with joy and pleasure, my dear friends throughout the universe, who surround me with unconditional love, laughter, and insight to accomplish this work!

Introduction

*"Your skills with animals go back to the time of Egypt ...
and you have in many lifetimes used those same skills."*

—Prior reading by Trance Channel Robert Petro

I DID NOT KNOW ABOUT THIS READING when I began to work with Barbara on this book. We had become reacquainted after almost ten years, when we met through art classes we were taking at the local community college.

At that time I had recently moved to the desert and was trying to build a new life, but it was not easy. I had too many dogs, was living in a small trailer without a lot of fenced yard or shade, and the dogs were not very happy. My plan to build a wonderful house for people and dogs to live in, did not make the present conditions easier.

Barbara had shown an interest in one of the small hairless dogs I wanted to find a home for, and had come to visit. I thought she had formed an attachment to the animal, but she left without the pup, to think it over. I remember praying that she would decide she wanted the pup and call me back. When she did I took the pup to her home to make sure it fit in with her other pets, and I remember it looked with great interest at a large bird she had that was climbing on the outside of a cage.

A few days later Barbara phoned me because Tigger, a good name for the hairless pup with wispy blond hair around its face, seemed to be unsatisfied with things when it was time for everyone in her human and animal family to relax together in the evening.

"Do you take the bird to where you all sit together?" I asked. "When I was there, Tigger was very interested in the bird and probably thinks it ought to be included in the family gathering."

Barbara phoned a few days later and told me that bringing the bird to their gathering had seemed to solve the problem.

For a few months Barbara and I had done some social things, but had not become fast friends—our lives were too different. She had an orderly life with everything in place, or so it seemed to me, and I was living in a heap where I hoped to make a home, with my belongings spread out in the desert around me, waiting for a place to be. I was not used to women who were always well groomed and employed, understanding or sympathizing with the mess my life at that time seemed to be.

I sometimes see patterns of people meeting who seem to have little in common, but are later meant to do important work together. When they meet again things have happened to change them both and bring them closer to the work they need to do.

I met Barbara again in Builder's Emporium, when it was closing. Everything was on sale, and people were sorting through disorderly heaps to take advantage of the bargains. She gave me her card, which said she was an animal psychic, and I told her about my trials in trying to get a registry for the hairless breed I work with. She offered to help me do it, but I didn't believe her offer would survive the difficulties I had run into before when people wanted to help.

It was another year or so before Barbara called me to relay a message from another friend who had one of my dogs. But this time we began to talk and found out we had many things in common. At some point she told me she was supposed to write a book about her work. I told her that was easy and that I would help her. She didn't believe me any more than I had believed her offer of help in doing the registry.

It is hard to pinpoint exactly what happens to make acquaintances into friends. I have an idea that it is when we share the things in our lives that are not so great, the things we worry we can't make right, and the things we feel insecure about. Perhaps it is when we know the other person's shortcomings and faults, but still decide that we have enough in common for a friendship. Or perhaps it is because our shortcomings and faults are so similar, or that our strengths are opposite enough to help the other when they are unable to proceed.

Barbara's strengths brushed away the blocks that had seemed insurmountable to me, and suddenly there was a registry. I told her what she needed to do to get her tapes of animal readings into shape to become a book. At first I didn't understand why she was so unwilling to include many details about herself and her own feelings in the book. Finally I realized that she doesn't think she is interesting, and has no desire to talk about herself—she just wants to share her work.

In helping her with the book, I had to edit out a lot of repetitive phrases that Barbara never used in conversation. It was clear to me that there were intelligences working through her during her readings, and I got to know them by their patterns of speech. Cleaning out the unnecessary phrases and hesitations of an oral reading is necessary, so that a reader can gain from the important things that have been said, while not being distracted by the repetition and detailed discussions or minor details needed to get through to the person who is dealing with the problem.

Barbara has a knack of getting in touch with the critical issues affecting people and their animals, even when those people keep insisting that the problem is really something else. So often the people share details or later events that confirm Barbara's reading to be correct, that I suspect "someone up there" is making sure that the readings happen in a format that makes it easy for a book to be done about them.

It became increasingly clear to me that this book was something that needed to be written and would give people important information that they could not get anywhere else. I am very proud to be a part of this work. I do not think Barbara has any idea where it is going to take her.

—Patricia Weissleader

Foreword

AS A CHILD I COULD ALWAYS UNDERSTAND ANIMALS but had a challenging time understanding people. So I decided I could do the most for humanity by working to bring people a better understanding of their beloved creatures.

I was born in San Francisco. In my early years I loved to visit the museums and other wonderful places in the city by the bay. As a teen I began to spend my Saturdays in the De Young Museum, looking at paintings and tapestries by old masters. I spent many hours at the Museum of Natural History and Planetarium, longing to know everything about the world and Universe.

I lived a conservative life style until, after the ending of a fifteen-year marriage, I wanted to make my life more fulfilling. I began to study many aspects of metaphysics. Not completely neglecting my conservative side, I also acquired my Masters Degree in Business Administration.

After a few more false starts I found myself at a standstill and sought spiritual guidance to know what work I came to do in this lifetime.

From birth I had suffered with chronic asthma. It grew worse during a period of my adulthood. I realized I had to conquer it, or I was not going to have much of a life.

I went on a quest for understanding of the condition, and finally got rid of it with energy-balancing techniques and herbal supplements. The process made me aware of Universal Laws in everything I saw.

Over the years I have shared the companionship of many pets. In the mid-Seventies I imported a Whippet from England. Darby was nine weeks old when I got him, and we formed a special love. At the age of four, Darby began to have seizures.

I researched alternative healing, and was able to arrest this condition with supplements. Darby lived to the age of fourteen, and was my emotional caretaker through many difficult times. I have always felt that he took on my pains and stresses, to give me relief from them. Darby was the most precious gift one could ever receive.

Darby's daughter, Allison, seemed to take over his job of helping me through life. Then, at the age of nine, she acquired Addison's Disease. Once again, I searched for alternative treatments, which I believe helped to arrest her illness so that she could move through life for a few more years. Her disease was one problem, and she acquired more challenging health issues which we worked through until her kidneys gave out. Our time together was priceless.

While treating animals with alternative methods, I began to feel that they were communicating with me spiritually, to give me clues as to what was wrong with them. In recognizing that the animal had a voice I should listen to, and by understanding the unique point of view of a wild creature, I could see a more complete picture of what an animal needed for well being.

I have always looked to spiritual understanding where human issues are concerned, and when I let an animal know I was listening to them, they often had many things to say about life that had to do with more than physical health. Their frustrations, fears and concerns were often clues to behavior problems or depression.

Sometimes it seemed reasonable to talk to a pet owner about things I felt their pet was concerned about or needed to be attended to. I was hesitant at first since so many people do not believe in such things. But after a while it seemed to be something important that I could do for others.

Since the time I decided to share this gift, I have been on a wild ride. I have received far more than I have ever given, in the work I have done with so many wonderful animals.

In recent years, during a session with an entity known as Ophelia, who is trance channeled by Elizabeth Medearis, Ophelia told me firmly, "We are told to tell you it is time to start your work."

And so it begins!

* * *

I have participated in many animal activities over the years. In the 1970's I was Racing Chairman for a local whippet club, putting on regional race meets, puppy and adult race training. As dog show chairman and chairman of the Regional Whippet Specialty, our event drew the largest entry in the history of whippets. I traveled to England to select and purchase a whippet who became AKC pointed, and have trained whippets in AKC Obedience—one of which reached the AKC Obedience Utility Level. I laso taught one whippet tracking. Along with my former husband, Robert Ortman, I conceptualized what is now commonly call AKC Sighthound Lure Coursing. Some members of a litter of whippet pups I bred have become AKC Show Champions.

At the time of this first publication I have an Anatolian shepherd, a whippet, and two Xoloitzcuintlis—along with my cats Sarah, Sabrina, Sirius Rising and Sam, my Eclectus parrots Emerald and Rosie, and Peter and Malinda, who are African Greys. In November 2000 my Anatolian Kada won his AKC Championship.

I am currently working on recreating historical records for the Xoloitzcuintli, in the form of a registry.

1: How It Works

WHILE MANY PEOPLE do not believe in psychics, most people have had an occasional psychic experience or know someone else who has had one that they believe is valid.

Most people are open to the possibility that a psychic is genuine if the information they receive is relevant and contains details that the psychic could not have known through normal means.

An important point about my readings is that I do not know anything about the client prior to the reading. The reading takes place over the phone and I ask my client not to give me information prior to the reading, so that when I start to talk to them about the animal, I am not feeding them back information that they have given me. Since I don't have physical contact with the animal, I am careful to make sure that the energy I am picking up is the animal they are concerned with. I ask the client to verify if the energy I am getting is the animal in question. This is why I always ask my clients to first give me the name of the animal. Before I answer the first question I tell them something about the personality or traits that I am picking up about the animal in question. Then we both know that we are talking about the same animal.

Sometimes there are elements of a reading that seem to be odd, since no two psychics do things the same way. Each is dependent on the connection they establish through their personal guides or helpers on the other side.

People ask me how the animals talk to me. Often they show me mental pictures that I have to interpret. Sometimes I feel I'm seeing things through the animal's eyes. Other animals seem to express themselves in words and sentences. Each animal feels unique and individual.

Another important issue has to do with what is an appropriate action for the owner to take. Some people who have lost pets need to be helped through the grieving process so they can move on. Others contact me for more insight on a pet's helath issue. Some have spent a lot of money on a sick animal and may need to understand that they are not to blame if the treatment does not go as they would have liked, and it is time to consider alternatives.

There are animals with behavior disorders. Some can be annoying and others can be funny.

One couple contacted me about their bird. They had talked to many behaviorists and still were baffled about this bird. The bird would chatter quite loudly, put bits of seed or food under a wing, squawk in a very loud voice, then lift up its wings and drop the food. It turned out that the bird was mimicking its owners! In the morning the husband would walk by, greet the bird, then go and get the newspaper and put it under his arm. He would always talk to the bird as he passed. While cleaning the house the wife would put things under her arms and hold them that way while she chatted with the bird. The bird thought that was the polite way you held conversations.

Sometimes an animal is not behaving normally, due to an illness or a discomfort. At these times I will read the energy of the body and see where the problem area is. A regular client contacted me the day before she had an appointment to check a lump on her dog's leg. As we talked over the phone I could see in my mind's eye that the lump was a fatty lump and of no threat to his health. But what I could visualize and feel was difficulty in his breathing, and perceived an enlarged heart. I felt this was a bigger threat to his life. A follow-up call from the client confirmed what I had visualized and felt the day before.

Some animals seem to be hampered by memories of expectations and conditions they experienced in other lives. A poodle who was behaving inappropriately to its owner's friends had been her guard in another life, and was continuing to behave as if the owner could be in danger from visitors. I had to explain to the dog that things were not dangerous for its owner in this life, and that the guarding was not needed. The dog's behavior did improve.

It is a mystery why sometimes I do not pick up problems animals are having. This was the case recently with my own dog, Tigger. She had not seemed ill, but a friend who is also psychic was holding her and said, "I feel there might be a problem with her thyroid." In the next few days, Tigger seemed to be very ill and I rushed her to the vet. There was no apparent problem but blood tests were done and came back showing a long-standing infection and a major out of balance condition. Tigger was put on antibiotics and thyroid medication. She got better, and is healthy and happy today. But I don't know why I was not able to pick up her problem in the same way I do for other animals.

* * *

Many people contact me about an animal that has passed on. They find it extremely hard to be without their cherished friend. They feel a great amount of grief, and often guilt that the animal was very ill and they did not become aware of it until it was too late. It helps the client when I talk about what the animals feel about leaving this life. People do not understand that an animal does not worry so much about the length of life, and sometimes is grateful to not have to continue in pain.

Animals who have passed on may also need counseling, so that they can rest from behaviors and beliefs that keep them tied to this life. From dealing with such cases I have learned that what happens to animals after death is just the same as what happens to people.

One problem people have is the grief they feel—due to the natural fact that animals do not live as long as people. They need to be reminded that dealing with the death of an animal is the reward for giving it a long safe life. In many cases the owner has had that animal in many other lives, and may expect to have it in future lives. In other cases the animal promises to return in a new body, later in the owner's present life.

When the reading rings true to what they already knew inside, they are able to accept it—even if their personal beliefs did not previously include such aspects of the afterlife. When a reading is beneficial, the owner, the pet, and I are all satisfied that the important issues have been brought out and addressed in some way.

There are some readings where what has happened is not so clear, and the owners may not feel sure that they received the value they were looking for from the reading. In some of those cases events happen in the days after the reading that confirm things that were said. In other cases, a clear knowledge of issues being settled is not possible.

Occasionally after a reading, I do not feel much was accomplished. Then I get a phone call from the person after a few weeks, saying they were very satisfied with what they learned from the reading.

I am learning and growing from this work along with the people and animals I work with, and I constantly ask for guidance to improve my ability to be of help to others.

* * *

The first contact with a client is to make sure that the animal in question is the one the client is concerned about. In all cases I make sure of this by describing some things about the animal to the client for confirmation:

BARBARA: Christina, how I'd like you to start is to give me the name of the first animal and your first question. I'm going to tune into the energy of the animal and then I'll move into the question.

CHRISTINA: Okay. My dog's name is Mattingly. We call her Mattie or Matt. My first question—is he okay?

BARBARA: Okay. Now, this is a dog that has passed on.

CHRISTINA: Yes.

BARBARA: All right. I just want to tune into the energy of Mattingly as you knew Mattingly, so we know we're talking about the same one. I'm picking up about a medium size animal. One that was very interested in you and very responsive to you and was always eager to please, was always wanting to do as you asked, always asking for commands. *What would you like me to do? I'd like to please you. What would make you happy?*

CHRISTINA: That's Mattingly.

* * *

In another reading:

ANA: I have a Shepherd, a Basset, a Coon Hound, and a Labrador Retriever. I have a Zoo. I love it and would not give it up for anything.

BARBARA: Please give me your question, and focus on the animal in question, so that I will be able to tune in on the right animal. Sometimes I might get another animal, if there is a grouping of animals.

ANA: Shan is the name of the animal. And my question is, is he happy?

BARBARA: I see a tail wagging.

ANA: That is what I am looking at.

BARBARA: Okay, that is what I see, a happy strong tail wagging. So my response would be yes.

ANA: We are talking about a horse here!

BARBARA: Then I am not tuned to the horse. Okay, let's tune in again. This happened another other time when a lady had two pets right in front of her. Okay—I get kind of a quiet animal.

ANA: Yes.

BARBARA: The animal that I get is—I would almost say placid, as to quiet.

ANA: Yes

BARBARA: This animal is not super happy, but not sad, just a regular kind of guy.

ANA: Yes.

BARBARA: It doesn't take much to please him. And he doesn't respond too much with displeasure to things he doesn't like. It just that he goes along with the program. Is the kind of energy that I am feeling.

ANA: Yes.

* * *

Sometimes an owner is afraid that if they don't get things exactly right it will affect the reading:

BARBARA: Is it T-o-n-n-i-e or T-o-n-y?

JULIA: T-o-n-y. Why is he sick? Or I guess that's a bad question?

BARBARA: No question is bad.

JULIA: We can't say that he's really sick right?

BARBARA: No—we can say whatever we like. There are no bad questions. There are just questions.

JULIA: He seems to be losing weight. He's not eating, so I'm assuming that he's sick. So I want to know why he's sick.

BARBARA: Okay. Let me tune into Tony, here. Basically, I get Tony is a quiet cat to begin with. Kind of laid back. I feel long hair. Does he have really long hair?

JULIA: Yes.

* * *

Since their spirits continue, it is possible to tune into the energy of animals that have died. But I still first tap into the personally of the animal, to make sure that it is the right animal:

JAN: My cat, McDuff, died on the fifth of May this year. It happened rather suddenly. There have been a lot of things wrapped around all of this, and I want to get, first of all, a sense of what you get from him right now. And how is he doing out there.

BARBARA: I'm picking up McDuff's energy, I'm picking up a cat in size and shape, one that's shorter-bodied in length. Kind of long legs. Is that—?

JAN: Yes. He was a Maine Coon cat. He was kind of a square cat. They have fur that is sort of varied in lengths so he was kind of a fluffy guy, and he had big feet, big square feet. He was a tall cat.

BARBARA: They get long-legged.

JAN: Yes.

BARBARA: And the personality that represents McDuff, he's—let me see here—I get loving, and I get not overly loving. He likes his time of being loved but not obnoxious—not in your face all the time.

JAN: Yes. He never was an in-your-face cat. He would lie there and look at you.

* * *

Many people write or e-mail me to check that a reading can be done about their particular concerns:

"I still grieve something terribly about two horses I had and lost and are now dead because of a lying horse trader, and would like to know if they are at peace and it they forgive me for what happened. This happened about twenty years ago. Can you help me, please?"

Another writes:

"My heart is absolutely broken. After two months of trying to find out what was wrong with my five-year-old kitty, I had to do the most horrible thing in my life by allowing her to be put to sleep. I had her at the most prestigious animal hospital and no one there or at my regular vet could figure out the problem. She did not recognize me, she was moaning, and miserable, and for the life of me I could not subject her to any more pain. My question is this: Do animals have souls? How do I know she is a peace? I need answers so bad. I want her back in my life and I don't feel complete. I took her in when someone threw her out three years ago, and she was actually my saving angel. Can you tell if their little spirits come back? How do I know she is at peace?"

*   *   *

It is important for someone getting a reading about a pet, that the reading actually is about the animal they need to know about, and that the information coming through is truly relevant and accurate for their present concerns. Sometimes this is established during the reading, but at other times details in the reading are not understood and the person later remembers things which confirm material that came through in the reading:

"Hi Barbara. After we finished our call Wednesday night, I was wracking my brain trying to figure out what crunchy food Aliska said she liked a lot during her last months with us. Finally, Liz reminded me that we had just started giving her these meat product snacks that were light, almost styrofoam in consistency, but were crunchy, and she definitely liked to chomp down on them. And there I was, thinking only of chicken or meat balls!"

The letter continued with some questions about getting psychic impressions:

"In all of our conversations, I've wondered if you see images, receive thoughts, or actually hear voices (or a combination of all three) when receiving information from your guides. Does Aliska have a voice?

"As some of your other clients may have experienced, the first session sparked additional thinking and questions. You have a special gift, Barbara, and we are grateful we found you. I found it comforting and encouraging, especially knowing that we will never really 'lose' Aliska, and may even be able to have her rejoin us. Thanks for all the communication and comfort you've provided.

"P.S. Our son, Jeff, more and more seems to have a special ability. Last Tuesday afternoon when he and Mom arrived home he was resting on the steps going from the garage to the kitchen, put his head down on the step, and without any prompting or prior conversation about Aliska, he announced 'Aliska's in the house.' He definitely seems to be aware of her presence."

My response back to the client:

"Darrell, that is why I tape the sessions. When a person is racking his brain trying to remember about things such as crunchy food, it may not come to you at the time—but sometimes hours or days later a person remembers. Thanks for the feedback. In our conversation with Aliska, she showed me the crunchy food. She gave me the sensations on how it felt to her and I could feel her pleasure. I get pictures that are mostly still life, and interpret what I see and the sensations I feel. Or I may hear words—it comes in a variety of ways—and each time can be different. I am like a pass-through energy—what you might call a Channel. I get information from Higher Energies and then I put it into human language. Maybe I could be called a Universal Interpreter? Your son is showing you, by using his trust, that Aliska is with all of you in spirit. He has a quality that allows him the ability to trust unconditionally. As adults, we have passed through the trusting innocence of childhood. We have experienced the first big dose of shame and betrayal in our life that makes us doubt and mistrust people and life, and we begin to doubt the impressions that could connect us with people and pets that are in a different dimension."

* * *

Another letter is concerned with dreams that may be psychic:

"Hi Barbara. I wanted to share with you something that happened last night. I don't know if I actually experienced a contact with Julie or if it was just a sweet little dream. But all night last night I dreamed a lot. Meaningless stuff. But right in the middle of one dream, it abruptly stopped. And a white cat, almost in slow motion but in absolute silence, Julie was at my feet and I picked her up and held her, and without saying a word we both knew we loved each other. It was the same way I used to pick her up and she would bow her head to me and I knew she was telling me she loved me. But that's all there was to the dream. Just this very quiet, lingering moment with her. It was so vivid this morning that I wrote it in my diary, and all day I have felt that Julie and I 'talked.' In your experience, was this just a wonderful and comforting little dream, or could I have possibly had that contact with her?"

My answer:

"Yes, I have experienced what you describe. From what I feel she is trying to tell you in her own way she is all right and she loves you so very much. In feelings of deep despair our love ones will come to us in our dreams. In the dream state we get the sent message, clearer. When our eyes are closed and we shut out the Illusionary world, then we are able to see more of the Real world. Bask in the love that Julie is sending to you, and allow it to comfort you and help you shift out of the heavier emotions. It was nice to hear from you, and thank you for sharing your intimate experience."

* * *

Sometimes a person has premonitions about dangers to their pets. Joyce expressed her worry about her bird not coming home, if she allowed it to be outside:

BARBARA: I like to work starting off with the name of the first animal and your question, and from there I'm going to tune into the energy of the animal, and then I'll move into your question.

JOYCE: I have to go pick her up. I just realized she's not with me, I don't know if that makes any difference.

BARBARA: None. No difference because you're not here with me here either.

JOYCE: Right. That's true. Her name is Nani. N-A-N-I.

BARBARA: And your question?

JOYCE: Well, I guess I want to know if she's happy. I let her fly outside. She always comes back, but she got frightened. And I want to know if I can continue to do that, to let her have that freedom when I'm not with her. She's such a free spirit. I want to give her as much freedom as I can.

BARBARA: Okay. As I feel Nani, I feel a bird who is always very observant, always looking around, is always very aware of her surroundings.

JOYCE: Yes.

BARBARA: Okay. I can see her head moving and her eyes shifting, just as if she were a sparrow in a way. She's always aware.

JOYCE: Right.

BARBARA: But this is not the case with her. She has a lot of nervous energy. She feels vulnerable, and I feel as if she's small—not tiny, but small.

JOYCE: Yes. She is a Quaker parrot and they are smaller. They're about the size of a cockatiel.

BARBARA: Because of that size, part of her chemistry is that she's concerned about being prey, so she's always alert. She's forever busy always remaining aware.

JOYCE: Yes. Right.

BARBARA: Okay. The question, is she happy by your letting her fly outside? As I feel it, letting her fly outside is an option that you would like her to have, but it is a risky option. So you're always going to have the feeling, "Something could happen and maybe this time she won't return." Not because she doesn't want to, but because she gets frightened. She's not aware of her whole surroundings. It isn't as if she was born in the wild.

JOYCE: Right. That's true.

BARBARA: And she doesn't have a big tree close to home. She leads me south, leads me to food, there's a lake over here. She doesn't have that upper perspective on the area, so she runs the risk of not having a sense of homing direction. It is nice to know that they can have a sense of freedom but freedom can also be with clipped wings. In other words, freedom can be out of a cage moving around but not necessarily flying.

JOYCE: Well, the other thing is I could clip her wings and

take her outside, or I can just leave them intact and keep her inside. I'm just wondering which would make her happier.

BARBARA: She does like to be outside. She likes the smell of the air. I feel like she sniffs the air a lot. This bird loves to catch the scents in the air. So she enjoys that time outside. Does she have to be able to fly through the house? If you choose to clip her wings it wouldn't change the quality of her life. In fact, it might improve the quality of life because she wouldn't have the opportunity to fly off and maybe run into unfriendly hands, and you not knowing where she is or being able to capture her. Do you see?

JOYCE: Yes.

BARBARA: A small parrot like that could become prey to a small hawk.

JOYCE: Yes. That's true.

BARBARA: So, you just weigh the options. I'm not going to say this is what you need to do, because we each have our own path and we each choose our own options. But at least it gives you something to think about as to what you want to do.

JOYCE: Okay. I just want to make sure she's happy.

BARBARA: There isn't any feeling trapped. We might think that in a cage we might feel trapped, but for some animals it's a form of security. It gives them boundaries so that they feel safe within those boundaries. She really does enjoy her environment a lot.

JOYCE: Is that right? How interesting.

* * *

A few months later Joyce contacted me for another reading concerning Nani:

BARBARA: I don't remember my readings from before, so we'll just go with what we get from now.

JOYCE: Her name is Nani, and I guess my first question is, is she alive?

BARBARA: Okay. Let's move into Nani here. Loves a sense of freedom. Loves her space and of course you pick that up and that's why you allowed her to move as freely as you did. As you asked the question, "Is she still alive?" the answer came back yes. I don't feel like she has passed on. I don't feel as if she has had an accident of some kind or run into foul play.

JOYCE: And then the next question would be, is she outside or inside?

BARBARA: Is she outside or inside? Okay. Let me see if I can trail how she went out. How did she leave? I feel that when she left, started to fly, she flew a little ways. She kind of came down low and then it's as if she hit a gust of wind and just lifted.

JOYCE: Okay.

BARBARA: Did she go out of a second story?

JOYCE: No, we were outside.

BARBARA: You were already outside?

JOYCE: Yes.

BARBARA: All right. I see looking down, so maybe that's her as she flies looking down—looking at the trees and things like that. Was it breezy that day?

JOYCE: I don't remember it being particularly breezy.

BARBARA: Okay. It didn't have to take much. As I feel it, she went down a ways and kind of caught a lift.

JOYCE: Well, that night after she flew off, a friend actually saw her and she heard her in a tree, and she was just chirping and chirping, so my friend went over and started kind of chirping back to her and then she just flew off again. The last time she got away she actually landed on someone's shoulder, but this time she seemed like, "No, I'm not going to do that this time."

BARBARA: She really loves her sense of adventure. It was like a great adventure for her and it was a whole new experience, but she hasn't had the birth experience. Do you see what I mean? She doesn't have the smarts to be out like that. So did she come down? I'm not sure why I feel this, but I feel that she went from tree to tree. Kind of moved on really, kind of had a good time and then the fun was over, but she had moved out in a direction rather than making a circle and heading back. She just kept hopping from place to place. Are you near a parkway or something? Is it a street?

JOYCE: Well, I live in a trailer park on campus. The last time she went to the reservoir, and that has a lot of trees and water. It's possible that she's headed in that direction again. I don't know. We are kind of on the edge of town, so she could have either stayed on campus or moved out. There are a few large houses farther north and then there's this reservoir which is east of where I am.

BARBARA: The reservoir's east.

JOYCE: Northeast, you could say.

BARBARA: I'm feeling like there's a row of trees that are planted straight. Is that by you on campus or in the reservoir?

JOYCE: Yes probably. Straight row of trees.

BARBARA: I almost want to say it's a street where they plant trees as a parkway. You know like in the median strip or between the sidewalk and the street.

JOYCE: Oh, I see. Well, it's not like a park where you go to a park in town. It's more kind of random, but north of here there is a new pathway that they made, and there are trees on either side. Now, I've walked down that pathway and called out her name but I got no response. I didn't go all the way cause it runs—

BARBARA: That's where I feel she went.

JOYCE: Okay.

BARBARA: I can almost see the trees on both sides.

JOYCE: Yes. There are trees on both sides with a pathway between it. Now there's another pathway that's at the reservoir, the same thing, and it goes into pine trees and it curves around. The other one is straight.

BARBARA: I feel straight. I'm definitely feeling straight.

JOYCE: Okay. So you don't feel any houses around?

BARBARA: I thought there were houses by the trees.

JOYCE: There are some, but it's just—I walked and she didn't respond when I called her name. I didn't go all the way. It kept going west and I didn't go all the way to the end of it.

BARBARA: I feel like she went tree hopping. They were close enough that she could almost hop from tree to tree. Are they kind of big and grown not together, but close enough?

JOYCE: Yes. They're wild trees. It's not like they were cultivated. They grew on their own. They made this path through those trees.

BARBARA: Okay. And that's kind of what they are showing me. I see trees on either side and it goes straight, and it's where, if she couldn't fly a long ways, she could almost get from tree to tree if she worked it out. Do you see?

JOYCE: Is there any way that you can draw her back to me? Is there any way you could do that, where she will be wanting to come home?

BARBARA: What I'm feeling is she doesn't know which way back home is.

JOYCE: Is there any way we can direct her? Or if I call her name she would respond to it?

BARBARA: I'm feeling like she's been out there long enough that if you called her she would respond to it. How would she have survived two weeks in the wild? Are there little seeds or fruits in these trees?

JOYCE: Probably. When she went up in a tree before, she would just pick all the branches off.

BARBARA: You see, I'm doing my logical thing rather than my intuitive thing. I'm wondering what she is going to eat. Where is she going to get this cup of seed? But there could be bugs and things that she could eat as protein.

JOYCE: Yes. So do you think I'll be able to find her?

BARBARA: I don't know. They're saying, yes you will.

JOYCE: Okay. So I should just go down that road, you think?

BARBARA: Yes. That's what I'm feeling. I'm trying to ask

did someone pick her up? Does someone have her? And I'm not getting any kind of yes answer with that. Do you know what I mean? Like someone found her, picked her up and took her home. I'm feeling that she's still out there. Maybe if you went out there and didn't call her, and just listened first.

JOYCE: Okay.

BARBARA: And then maybe on the way back call her or something, or call her and be quiet and see if you can hear her. It's been a couple of weeks?

JOYCE: Yes. Exactly two weeks from today.

BARBARA: What about the other bird? Have you brought the other bird out with you?

JOYCE: I have, and she doesn't respond. I did that the first time too, and she'd just gone too far and she couldn't hear him. And then he ended up flying off, so I'm not doing that again.

BARBARA: Well, I would take him out in a carrier.

JOYCE: In a cage?

BARBARA: In a small little carrying cage or something.

JOYCE: This path does cross a highway. Do you think that would be pretty far?

BARBARA: I don't feel that there's a highway between you and where she would be. I don't see the highway actually. It's a ways down. It's not like right across your street.

JOYCE: It would be north of me. I would go through the trailers and then there's condos and then there's this path.

BARBARA: Yes. That's where I feel—and I'm feeling more on the left side, if I were to feel where the energy would be, not on the—

JOYCE: If I'm walking on the path, it would be on the left side of the path.

BARBARA: Yes. Yes. I'm feeling like it's on the left. Maybe a little farther down then you expect.

JOYCE: I definitely didn't go all the way down. I stopped when it ended at the condos.

BARBARA: You might go out early in the morning, or just toward sunset when they seem to chirp and talk and make their most noise. You might be able to hear her better with that, and then maybe Boomer—Boomer, right?

JOYCE: Boomie.

BARBARA: Boomie. Okay. Boomie might be a bit noisy too, and could be helpful with that. It might draw some kind of conversation—

JOYCE: Response. Yes. If she hears something that sounds like her.

BARBARA: Yes, exactly. Kind of a similar voice, and your voice.

JOYCE: So we have a chance here?

BARBARA: I'm feeling like you do. I'm always very positive. I want the animals to come back. And I feel like she's out there and I feel like she stays up in the trees where it's safe for her. There's enough cover from any kind of hunting that might go on. It feels like it is enough camouflage.

JOYCE: Okay. She blends in.

BARBARA: Yes.

JOYCE: Well, this definitely gives me direction. And I kept going on that path the last few days, and I kept thinking she might be there.

BARBARA: Yes. It's always interesting how that happens. You feel that, but then you don't see them and you think, "Where am I getting this information? Why do I keep doing this, and I don't see them?" But it's like something that's there. There's a vibration there that you are following. Yes. I feel that she's alive. I feel she's just up in the trees. I don't feel that she's real worried.

JOYCE: Yes. I think she's probably having fun, but I'm hoping that she's ready to come in, because it's getting colder. I had to turn on the heat last night, and I have it on tonight again. She's a hot bird. During the summer when she'd come on my hand, her feet would be hot and her beak would be hot where the other bird, his feet would be cool and his beak would be cool. So she's hot you know, she can take—I think she's got a good thermostat going on inside of her.

BARBARA: Yes. And trees are insulating as well. Being under a canopy probably protects her from being out in the elements.

JOYCE: Okay. Well this definitely helps me.

BARBARA: Oh good. It feels like she would like to return now. She's had enough.

JOYCE: Yes. She says "Okay." And she probably needs a bath. She loves taking showers with me.

BARBARA: Oh, how interesting.

JOYCE: She's probably ready. Although it's been raining some, too, so she may be getting her own shower.

BARBARA: What kind of bird is she?

JOYCE: Quaker parrot. They're about the size of a cockatiel, a little bulkier though.

BARBARA: Okay.

JOYCE: So I'll take Boomie out with me and see if he can kind of coax her back.

BARBARA: Yes. Let me know.

JOYCE: Oh, I'll let you know. I will.

BARBARA: When you get off the phone, start to say, "Okay come on. Just come on home. Return."

JOYCE: Yes. "You've had enough fun now."

BARBARA: But I just don't feel any way to pick up the antenna part. She's too far out to know the way back, so she's just kind of hanging out there. She just hangs out in that one area.

JOYCE: Okay. Okay.

BARBARA: Almost like it ends out there or something.

JOYCE: Barbara, thank you so much for getting me in so quickly.

BARBARA: Oh you are entirely welcome. I always leave spaces open for the—

JOYCE: Emergencies, huh?

BARBARA: Oh absolutely. Because they come up on a daily basis, it seems.

JOYCE: Oh really?

BARBARA: Yes. It's a loss, or health, or death, and you always just like to get it resolved whether someone's been waiting a while or it's like, "Now I want to know."

JOYCE: Right. Right. You're done with the wondering part and you want to know, one way or another. Just let me know and then I can deal with it. It's just the waiting. That hopeful anticipation that maybe—. This makes me feel better. I'll just go along that path and I'll take Boomie with me, and we'll just see if we can remind her of her roots.

BARBARA: She is enjoying it out there actually.

JOYCE: Well, that was the feeling I got. There's just something in her. In the house, she gets so frantic. I have three rabbits and a guinea pig and she was always biting them and picking on them and picking on me and just wanting to move and do something. All this energy and all this intelligence and she just wanted to use it. I have them in this large dog cage when I'm not at home so that she'd have the space. This thing is meant for a collie. So I've been trying to make her happy but she definitely wants more. She wants to interact. She wants to learn. Boomie is more happy to be on your shoulder.

BARBARA: Oh yeah. He's just happy. He's a homebody.

JOYCE: Yes. Very much so. He's actually become extremely affectionate since she's been gone. He'll kiss me and he'll snuggle with me.

BARBARA: Well, he now has a chance to get closer to you. He doesn't have that competition.

JOYCE: Right. So it's been good for him. I don't know how he feels when I'm not here, but he seems okay.

BARBARA: He's pretty self-contained. I feel like he's fine. Birds can get attached, but not like mammals.

JOYCE: Huh. Interesting.

BARBARA: Yes. I don't feel like they get that kind of attachment. Well, I mean the birds that I've come across. It's kind of a different feeling.

JOYCE: Interesting. I hear your babies.

BARBARA: Oh yes. I've got four. I've got two Eclectus and two African Grays.

JOYCE: Oh, that's right. Well, it's time for them to go to bed pretty soon huh?

BARBARA: Oh no. As soon as it starts to cool down here they go through the whole repertoire of all kinds of things. Sometimes they go until I turn the lights off, or maybe if I watch television they'll quiet down. Joyce, I wish you the best of luck and I hope that you can get her back.

JOYCE: Yes. And that she'll be happy, she'll be content.

BARBARA: She's pretty happy with what she's doing right now.

JOYCE: You mean that maybe being free is better for her?

BARBARA: Yes. It might be.

JOYCE: So we'll just see.

BARBARA: It's just—the winter might be a little bit hard to deal with. So it might be good for her to come back for the winter, anyway.

JOYCE: Right. Then she can go back out in the spring! Thank you Barbara.

I am still hoping to hear that Nani has been found and is in good health.

* * *

In the following case, there was a behavior that was perplexing to the owner, and the issue was confirmed during the reading, but took a bit of time to sort out:

MARY: Her name is Francis. My question is, what is scaring her so badly at night? Why is she shaking?

BARBARA: Okay. Let me tune into the energy. Is there something below you? Are you in a house or is something below you?

MARY: In a house.

BARBARA: My first impression I get is that something below her is scratching. Like the rodent in the frame of the house or something.

MARY: There have been squirrels under the house before, but they make a different kind of noise. And I hear those noises, too. It is something else. I think it is something else. She is looking in a different direction than she would for the rodent.

BARBARA: I am feeling like it is underneath. Not the side wall but more under the flooring of the house. That was the first image I got. I feel like Francis is timid, and safety is a real issue for her. I feel that if she were approached she would run behind you, or stick to your side for this security. That she would feel comfortable with you, before she approached something or something approached her. Is that how she is?

MARY: Yes.

BARBARA: I need to tune into the energy.

MARY: The word that I would use to describe her is skittish. I can't seem to make her secure. For this one problem. I usually am able to.

BARBARA: I feel she really relies on you for her security. She runs to you and then she feels safe. If you say that she's okay, then she's feels safe. Safety is a major issue with her. Trust is the other issue with her. She trusts you. And what I'm hearing is that there is a scratching or gnawing going on at night. Did you say it was every night?

MARY: Yes.

BARBARA: Okay. Is it possible that there this something bigger than a squirrel that would be under your house, or in a sub-basement or something like that? Something that would use the basement as a place to go in the evening. To sleep.

MARY: I don't think so. I could look for it. It's a small crawl space under the house. There is no basement.

BARBARA: Is there any way that you could actually put a piece of wire in front of the crawl space?

MARY: A cat or small dog would be the biggest that could get under there. The way she looks, is out into the yard. The way her ears are at attention and the direction she looks is out in yard. I can turn on the TV at night and it drowns the sound out. But meanwhile, I can sleep.

BARBARA: It is the sound. This is very unusual. That is what they're showing me. It could be an animal—something that's under the sub flooring. I feel like she hears the sound and the sound is not directly under her, but it's under the house. So she is listening, looking out into the yard. But the thing is, the direction the sound is coming at her, and she's— I feel, is not tilting her head to listen to the flooring. It's a level sound she can hear, and I thought of a rodent with babies, maybe something nesting under the floor. Sometimes they go and nest under there. The sounds of the day drown out a lot of the noise.

MARY: It did start around the time of the earthquake. And my vet thought that it might have been the earthquake of a couple weeks ago.

BARBARA: It was a very scary earthquake.

MARY: We went thought the Northridge earthquake and she had no lingering after effects. And there is also a subway station being built nearby.

BARBARA: A subway. Underground! That gives me goose bumps all over. Something underground. So they build at night?

MARY: Yes, but it is not every night. That is the weird thing. Suppose the construction goes from 6 p.m. to 6 a.m. But she doesn't get nervous at 6 p.m. or 9 p.m. or 11 p.m. It is more like she gets more nervous at 2 a.m., 4 a.m., 6 a.m. So I did think of the subway construction.

BARBARA: That would make more sense. Animals are sensitive to vibrations, sensitive to sound. Sound carries, but because of activities of the day or maybe the early evening, so much is muffled you don't hear it. Until the dead of night, the very early part of the morning, when most people are sleeping, sound will carry intensely.

MARY: Is there anything I can do to make her feel protected and not scared?

BARBARA: She feels the vibration of the ground, she feels the sounds coming from under her. So to her, every night feels like an earthquake, because she is sensitive to the vibration. As it becomes earlier in the morning it becomes more intense. What do you do about it? What came to me was, Rescue remedy. Have you ever used any of the flower essences? It is a vibration. They take flowers and put them in water and put them in the sunlight. The water absorbs the vibration and then they take some of the water and add it to alcohol, which is usually brandy. It has a very calming effect. It is used for rescue or trauma. For traumatic experiences. You mist the aura for a minute or two, covering the coat of the dog. All over the dog. Then wait about five to ten minutes and do it again. How long you mist or how long you wait is not a critical thing. It is what you are using that will help. It is calming for the aura. I feel that her hearing is very acute, and she is very sensitive in her paws and her body. What does she sleep on at night?

MARY: She sleeps on the bed with me at night. It's a big bed.

BARBARA: I thought about something that was insulating as a big bed, which is insulating. But, it is the sound. Another thing that might help in soothing her is classical music. But, I am not sure if you want to play classical music all night. Maybe a classical station that plays music without commercials might help.

MARY: I had her on Valium for a week to take care of this. And she seemed to do well on it. I don't want to have her on Valium for the rest of her life.

BARBARA: Right, right. This might be a time when you are going to have to compromise a little bit. Until this underground project is done. To put it mildly, it is freaking her out. She just is beside herself as to understanding what is going on under the ground, and this really bugging her. Her eyes just gloss over. She gets into this fear and she doesn't hear anything else. There isn't anything that consoles her. I was trying to think of what you could do to get to where she doesn't hear the sound under her. Is the bed wood, on a wood floor?

MARY: The bed is wood on carpet.

BARBARA: So it has an insulating factor. I was feeling like it maybe it was wood on wood. And something in between might help insulate. But she's just very sensitive. Her whole body is sensitive. The rescue remedy would help. A little will help calm her, and over time it starts to have a more lasting effect. We use it for injured animals a lot. You just grab the Rescue and start spraying. You could put a few drops on her tongue, open her mouth and spray it into her mouth. There's nothing that would really harm her.

MARY: Where can I find Rescue?

BARBARA: You can find it at any alternative food store or health food store. Classical music is very soothing. If you turn the radio on and turn down the volume, maybe to where you might not hear it, she will still feel the vibration. Even having the classical music on will calm her down. The music is so very healing. This would be another way that would help.

MARY: I could put a portable radio on and keep the sound very low.

BARBARA: You can have the radio on and the sound off. You could put it under her pillow. It might be that the vibration would be enough. Test it out and see what works for you. Anything that would distract from the total still of the night would help. Then find out when that project is going to be completed.

* * *

The best kind of confirmation that a reading is accurate and useful is from letters after an owner makes decisions considering the information that was gained from the reading, as is seen in the following two letters I received:

"Dear Barbara: I want you to know that I called John Lyons' Resistance Free Training Riding on Sunday and a woman came out and worked with my horse for three days. She is like a different horse now. You were right. The saddle was not fitting correctly, as it was pinching her and was causing her pain in the withers and her shoulder. My thanks—you were so incredibly on target with this."

And this one:

"Hi Barbara. Thank you, thank you, for helping me deepen my connection with Chelsea—I mean, the Princess! You are so talented, both with seeing and with interpreting and offering advice. You were right about everything I know about, thank you! In fact, I felt that you knew what I knew, as though we had talked for hours, or had known each other for a long while. You knew what I was referring to without asking, and referred to things I hadn't told you. What a special talent God has given you!

"I visited the farm where Chelsea's old stablemates are, that I told you about. It was EXACTLY as you described. The barn is in a little valley in the woods, and you walk through the woods on a gravel lane, over a wooden bridge and the woods open up to lots of roomy, green turnout paddocks, small fields, and the riding ring. There are 116 acres to ride out on. The owner is super-laid-back and I instantly inquired about a stall. We move in on Saturday, and I am very excited about being back together with those four people and horses. Thank you for reading ME and knowing my emotions were so torn about this. Incidentally, the horses there are all pampered show horses, and I think my special Princess will be back in a herd of special horses.

"I haven't made much progress with the gate work yet. I think Chelsea and I are on the same page, but Cynthia's not too happy with me leaving her barn, and hasn't even wanted to talk about this. The new person, Morgan, seems very interested in working WITH her instead of against her. (It's interesting—your descriptions started me thinking along other lines and seeing things a little differently.)

"Oh, I bought some turnips and took them to Chelsea. She was so cute with her immediate, intense response (Oh, oh, oh, hurry! Feed me NOW! oh, yummmmm... MORE! Give me more!) and acted as though they were long lost friends. (Thanks a lot. Now I can buy TURNIPS along with the carrots and apples.) Really, I am thrilled to know that much more about her, especially something that pleases her so much.

"I have been telling EVERYONE about what a great bridge builder you are. I'm sure we'll be talking again!

"Thanks!

"Judi and Ch— Princess."

2: Zoning In

WHEN A PET IS LOST, it is best to get in touch with the animal to receive impressions. But I must try to determine the location of the animal in relationship to landmarks and compass directions, so the owner can use the information to go and find the pet. This may take a lot of discussion, since the feedback about landmarks may help to further zone in and describe the exact location of the pet.

Otto is a dog who went out to play with a companion dog and didn't come home when he was expected:

JEANNIE: Otto is a schnauzer. I lost him today. He hasn't turned up yet and I feel like he probably won't. But if he is somewhere, I'd like to find him.

BARBARA: Okay. I feel like Otto is very, very active—an exceptionally active dog. Almost to not paying attention to you and to being wild at times. Is that him?

JEANNIE: Well, he is frisky. He is, but kind of fun.

BARBARA: Oh sure, it can be fun. I'm not meaning—of course the word "wild" can be misunderstood. I feel like he's a selective listener—that he listens and he hears what he wants to hear when he wants to hear it, and other than that he's doing his own thing.

JEANNIE: Yes.

BARBARA: Okay. I just want to make sure I get the right animal, that we're talking about the right animal as I tune into this particular one. If I remember from your e-mail, you said he went out with someone?

JEANNIE: Yes. With Sheba, our other dog. Someone just dropped her on the road. She came in and adopted us. She's a beautiful dog. They never came to pick her up. They didn't want her, and I'm glad she's here.

BARBARA: And she seems like a very maternal, motherly kind of energy. She has a lot of personality but she's very soft.

JEANNIE: Yes.

BARBARA: Very feminine, as I feel it.

JEANNIE: Yes.

BARBARA: Okay. So let's see where Otto went and what he's doing, how he left. You live out where it's open.

JEANNIE: Yes.

BARBARA: I don't see a lot of buildings close together as I get what I'm feeling here, so it's rural. I feel like Otto likes to chase small things—rabbits and squirrels. It's a big pleasure of his, and he can get very distracted with that. I feel like they went out together running. They didn't just walk. They ran, and they were in pursuit of something small, and where they went they found a lot of small things to chase, so then it became like, "Which one do I chase? Which way do I go?" And I feel like Sheba got tired. It became boring to her after a while, and she just headed back. But for Otto, it didn't. Okay—so which way did he head out? They're showing me, if I were looking at twelve o'clock, they're showing me about one o'clock. Do you know what I mean?

JEANNIE: Twelve o'clock would be north, then?

BARBARA: Let me see. Yes. Twelve o'clock would be north. So they headed out to the right. Out that way, is what they're showing me. And I see wherever they went, it does have—you have some trees around you, but there's an open area. I'm not sure if you call it a meadow, but it's an open area where the brush is low. It's a big clearing, maybe a meadow. It's not just soft grass. It's a little more scrub.

JEANNIE: Okay.

BARBARA: Does that describe part of the area?

JEANNIE: Yes.

BARBARA: Okay. That's where I see him heading out, and he's running. He's just chasing everything that moves, and he's gone a long ways out, because he kept going out in that direction. Sheba was having a good time with this, but she doesn't hold her enthusiasm for it for a long time. But he is just full of energy and spit and fire so he just—. All these different things are moving, and he's not sure which one to chase but he's got himself a ways out there. I'm asking why he won't send himself home. A lot of dogs will go hunting and they'll just follow their own scent back. He won't calm down enough to do that. He's kind of wiry, as I feel it. Maybe he calms down when he sleeps. Is that a little bit like him?

JEANNIE: Yes. He does, but he's busy, you know, when he's on the go. He's very affectionate and loving, and he's not really brave.

BARBARA: Well, he didn't think about bravery when he was moving and chasing things. I guess it didn't come into his head, "Oh my God, I got too far away now, do I know where I am?" These small things just kept moving out there. Little squirrels, rabbits, or it could be anything in the brush. He might even see a bird fly over and think it might be interesting to follow that. He likes to chase things a lot doesn't he?

JEANNIE: Um-hmm.

BARBARA: Yes. I feel like you have to go out there to get him, to help bring him back in. Is it an area where you can go on your own?

JEANNIE: We've been all over the place. I don't know where to go. My friends were riding out there and my husband looked everywhere. I was looking through bushes and trees, and I went down to where my sister lives on the property that's adjoining us, and I saw two rottweilers down there. I found somebody's rottweilers, and I called them to come pick them up. And, I thought it was him. I just saw a little shadow and it ended up being them. I thought maybe he would be following, but it seemed so far for him to go.

BARBARA: I feel like he's gone out quite a ways. He's out there quite a ways—

JEANNIE: Because the weather's just terrible here.

BARBARA: Oh, is it? Snowing or freezing or cold?

JEANNIE: Well, it's cold and raining, and a bit of a thunderstorm.

BARBARA: Okay. If I were to say north was twelve o'clock, and look between one and two o'clock, if you were to head out in that direction. I'm feeling like at the front of your property not the back. I don't know what that means.

JEANNIE: Is it by a road?

BARBARA: Is it by a road? Not real close to a road. No, I don't feel a road right next to it. I feel a road's closer to you. If there's a little road, the road's kind of going at the edge of your property. If your house faces the front, is a road at the end of your property that goes between three o'clock and nine o'clock—that way?

JEANNIE: Yes.

BARBARA: Is there a road there?

JEANNIE: There's a road that goes from our house straight towards the barn, and it's Nashville Road and then it turns left, which would be three, at three o'clock, and goes down a hill.

BARBARA: Well, from there, from that road, if you look at two o'clock, that's where I feel he's out—between one and two o'clock. Out there. Is there an open meadow or an open area out there? Or is it so vast that it's more open than that?

JEANNIE: Yes. Well there would be sort of an open area.

BARBARA: That's what I'm seeing. That's where they're pointing me, in that direction. And I would take Sheba with you tomorrow, because she might help pick up a scent. But if it's rained, that would make it harder to pick up a scent. But I think she would help you.

JEANNIE: Okay. Between one and two o'clock. Is he by any trees, or is he right in the middle of the meadow?

BARBARA: I feel like he's gone out into the meadow. There's a stand of trees on the right side, but as I look into the meadow, or whatever that open space is—it's open for a long time.

JEANNIE: Yes. Okay.

BARBARA: And if there are any trees, they are way in the back. But I do see trees to the right. It's an opening between two stands of trees, and you can see this huge open space. I don't know—there's no trees in front of me. Do you see what I mean?

JEANNIE: Yes.

BARBARA: I don't feel any streams close by. Sometimes I can see a stream or something he'd have to cross, or some other landmark, but I don't see it. I see a huge mountain range. Is there a mountain range back there?

JEANNIE: No.

BARBARA: No. It's flat?

JEANNIE: No, but on the other side of the meadow there's trees.

BARBARA: It's flat terrain though?

JEANNIE: No, hilly.

BARBARA: Hilly. Okay. I see rise, maybe not mountains. I see the land rise up, not to 8,000 feet or anything that high, but I feel like he's out in that area. That's where he headed.

JEANNIE: Is he alive?

BARBARA: I feel like he is. You'd be surprised how resilient animals are.

JEANNIE: I think I know. Can I say where it is?

BARBARA: Oh, of course.

JEANNIE: I'll repeat it back to you, okay? So I'll go up, take the road out to the barn, which is sort of like going south from my house, then I'll take the road going down, which is still the asphalt, which is three o'clock, then I'll get to the bottom of that hill. And it sort of winds around. It's a dirt road, and if I go out to the left, there's a stand of trees on the right and a few sort of scrubby ones on the left. You know—orchardy almost. There's not really a whole stand there. Does that look familiar?

BARBARA: I see bigger trees on each side.

JEANNIE: Bigger trees on each side?

BARBARA: Pretty tall trees, not in the open space but on the side of it. It's almost like it was maybe a stand of trees and they clear-cut it or something. Is that kind of how it is in your area? And the scrub has grown up and the trees haven't grown up or something. I don't know what that means.

JEANNIE: It's not in a nursery is it?

BARBARA: No, I don't see a nursery.

JEANNIE: All right. Okay. Because we've got a nursery with trees.

BARBARA: No, I don't see that. Instead of going south, what happens when you go north?

JEANNIE: Okay. If I go north, I look right into fields and then over two fields there is a stand of trees that goes all the way along and runs east and west.

BARBARA: Runs east and west. Runs east and west. Yes.

JEANNIE: But if I go out there and then I turn right and I look to the right there's a stand of trees there. And there's also a place where we put new topsoil in the meadow there. Is that anywhere in there?

BARBARA: I feel that's closer. I want to say go north. If you go out your front door, that's the south. It's facing the south?

JEANNIE: Yes.

BARBARA: Do you usually go out the back door more than the front door? Is the back door more heavily used than the front door?

JEANNIE: Yes.

BARBARA: Maybe that's why I'm turned around. I feel like it's an entrance that you come and go the most. I feel like it's more north.

JEANNIE: It is more north.

BARBARA: And if I were to be facing the north, then I would, on the clock, be going to the right, you know, sort of to the right.

JEANNIE: Oh, okay. To the right, there's some trees. If I go out that door, walk along, there's a hedge, and go along the other side of that, it's sort of scraggy, then there's fence, and on the other side of that you go down a hill. To the right, there's a stand of trees.

BARBARA: Is there an open meadow?

JEANNIE: To the left.

BARBARA: I don't know why I feel like it's in that direction. I feel stronger with that.

JEANNIE: Okay. Is he by any buildings or anything?

BARBARA: I really don't feel that. I don't feel any buildings. I just feel he's out and he's a ways away. He's not just sitting under the porch or something, as I feel it. I feel like he's kind of found some trees or something to nestle in or some leaves to lie in to rest. But I think he would be eager to return. He's had more than his share, this time.

JEANNIE: Oh, this time. You knew there was another time. I'm concerned because we had a fox out here a couple of days ago, and there are coyotes around, and he's little you know, and he sort of looks a bit like a rabbit.

BARBARA: Oh, he's a miniature?

JEANNIE: Yes. He's a miniature.

BARBARA: Okay. I feel like he's resting now. He's sleeping now. He's found a place to lie down, but he's had enough. He'd be really thrilled to find his way back home.

JEANNIE: Okay.

BARBARA: And I think the thing to do would be to go out with—

JEANNIE: Sheba.

BARBARA: Yes. Because she may be able to pick up his scent, you know. She can pick it up in the wind. And help guide you in some way. Sometimes it's hard. Sometimes the other animals are so subtle in what they do, you think, "Oh no. That doesn't make any sense. Why would she want to go there?" I would let her kind of wander about with you.

JEANNIE: Was he—is he on a hill?

BARBARA: No, I feel it's pretty flat. That's what I'm seeing. More flat, not hilly. There might be a little hill to the left of him. He has nestled in the trees or something to rest. After his running around with wild abandon.

JEANNIE: Yes. He doesn't usually—he usually comes back.

BARBARA: Well, he just got into a spot that had so many things jumping up and moving around and doing, doing, doing, that he just couldn't stop. He was just beside himself. Like, "Which way do I go? Oh boy, what's next? Oh boy!" He didn't pay attention to anything around him, just what he was doing.

JEANNIE: Okay. Well, between one and two o'clock at the front of the property. I'll head out between one and two o'clock.

BARBARA: Yes. And I would take Sheba with you, and I'd try calling for him. Maybe earlier in the morning, when the day is quiet.

JEANNIE: Okay.

BARBARA: I don't know. I'm feeling like he'll hear you.

JEANNIE: It was really windy today and stuff. The rain, you know. It was raining, and it was hard to hear, and I went to the south, into the trees.

BARBARA: Yes. I've had people who have hunting dogs, and they went out and ended up—. A storm came and a dog got too far out, and it couldn't hear him, and actually the dog returned about a week later, and was not too bad for wear. It was amazing.

JEANNIE: I had a little dog that left in a blizzard and ended up about three quarters of a hour away from here by car, and it was just luck we found him. Anyway, I decided after that I'd better get him fixed. He was just a bit on the road too much. He was a beagle cross. Another interesting character.

BARBARA: Oh. A good nose.

JEANNIE: Yes. He was a great dog. All my dogs have been great.

BARBARA: This one's a wonderful little dog. He's just full of personality, there's no doubt about that.

JEANNIE: Well, this is giving me some hope. My husband said, "I think he's gone."

BARBARA: I don't feel like he's gone. I feel that he's moved out too far for him to find a way back. Hopefully, the wind will go in your direction. You'll be shouting into the wind, if there is any, rather than have the wind come at you. Maybe bring a squeaky toy, something that the sound would carry.

JEANNIE: That's a good idea.

BARBARA: I feel positive about it.

JEANNIE: I've been hoping to be positive, but with the weather and everything—

BARBARA: Well, I feel like there are some places where the trees get pretty dense, where the weather doesn't come in on you as much as it does in the open areas. The trees protect from a lot of wind and rain. There's some denser areas or something.

JEANNIE: Do you do horses as well?

BARBARA: Oh yes. I do all animals.

JEANNIE: I've got lots of animals here. Okay. Is there anything else you can tell me about Otto?

BARBARA: Not at this time. I really just feel like he's anxious to come home. I feel positive about the results. I always want everything to turn out happy. Sometimes, when the message is not good, I will say so. I have to say what I see. But this time I feel positive about it.

JEANNIE: Okay. So you would say if you didn't, wouldn't you?

BARBARA: Yes, I would. I would say that the energy is no longer in the form it was. Sometimes that does happen. They're taken by surprise, by a wild animal or something, and sometimes I can feel that. But in this case, I feel like he's fine and just resting—and using Sheba, you can go out there and find him.

JEANNIE: I will do that. Does Sheba know anything's going on or not? Or is she enjoying having the peace?

BARBARA: It's a little quieter. She's enjoying the peace. Yes. You're right she is. But it's not like, "Well, what happened to him?" They don't quite do that part usually, but I think she'll be helpful in helping you find him. She might go out in the same direction.

JEANNIE: I'm going to head out there. I don't think I went far enough out there today, so I will head out there tomorrow.

BARBARA: I just want to say, it's a ways.

JEANNIE: But he didn't cross a road you don't think?

BARBARA: There could be a road in front of your property that he crossed, but I don't feel like there's another road that he would have crossed way out there.

JEANNIE: Okay.

BARBARA: Do you know? I don't feel that there's another—

JEANNIE: There's only the meadows on our side. The other side has more trees. People don't farm over there, have cattle or anything, so the meadow is more on our side of the street, the road.

BARBARA: Okay. If it's any kind of a road, there isn't a wide road. It's a rural—if there is a road there, it's pretty hidden. If there are any more roads out there, I don't feel them. There would be, to me, trails or something. Nothing heavily traveled. It feels very wilderness like.

JEANNIE: There's a place that I was walking along the other day, where I think there were deer that might have been sleeping there. Does that sort of feel like it at all?

BARBARA: I feel deer would come into this area to feed.

JEANNIE: And he might have been there before, do you think? Or not?

BARBARA: I can't pinpoint any feeling of that. I pinpoint that deer would come to this area. It would be an area where deer could graze. It feels like lots of different opportunities to eat things, and they could still look out. They wouldn't get blasted by something because it's open.

JEANNIE: Yes. Okay. Do you feel it's anywhere near a fence? Like even a wire fence?

BARBARA: I don't feel any fences. The only fences I might feel are fences around your property, or around your house. Do you have fences?

JEANNIE: Yes. I have a fence, sort of between the meadow and the house.

BARBARA: I can see your fence, but it's a big fencing as I feel it. Not small fencing. What do I want to say? The area that's fenced is a good size.

JEANNIE: Right.

BARBARA: Yes. That's what I want to say, but it's past that.

JEANNIE: Can he see us from where he is or do you know?

BARBARA: I feel like he's really a ways out there, and he's kind of little, so he can't. I'm feeling like that's the problem. He's not sure which direction now. I mean, if he was a deer he could look up and say, "Oh, that's the house, it's over there."

JEANNIE: I think I know a part of the area that he might be in. It gives me a clue.

BARBARA: I would call him. A squeaky toy—the sound would probably carry quite a bit.

JEANNIE: A squeaky toy is a great idea. I called Fred, do you know Fred, the Indian?

BARBARA: No.

JEANNIE: Years ago, a friend of mine was calling him. He did horses. He was a horse psychic, and movie star I think, too.

BARBARA: Was he Canadian?

JEANNIE: No. He was from California. He was old and in his nineties, and he died a few years ago. He was very interesting, very bang-on. I was talking to him and it was really interesting. Well, I'll go out first thing in the morning. I'll take a squeaky toy and I'll take Sheba.

BARBARA: Yes. Let her see if she can pick up some kind of scent and lead you out.

JEANNIE: I really appreciate your help. I will e-mail and let you know if I find him.

BARBARA: Thank you. I would appreciate that.

* * *

A follow up phone call:

"Otto returned! He's back! I just can't believe it. He just walked up the driveway a few moments ago. He's back! I just want you to know he returned. Thank you so much."

* * *

Mustard is a dog who got lost after a fox hunt. This owner searched for him two weeks, before calling for a reading. This was their last-ditch hope to help locate the dog.

MAX: We are wondering where Mustard is. He got left out, or didn't come back, a couple of Saturdays ago, after a fox hunt. The hounds are taken out on Saturdays in a pack, and they are trained to follow the hunt, and to obey the huntsman. They come to voice command, and to a horn. So when he blows them in, they are suppose to come in from wherever they are, no matter what they are doing. And 99 percent of the time they all come in. Particularly, Mustard. It is very unlike him not to come in.

BARBARA: Is he the dog that follows by the horse? Are you on horseback?

MAX: Yes.

BARBARA: Does he follow more to the left side of the horse? Do the dogs stay with you, or do they run ahead of you?

MAX: They go all over. I do have some that I can pretty much count on to be to the left or right of me. My impression is that Mustard is usually on my right.

BARBARA: On your right. Okay. But, does he stay fairly close to the horse and to you? Or does he run and point or something like that? What I mean to ask is, whether he stays ahead of the rest of the pack. Is he more of a dominant energy?

MAX: He is more of a team player. The pack does have a personality of behaving like that. He is a very self-confident hound, but not a leader. He is more independent—part of the pack, but he's kind of a free thinker.

BARBARA: Okay. Okay.

MAX: I have a hound that really stays very close in, close to me a lot, that is Peptic. They do have some similarities, as they are both real big hounds. You might be picking up on Peptic.

BARBARA: I am getting someone that is Mr. Do-gooder—"Am I doing good? Is this what you want? I can show you I can do this!"—kind of a performer.

MAX: That is Mustard.

BARBARA: Okay.

MAX: He is a team player. He tries hard. That is why he usually comes right back. He is not disobedient, and would not normally ignore the horn or the command. He is not rebellious.

BARBARA: He tends to range out farther than the others?

MAX: Sometimes. That is a good trait in them, by the way. If they are obedient and come in. That is a very good trait.

BARBARA: I get a feeling that he has ranged out farther than the call back could carry—so he could not hear the command to come back. I feel it was very cold. Was a wind running the wrong way, so that the sound came back at you rather than going out to him?

MAX: Yes. It was very, very windy that day. The wind was in the direction we were going. We were on a large ranch and we go different directions. If they are upwind of me, they have a very difficult time hearing me. They know this ranch pretty well. They know their way back because we always start out from the same place. That is the other thing that has us so worried. Some hounds will be out a while after we come back, but they always find their way back from where they started.

BARBARA: I have Whippets. And Whippets go out hunting in the field, then backtrack by their own scent.

MAX: These are scent hounds. They can follow the scent of the rest of the pack back. We have been to this particular place enough times that they know their way around. They know where we start out.

BARBARA: I just feel like he headed out straight. Way out. And the wind was blowing the wrong way and he never heard the command to come back.

MAX: Let me ask. Are you picking up that he is still alive?

BARBARA: Yes. Actually I was getting a strong feeling about where this dog could be. I was getting that either he has gone to a barn where there are horses, or that a neighbor or someone who lives close by has picked him up.

MAX: That may be.

BARBARA: The people that picked him up, they don't plan to keep him, or to not let anybody know. They just don't know where he came from.

MAX: He has a collar with our name and phone number on it.

BARBARA: He does?

MAX: The few times that we have had a hound be out overnight, we have had people call us, and say, "Your hound has come to our place." It has been very, very cold in Tulsa. That is what got us so worried. The day we hunted was chilly, and that night was fairly cold. Then the temperature really dropped and we have had temperatures at nine or ten degrees. If he has gone someplace like a neighboring ranch, it would be good. We are just afraid that he will freeze to death.

BARBARA: I am not picking up that he is gone. If I were facing north, I see him going out northwest. In a northwesterly direction headed straight out.

MAX: Well, that is certainly possible. He could have gone in any direction of the compass, where we were.

BARBARA: Okay. I do not know which direction you were hunting.

MAX: The last time I think we saw him, the dogs were headed north. Into a north wind. If we blow the horn and they were running north it would be hard for them to hear.

BARBARA: That is what I was feeling, that he was doing his job and he was out there and he never heard the call to come back. He didn't feel stranded or afraid—I guess that is part of it—and he is used to being out there, and doing whatever he is supposed to be doing.

MAX: They are trained to follow coyotes. They are fox hounds, but there are not many foxes in our part of the world. When we ride to the hounds they chase coyotes, following them by scent.

BARBARA: I feel he is in a place where there is straw, in a barn with horses, someplace like that.

MAX: That is what we would hope. I hope I am not the one giving you that feeling, because we are hoping he would be in a situation like that. And there are some barns around there, exactly as you described. The closest one is the ranch from where we started. I have gone back to that barn to look for him—and again, I wonder if you are picking up on me doing that. Every time I go to look, that is the first place I go. In that barn where the horses are. It is a place where he could get in out of the weather.

BARBARA: That is what I am feeling. Whether I have picked it up from you or not, I feel like he has gotten in out of the weather, where there is heavy straw on the floor. I don't feel if he has eaten or not, and you say it has been a while. I don't feel him starving, I don't feel hurt.

MAX: In good weather these hounds can survive on their own for months. It is amazing. I didn't know. We have some shy hounds. We had a shy hound that got away from us one time. She was on her own for three months. We knew where she was, but no one could catch her. She just survived on her own and wouldn't come to anybody.

BARBARA: They eat rabbits?

MAX: They would eat anything. They would go to ranch houses where people put food out for their own dogs, or eat cat food, or they would eat whatever they found. We finally had to trap her with a wild animal trap. Today, she is just wonderful. She goes with us and she is one of our most trustworthy hounds, but she just got scared. We knew she stayed within a two mile area. But he is not like that. He is so gregarious and so friendly that he would go up to someone. See, they will hang around a place, and they won't let some of the people get close enough to them to read the collar, until after some time goes by—and then they will call us.

BARBARA: I don't feel like he is going to beg at someone's back door. The energy I feel from him is more self-sufficient—he can take care of himself, does not feel frightened. I don't get a fear at all of just being out there by himself. He is that way?

MAX: Yes.

BARBARA: I get a male energy, but it does not necessarily have to be a male dog. Sometimes that's how it is.

MAX: He is a big dog, even for the breed he is a big dog. He weighs close to one hundred pounds.

BARBARA: Oh, he is big!

MAX: He is very self-confident.

BARBARA: I get that, and I get that he is not scared of people, he almost doesn't need people. He has the air about him, that he is his own man.

MAX: That is certainly true, though they have a tendency to bond to the people they are with all the time. They really are a pack animal, and bond inside the family group. They bond with me and with Barbara, because we work with them. I could see that he would not just go up to a rancher or ranch hand or someone like that.

BARBARA: I feel that this barn is close to a house. It is a good size house.

MAX: Sounds like the Long's—or the Nelson's, maybe.

BARBARA: He is in the barn sleeping in the hay, because that is what he knows to do. He is not asking to get into the house.

MAX: He does not live in a house.

BARBARA: And he doesn't know how that works. Somehow I get the feeling that the barn door was open and it is safe and comfortable.

MAX: We should call the Nelson's tomorrow and ask them to look around.

BARBARA: I get that there are mice in there, too. Would they eat mice?

MAX: Yes—well, our barn dogs do. I guess our kennel dogs would, too, if they were out. I have seen our barn dogs catch mice.

BARBARA: I get little gray things running around.

MAX: Those are mice!

BARBARA: I get that he may catch them to eat something. He knows he needs shelter most of all, and right now he is staying where there is shelter.

MAX: It is so cold, that would be like him. The Nelsons are north and west of the place where we were. They have a horse barn.

BARBARA: The guides just point that way, like that is the direction he went. He went straight out that way, is what they are saying. Straight as the crow flies.

MAX: I wonder if he still has his collar on? Could he have he pulled it off or something?

BARBARA: I am not sure if the people know he is there.

MAX: That could be.

BARBARA: He is staying quiet. He went into a strange barn and he would just be quiet and stay out of sight.

MAX: I think so.

BARBARA: He wouldn't go up to everybody and go, "Oh, hi, here I am." I don't get that from him. He is not scared of them, but he is just not going to approach them. He will be quiet and stay still. Like a little deer hides in the brush when there is danger around.

MAX: Maybe 'til he got more comfortable.

BARBARA: He is just lying down, being quiet. Not letting anybody know that he is there. The horses are a familiar thing to him.

MAX: Well, he is around horses all the time.

BARBARA: Okay. They make him feel safer.

MAX: There are two places he could be that sound like that, and we can call both of them tomorrow.

BARBARA: Is one of the houses gray?

MAX: I don't know if the Nelson house is gray. I can ask them tomorrow, when we call. It is a neighboring ranch. It is a pretty good size place, thousands of acres. I have talked to the Nelsons on the phone, but I haven't seen the place. I know they have horses—we can see them across their fence, and our place goes up to their boundary. In fact, we are talking to them about permission to ride and hunt on their property. Do you see anything about the barn?

BARBARA: I don't actually see the outside. I feel like, if I were to see the barn and the house, and I were to be looking north, I would see the barn first and then the house. So the barn would be on the south side of the house. That is where I feel he is. It is very flat land.

MAX: The Nelson property is flat land. Particularly where their pasture and their barns are. As I remember it, it has some very large pastures. But it sounds a lot like Long's, too. She is out of town for two weeks. She left town the day after our hunt. and she has someone coming in to take care of things. But not someone who would know Mustard didn't belong there, if they noticed him.

BARBARA: I see him in a corner and out of sight, not visible in the hay.

MAX: She has a veterinarian coming to feed the horse and

take care of her dogs. She has some dobermans that she keeps around there. They have these collars on them so when they are outside they don't leave the set boundaries. The dobermans have been inside, because it has been so cold. I will call the vet and have him look in the barn when he goes, and call the Nelsons and have them look in their barn. Those are the two horse barns. What concerns me a little bit is that I wanted to find him so much in that one barn where we go. Because that is a place with good shelter and protection.

BARBARA: Lots of time the animals pick up things on another level, and it seems like you can direct them without talking to them. You have projected that would be the best place for him to go, and that is what he has picked up.

MAX: We were concerned that he got caught up in a fence or fell in a well hole or something. Because we thought that if he were safe he would be more inclined to go right up to someone, not act like one of the shy ones and hang back.

BARBARA: I am not getting that he is hung up or has fallen in a well. He is not going to go right up to someone. He doesn't need them! That is his attitude. "I don't need them. I'm okay, like I am! I can take care of myself. I'm a big boy."

MAX: Oh yes. That is exactly what he is like. He is very independent. He is comfortable in the pack and he likes the pack, but he is self-confident. But, for the very cold weather, I feel he is the kind that could take care of himself on his own. If he has not had an accident, or anything's happened to him. He is a pretty strong guy and he is in strong health. Very well fed. And has a good coat.

BARBARA: I feel that he is still in a good health.

MAX: Will there be a time that he will seek someone out so they can read his collar?

BARBARA: If someone came up and talked to him I don't feel like he would shy away. He would just say, "Okay, hi, I am here! Who are you? This is me!" I feel that they could walk up to him and read his collar and I don't feel that he will run away. He is just hanging out.

MAX: Well, if he had something to eat, it may very well be a barn like that, that people are putting food out like that for dogs or for cats. They would eat cat food or whatever. They are not that discriminating. He could catch mice.

BARBARA: I don't feel the body is in any discomfort. I don't feel any stress about food. I feel like he is hanging out in the corner in the straw waiting it out. He is not worried about if he should leave now, or wait.

MAX: With the cold weather he may be keeping a low profile, and when it warms up he will come out where they will be able to see him.

BARBARA: He just knows that it is real cold out there and not real comfortable, and he is fine where he is. He will just hang out there until there is a break in the weather, or it is good for him to travel. I feel like he will travel back the way he came.

MAX: The frustrating thing is not having any direction to go or think about.

BARBARA: It is one of those gut wrenching things.

MAX: We have started putting tracking collars on the dogs—because of him mostly—we have started, and we have about enough for the pack. We have decided after this last weekend that we are going to bite the bullet and get tracking collars for the rest of them. It costs $140 for each collar. With twenty hounds, it is expensive. But losing one like this is, too, considering the worry—plus the time and effort we take to go up there and try and find them. The ranches are an hour away from the kennel.

BARBARA: It is like looking for a needle in a hay stack.

MAX: I can be looking on the east side of the ranch and the dog is on the west. It is four to five miles different. Then you start to worry when you go out, who might not be going to come in this time. So you corral them in too close, then they feel a bit stifled for what they are suppose to be doing.

BARBARA: A lot of times the animals have a different feeling. A lot of times we project how we would feel if we were lost. The animals don't feel like that. Sometimes they wander off for the experience. Some are pretty self-sufficient, or they want a new experience.

MAX: Sometimes when they wander off for a few days, when they get back in the pack they are very well behaved. They are the first ones back when we call, and it seems like they hang pretty close and they don't want to do that again.

BARBARA: That day, were there two different scents? Oh — how would you know? I was feeling like he picked up a scent on his own.

MAX: He could have. The object of this is to scent the hounds out, and they hunt on their own. They find coyote scent and then open. Open is when they start barking, and the rest of the hounds will honor the one that has found the scent, and they will go together in the pack following the scent, and we will follow the hounds. That is what riding to the hounds is all about. It is not a sport that kills the coyotes. It is a sport to get a chase. He could have found scent that the rest of them didn't find in a high wind. He could have gone off on that scent. He could have even opened and they could not hear him, and he could have gone off and followed the scent on his own, and the rest did not honor it and we didn't know because of the wind.

BARBARA: I feel it was the wind. It set up a sound barrier kind of a wall. The sound didn't carry for any distance.

MAX: It was probably a twenty to thirty mile an hour wind that day. It was bitter.

BARBARA: I get that it was bitter cold.

MAX: It was cold in the open, but when we were in the woods it was pretty comfortable. Out in the open and the plains, and in the pasture it is very cold with the wind chill. The temperature was thirty-six degrees, but with a wind of twenty-five miles an hour you are probably talking about zero.

BARBARA: Was it kind of foggy?

MAX: High humidity. It had rained.

BARBARA: I get that there was less visibility than what you usually have.

MAX: Pretty heavy clouds. Gray day. If you get any other thoughts please call us.

BARBARA: Okay, I will. When you find him let me know. I do appreciate the feedback.

* * *

A follow-up phone message from Max:

"We wanted to let you to know that Mustard is home. We got in late on Tuesday night and the first call we got Wednesday morning was someone who had Mustard. He had come up to them. He was north of the ranch. He's healthy and well, but a bit skinny. But he is back in the kennels and looks good, and we just wanted to let you know. So this had a good outcome. Thank you very much. Bye, Bye."

A later communication from Max:

"I know that anyone who has animals, and it does not even have to be a loss situation, and you feel there is something wrong or has gone wrong, there is incredible stress on a person. Our dogs are like family members to us. Even though we have forty dogs, they are all like our kids. Since the time that Mustard was lost, we have gotten tracking collars for all our dogs. Actually, Mustard was the reason that we got tracking collars. We don't want to go through that again.

I feel that you should mention in your book that obviously men are more skeptical than women, and I feel men are less intuitive. And most people believe it. I feel women are more intuitive and less skeptical about things. So I was skeptical about it. But, Barb and I talked about it and if we were going to have any chance at all we had to have faith in the possibility that it was going to work—of finding Mustard through an animal psychic. The most important thing was that Barb and I had the same emotional reaction—for use of a better word—to our phone call to you, and that was that we felt a great deal of relief. Even though we hadn't found Mustard at the time. We didn't know if we would find him or he would ever come back. The very fact that we talked to you about him and you saw him still out there and healthy—that was a big concern of ours. It was bitter cold and the temperature at night was zero. One of the things you said was that you saw him getting inside. And he was not in any great stress. And for some reason the connection between you and us caused us to be reassured."

3: Animal Illness

IN MANY READINGS, owners are concerned with animals that are unwell. Sometimes the veterinarian is treating a pet which does not seem to improve. Other times the owner is worried about an animal that does not have any clear symptoms of illness, but seems to be not as well as it should be.

* * *

KARLA: His name is Waldo. My basic concern and question is, what can I do, so that he feels better?

BARBARA: Okay. My first impression is, I'm getting a dog that's concerned about you.

KARLA: Yes. That's my feeling, too.

BARBARA: Usually I get a little bit more about the animal's personality. I get him watching you, him looking at you, him observing you. It's like—it's like he is waiting for you to make a move. He's preparing himself to do things as you would like them. What can I say? An animal that above all else wants to please you.

KARLA: Yes.

BARBARA: And so that's why he is watching you and paying attention to you. So your question is, what can you do to make it so he can feel better. Maybe you would feel better if he were more relaxed, not so concerned about you, not following you on your heels. Is that what you would like?

KARLA: No. What's going on with him started a little over a year ago. I had two animals, within a couple of months of each other, get sick. He's the one that is having the most trouble. He has some kind of skin thing going on, and he's just itching all the time.

BARBARA: Okay.

KARLA: I've taken him to the vet. It didn't help. Well, they had him on Prednisone and that helped, but you can't keep him on Prednisone. Now we are going to a homeopathic vet and he is still really itching. We've been doing that since February. He just had an allergy test, and there is nothing that he is allergic to, so now we are doing the food test to eliminate all the foods that typically cause allergens. It's just so frustrating to me that he just scratches and bites himself so much, and my feeling is that it has something to do with me. That somehow it may be because of my general attitude, which he is picking up on. I just don't know what to do and I'm just so frustrated. And he's sitting right beside me scratching like mad right now.

BARBARA: And I can feel the itchiness of the skin. It feels like the skin is very dry and taut.

KARLA: The skin is better than it was. It used to be flaky.

BARBARA: Okay.

KARLA: The improved diet I have him on—the special foods and supplements and that, have helped a lot. But, he's still itchy and he just scratches and bites.

BARBARA: And there are no parasites, fleas or anything.

KARLA: No. No. He gets frequent baths.

BARBARA: I'm feeling he is itchy from underneath, like an allergy rather than something topical. It's like if you get a bug bite and you scratch, it feels good when you scratch because it just has that great feeling. But the more you scratch the more you irritate it.

KARLA: He is very sensitive to temperature. He gets hot easily or he gets chilled easily.

BARBARA: Okay. That could be the thyroid. Have you had his thyroid checked?

KARLA: He has had lots of blood tests. But he—I don't think that was elevated—I'll check the last one.

BARBARA: Okay. Sometimes a sensitivity to temperature changes is thyroid. Usually an underactive thyroid, rather than an overactive thyroid.

KARLA: Yes. I've always thought—he's a purebred—and I got him actually fourth hand. I think I was his fourth owner. But I've always felt like the purebred dogs have a harder time with immunities and stuff.

BARBARA: No, not really. It depends on the breeding.

KARLA: I have a mutt too, and I've never had any problems like that with him.

BARBARA: The first impression that I got was that he has a weak immune system.

KARLA: I have him on a supplement called Immuplex from the homeopathic vet.

BARBARA: The immune system needs to be built up, so he's less sensitive to everything. You could try to get four different kinds of food. Each day give him one food and then don't give him that food for three days, and then the fourth day give him that food again.

KARLA: That is interesting. I've never heard of it that way before.

BARBARA: It's the same with people in that if you don't eat—

KARLA: Because you're not over-stimulating on one thing.

BARBARA: Right. If you are sensitive to something, and you eat it once every four days, you are less likely to stimulate a reaction from the immune system.

KARLA: What I'm doing right now is feeding them the same thing in a very limited diet. And a lot of rice. And I actually mix rice and vegetables and supplements together, and then he gets—when we decided to do the elimination diet, they told me to get something he never had before. Canned venison is what he's eating right now. He's been on that for nearly four weeks and I don't see any changes for the better at all. I would have expected to see at least some minor improvement, but I've not seen anything.

BARBARA: Do you have him on any kind of wheat products whatsoever?

KARLA: No, not right now. All he eats is brown rice. It's a mixture. Have you ever heard of Dr. Pitkaren? He's got a book out with some recipes in it.

BARBARA: No.

KARLA: It's kelp, bone meal, nutritional yeast and some mineral supplements, and then there's a thing I get from the homeopathic vet called the "missing link." It's like omega fatty acids and stuff, and then I add olive oil and carrots and he gets the canned venison. It may have potatoes in it, but I'm not sure. But there's no wheat, no corn, no soy, no beef except for that bone meal, which the homeopathic vet said would be all right.

BARBARA: Bone meal shouldn't be a problem. The yeast may be a problem.

KARLA: He does have a tendency to have yeast infections in his ears. And because of the itching and scratching, he's got a bacterial skin infection.

BARBARA: Yes. That's the yeast. It's too much yeast.

KARLA: So get rid of the yeast?

BARBARA: Yes. I don't feel his tolerance is really good with it, and I would recommend that he have different foods in rotation. If the same food is not given more often than every fourth day, the dog may avoid having a reaction to it, even when he is somewhat sensitive to the food.

KARLA: Okay. What about when I took him to do the allergy test—that was a different vet because the homeopathic vet that I use doesn't do conventional veterinary medicine, so I have to work with all these vets. This one wanted to put him on antibiotics, but the homeopath didn't want to do that. Since I don't really see him improving, I'm wondering if the antibiotics would harm any progress we might have made with the immune system.

BARBARA: Sometimes an antibiotic will make a dramatic improvement in a short time. Sometimes you need a leg up because of the severity of the problem. I almost feel like that wouldn't be a bad course of action. And I don't know why raspberry leaves keep coming up, but that's what I'm getting. Maybe you need to look up the properties of raspberry leaves.

KARLA: Raspberry?

BARBARA: Yes. Raspberry leaves. Raspberry leaves. That's what they are telling me.

KARLA: I have an holistic herbal book. I'll look it up. And I'll call the vet back who wanted to prescribe an antibiotic after the allergy test, and see what he says.

BARBARA: Let's try and find the cause of his skin problems. He always stays near you?

KARLA: The way I describe him to other people is, he's a momma's boy. Follows me around. Waits by my feet when I work at home. He sleeps right beside the bed at night.

BARBARA: He is a guardian. That's his job. He is the guardian.

KARLA: My guardian.

BARBARA: Yes, he really is.

KARLA: And it's funny because when he started having—he's had little problems with his skin off and on. This started when I started dating someone last year, that was a lot like my dad, who was not a good person.

BARBARA: Interesting.

KARLA: I have a cat who started having some problems, and he has totally evened out. But I keep thinking it's got to have something to do with me.

BARBARA: Actually, it really doesn't. You are feeling pretty guilty here. I would definitely drop the guilt. Just forgive yourself, let go of the past, move forward. You know—we all make mistakes, and we've all been there and done that. And we can beat ourselves up on a daily basis, and say, "Why did I do that? I shouldn't have done that?" You made a mistake. And we all make mistakes and that's how we learn. The dog is not upset about the mistake. He's worried about you.

KARLA: Um-hmm.

BARBARA: You are so into him, worried about him, and he's so into you, worried about you. It's like this little dance that the two of you are doing. "Okay, you want me to eat this?" Oh okay, he'll eat this. "Yes. Okay, now what? What should we be doing?" So it's like you two are having this great time, actually. He's getting all this wonderful attention. It is time to let all of that go—"I'm moving on. I'm not staying stuck in this." And Waldo is connected with you, and he is the guardian. And so he will do anything to please you. Just anything. And he'll eat anything. He'll act any way. So just give him the word, and he'll just do it.

KARLA: Yep.

BARBARA: Yes. And it feels like he is up on his toes. Any minute now, you just might give him a command and he'll be ready.

KARLA: Yes. He's getting older so it's hard, too, to see him slowing down, because he still has that desire. He's so eager, but then like on a walk, he'll get tired sooner. Was there something that happened when this problem just suddenly came on? Because he was fine.

BARBARA: Sometimes the immune system can get weakened, for whatever reason, and it can come on.

KARLA: So maybe it was the stress of what was going on back then?

BARBARA: It could have been.

KARLA: It could have been that.

BARBARA: But don't go down that road, you know. Don't do the guilt thing.

KARLA: Yes, I don't think that I had altered his food at that time, or I hadn't—. I had been living in the same house for a year and a half at that point, so I know it wasn't the environment. I hadn't changed the environment.

BARBARA: Um-hmm. It's just something, that the immune system got weak. As animals get older, it can happen too.

KARLA: Yes, that's what I'm thinking, too. He's about eleven, I think.

BARBARA: And he's about medium size?

KARLA: He's a bassett hound. He weighs about sixty pounds.

BARBARA: Eleven years old is doing pretty good. Once you get him stabilized to the yeast. B-6 is great for joint problems.

KARLA: Okay. Yes, because he has been not wanting to go down the stairs very readily, lately. That's sort of a secondary thing that's been going on, and I didn't know if it was his joints.

BARBARA: Actually it is. They're getting some arthritis in them.

KARLA: What about aspirin? Like just putting an aspirin in his food?

BARBARA: You can. The aspirin's hard on the stomach. You could get glucosamine but check the supplement. No sugar, no yeast, no anything like that. I feel like there's some arthritis setting up in the joints there, and it gets a bit crusty.

KARLA: It's worse right after he gets up in the morning, when he hasn't been moving around much.

BARBARA: Yes, yes. It's going to be a little harder for him in the winter. A heating pad or something he can lie on would keep the joints sort of warm—but not too warm, to where he would get chilled when he went outside.

KARLA: The itching is all over his whole belly, now. When it first started it was just his armpits in the front, and it goes from his armpits in the front all the way to his armpits in the back. And it's not like a solid thing, but there are spots all over him, on his belly, that are real irritating to him.

BARBARA: Is there anything that feels a little firm on his sides or on his ribs or anything? Have you checked him to feel to see?

KARLA: You mean like a bump or something?

BARBARA: Yes.

KARLA: Yes. There might be. It's hard to tell. His ribs do feel kind of bumpy to me.

BARBARA: Check his rib cage. Under his arms.

KARLA: I don't know what dog ribs normally feel like.

BARBARA: Just little bumps. It just kind of comes to mind so I put it out there—just something to keep an eye on.

KARLA: Okay. Well, is there anything else that I need to know from him?

BARBARA: He tells me, he doesn't want you to feel guilty. He wants you to feel happy, and he's happy. The two of you together is happiness.

KARLA: Uh-huh.

BARBARA: That's what he feels—the two of you together is just absolute happiness for him.

KARLA: Yes. He was definitely in a worse place before.

BARBARA: Yes. And he really just loves to have the two of you together.

KARLA: He's just with me all the time and when I'm sitting at a chair, like at the dining room table, and he'll poke me with his nose or poke me in the butt with his nose, "Here I am." Or lie on my feet. He's really a sweet boy.

BARBARA: Yes. And lying on your feet is like, well, if you move, he'll know, so he can go to sleep and rest.

KARLA: And I try, because I know that he's like that, and that he likes to be with me like that. If I go somewhere—because he's starting to get a little hard of hearing, and doesn't see as well—I always try to get his attention, so he knows where I'm going. Especially if I leave the house. I want him to know that I'm leaving the house, so he doesn't wake up and freak out running all over looking for me.

BARBARA: Yes, that's good. Then you can say, "Now I'm leaving through this door and—"

KARLA: "I'll come back through this door."

BARBARA: Yes. And so he doesn't panic. That's really good, what you're doing. Because then he doesn't panic about, "Well, where did you go all of a sudden? I woke up, and I didn't see you," or, "You forgot me."

KARLA: Uh-huh.

BARBARA: His memory's going, a little bit. He doesn't remember as much as he used to, so he's not quite sure of himself. Does he get a little bit confused?

KARLA: Um-hmm. And another thing. All he wants to eat is chicken. That's it. Chicken, nothing else.

BARBARA: I don't see where chicken would be a problem.

KARLA: Yes. I've done this other diet for four weeks, and I have not seen any change at all for the better. I don't think the food thing is making an effect at all.

BARBARA: No, because some of it's not the right foods.

KARLA: And can I ask you about my other animals? The other animal that I had the problem with about that same time was my cat, and his name is Garp. He was rescued from a shelter when he was a kitten, and he had tar on him and he was stuck to a fence.

BARBARA: Oh, my God.

KARLA: And they are pretty sure that someone did that to him.

BARBARA: Oh, gee.

KARLA: So they named him Tar Baby. I got him about the same time that movie, *The World According to Garp*, came out. So I named him T.B. Garp because he is an orange tabby, and he was real—had an attitude like that character in the movie.

BARBARA: Oh, that's wonderful!

KARLA: So that's his story, and he's eighteen this year.

BARBARA: He's strong. He's solid-bodied, and he has a real attitude.

KARLA: Oh yes. What happened is, his eyes filled up with blood, and we couldn't figure out what was going on. Well, after many vet visits—and I took him to an eye specialist—we kind of think that over the course of his life, being overmedicated, it caused a thyroid condition, which the thyroid doesn't show elevated on the blood test, but the bleeding in the eye is from high blood pressure, they said.

BARBARA: It could be.

KARLA: Then he was starting to have kidney failure, also. So I'm doing the homeopathic remedy, and he's on a human blood pressure medicine. And he's doing very well. I know he's old, and you know, one of these days he's going to say, "Well, time to go," but—

BARBARA: Yes. That's kind of a natural progression and rightfully so—the gift of leaving, as well. I was getting something about the eye. Did he have any glaucoma in that eye?

KARLA: They told me when I took him to the eye thing that he had some retina damage, and he's got a big scar in that eye now. But he seems to be able to see out of it, somewhat. And because of his age, I wouldn't do anything with it.

BARBARA: No, it's maybe better to just to leave things be. The anesthetic and the procedure may be harder for him being he is up in years and it could be best just to let it be. And the other problem I feel is the kidneys. I would recommend no fish for him. And he doesn't see well at all.

KARLA: Yes, but he is happy lying around, and he's an indoor cat. I have a dog run that's covered, and he can go outside, but he can't run free, and nothing can get to him.

BARBARA: Oh, that's perfect. I think you are doing fine with him.

KARLA: He seems fine.

KARLA: Then my other dog, his name is Rufus. He's about five or six.

BARBARA: He's pretty active.

KARLA: He's a chow-terrier mix, but he's mostly terrier. He's about thirty pounds. He looks like a little sheep dog, but he's got the curly chow tail. He wasn't abused, but he was neglected. And I feel like he didn't get enough love when he was a baby, so that's what he wants.

BARBARA: He's just pure love. And he's just—he just can't be any happier. He just—I feel like he smiles all the time.

KARLA: Um-hmm. He's just—I just bought this house that I'm in now, I just bought it in August of last year, and he just loves it here so much more than where we were before. It's a good yard for him. He can see what's going on out on the street. I live on a corner lot, and he just loves to be outside, and he loves the dog run. He sleeps out there half the time.

BARBARA: His instincts are, he wants to be guarding or protecting things.

KARLA: Yes. They're both very protective. I never worry about anybody sneaking up on me. And I like that because I live alone.

BARBARA: Right, and you can feel safe. Waldo, just—he is your guardian, and Rufus is, he is just a protector.

KARLA: Um-hmm.

BARBARA: He wants to protect the whole perimeter of the property. And that's why he's outside. He's watching to see that nobody sneaks up from another spot.

BARBARA: What you could say is, "Thank you."

KARLA: Yes. I do. All he wants is to be outside. He wants me to feed him on the back porch. That's been our funny thing this summer. He wants to have patio dining.

BARBARA: Oh, isn't that fun? Well, that's just because he just enjoys the outdoors.

KARLA: Yes. He just loves to be outside. When I first got him, the first nine months of his life, I don't think he ever was indoors. He couldn't handle being inside. So now that I'm in this house, I've built the dog run so he can go out anytime he wants to. He just loves that.

BARBARA: Oh, that's wonderful. Yes. He does. He would be like someone who would guard sheep, be some kind of herd animal. A bunch of ducks. You know.

KARLA: Actually, I think he's kind of a bird dog. He might want to eat the ducks.

BARBARA: Well, maybe not.

KARLA: My neighbors had chickens right next to the fence for a little while, and he was over there all the time, and sometimes they would kind of get out of the enclosure, and it's a chain link fence, so he could see them. And he would just be sitting over there, quivering. It was just so funny.

BARBARA: Sometimes it's almost like a mothering instinct. "What can I do? How can I care for you? I can't reach you. I want to care for you."

KARLA: Yes. That's funny. Maybe I could ask you just one last question about Garp?

BARBARA: Sure.

KARLA: Sometimes he walks around meowing. And I used to have another cat, and I had to put her to sleep, quite a few years ago. And they were buddies when they were little, but not as adults really. But I was wondering if getting another cat would be too disruptive, or if he would like that.

BARBARA: I feel like, the walking around and meowing— he's calling.

KARLA: That's what it seems like.

BARBARA: Yes. He's calling this other cat. If you get another cat for him, you would have to get one that would be very soft and loving, and not real wild. If you were to get another cat, and you still had Garp around.

KARLA: But would he be okay with that?

BARBARA: Oh yes. He's calling because —when he goes to sleep and he's in his other realm he can feel this cat. It's around. It's right there, and he opens his eyes and it isn't there. So he calls, "Where'd you go?"

KARLA: Okay. If he really wants one, I'd get one, but if I'm misinterpreting it, and it screws things up, that would be a real drag.

BARBARA: Yes. Well, he's calling the one he's seeing in his imagination. Was it female?

KARLA: It was female.

BARBARA: Yes. He liked her a lot.

KARLA: She was the boss cat. When they were little, I have pictures of them all cuddled up together, and they were good. And she only lived to eleven. I know so much more about food and nutrition than I did then.

BARBARA: No matter what you do, sometimes you can never find what it is that they really need. If you want to get a cat, it's okay, just get one that's quite mellow. Cause he's not up to sudden moves, or being leaped upon.

KARLA: Yes, especially only seeing clearly out of one eye.

BARBARA: Yes. He would feel very vulnerable.

KARLA: If he's okay without, then I think I will wait. I have so much to do dealing with their health issues as it is. I sure appreciate your information.

BARBARA: Oh, thank you.

KARLA: And I will let you know how it goes.

* * *

A follow up e-mail from Karla, who has been doing her homework:

Hi Barbara:

I'm doing some web research and I found this: "Blackberries, cranberries, blueberries, bilberries, strawberries, raspberries. Yum! Eat them plain, eat them juiced, eat them on top of shortcake, or with cream; any way you eat them, you'll be getting lots of berry good nutrients that contribute to your health. Berries are used to treat arthritis, candida, urinary tract or bladder infections, or irregular or painful menstrual cycles. Because of the antioxidants they contain, they may help to prevent some of the negative effects of aging. Healthful compounds include vitamin C, anti-cancer ellagic acid, and the essential fatty acid, GLA. Use strawberries to keep your teeth free of tartar, raspberries to avoid cancer and bilberries to strengthen blood cell tissues and improve vision. Actually, choose any berry: Go overboard in your berry consumption this summer, your body will thank you for it later. And remember, life is just a bowl of—berries?"

Thanks for helping us,

Karla

* * *

Barb and Tim adopted an ex-racing greyhound which had a lot of pain. This is the e-mail that was received prior to the session:

Hi Barbara,

Can you please help my dog? Eunice is a retired greyhound, seven years old, and sweet, lovely, and kind. She had an accident two years ago, in which she tore her shoulder area skin and muscle. Over eighty stiches later, it appeared she recovered wonderfully. It has been nearly two years since her accident.

Since April of this year, she is in daily pain. Cries every night. We have had standard veterinary care along with chiropractic, accupuncture and homeopathy treatments. Nothing seems to help her. The vets believe that the scar tissue growth from the accident is the cause of her pain. I tend to think there is something else, something hidden. All X-rays and blood work show nothing. Eunice is on daily steroids which have other serious side effects.

Can you help us? We saved her once, and have vowed to ensure a good life for this wonderful dog.

We live in Virginia. Is this something we can do telephonically?

We look forward to your reply.

Regards,

Barbara and Tim

* * *

TIM: The dog's name is Eunice, and she's had a lot of pain the past four months. We'd like to know the source of it. It is very elusive, and as I said in my message, she's been going to therapy.

BARBARA: Yes, you did tell me Eunice is a greyhound. As I pick up Eunice, I pick her up as being a bit shy, and you said she ran on the track. I feel like she's pretty aggressive when it comes to running, but she's timid when it comes to strangers. She's wary of people. Is that a little bit as Eunice is?

BARB: Yes, she very much is.

BARBARA: Okay, good.

BARB: She's very timid. She's very gentle. She prefers to be out of the way of noises.

BARBARA: Right. I feel that part of her timidity has to do with sensitivity, and very much to sound. She has very good hearing and is sensitive to loud noises. They startle her. You e-mailed me that she had an injury a couple of years ago, and it had to do with her shoulder, and right now she's in a lot of pain.

BARB: Right.

TIM: It comes and goes.

BARBARA: And you indicated, more in the evening.

BARB: We are around at night and we can hear her and comfort her.

BARBARA: Okay. Well—as I'm starting to go through the body, I'm feeling the neck and the vertebrae on the neck feels stiff. I feel she doesn't have as much range of motion as she used to. Feels a little stiff down across the shoulders as well. Feels like a bit of arthritis in her spine and in her neck. Do you notice that she doesn't have as much range of motion with her neck?

TIM: She doesn't. We've been going through chiropractic with her. She doesn't have as much range of motion as she used to have.

BARBARA: Okay. Okay. I feel it's arthritis. She's only seven. It can be her own chemistry. You know—sometimes we do get things just based on our own chemistry. One being the arthritis that sets in.

BARB: Can you sense whether it's an injury, or whether her parents had something to do with it?

BARBARA: I was just trying to go there to see if it had to do with just her particular chemistry, or if it had to do with injury. I'm feeling like she's taken a few tumbles in her racing experience, and it's compromised the vertebrae. When they get out of balance and they function wrong, then arthritis gets in there.

BARB: Do you feel that it's the base of her neck, or the vertebrae farther down?

BARBARA: About an inch down from the head to the shoulders, and then down over the back about half way. In that particular area I feel that it's pretty stiff.

TIM: And is that stiffness leading to pain? Do you get a sense of any real pain? Because there are times when she cries.

BARBARA: Yes. I'm trying to see if there are any nerves that are set in here that are compromising this as well. You know—like you get little twinges, and things like that. I'm feeling that cold would affect her.

TIM: As far as even being outside in the cold?

BARBARA: Well, being outside in the cold, or just the temperature changing to cooler—it would have a tendency to affect her. What I'm feeling that would work real well for her is something with a deep penetrating heat.

TIM: Okay.

BARBARA: They've got things like Tiger Balm that penetrate in to the tissues. And if you do use that, wrap her to draw the heat down in. Don't let her out while it's still working, so she doesn't get a cold where it's heated up.

TIM: Right.

BARBARA: I feel that would help. Still trying to tune in to why she's crying at night.

TIM: Early in the morning, like five o'clock, is when it seems to bother her.

BARBARA: As you say that, I'm feeling that it's when she starts to move at the beginning of her day. Is that about when it starts?

BARB: It could be, but yesterday, she was crying in the afternoon.

TIM: Yes. She was in such pain. She's not very active. She pretty much lies around a lot.

BARBARA: That's because it's not comfortable for her to be real active, and I feel that what's going on here—I'm feeling that when she starts to move, after not moving for a while, her joints are hurting her.

TIM: Okay.

BARBARA: So if she's been quiet for a while and then she moves, I feel that she's pretty stiff. She gets pretty stiff, so she stays still—because it's more comfortable to be still. But when she starts to move, there's a lot of stiffness in the joints.

BARB: All over, or just the joints like down the neck?

BARBARA: No, I feel more in other joints as well. I feel in the knees—I don't know if you call them knees—let me see, the front legs where it bends at the wrist, you might say. I feel that's a bit stiff as well. I don't know why I'm not going to the shoulder, so that's interesting. I'm going into, and I'm hitting all these other areas. The bones where they have motion.

TIM: Can you tell if anything we're doing for her helps her at all? As far as drugs or traditional medicine, acupuncture, chiropractic?

BARBARA: What I get is that if there's an ultrasound treatment—you know, where they go in there and they take the stress off tight muscles and bring them down—that type of thing would work very well for her. I'm not feeling that the acupuncture is helping the arthritis. Chiropractic would help balance the body, because this is an out of balance condition.

TIM: Okay.

BARBARA: I feel like it's pretty advanced for her age, and I don't know why that is.

TIM: Well, I think Barb mentioned she did have an injury about a year and a half ago.

BARBARA: Yes. I think that's part of it, but I think part of it's her chemistry. B-6 is something that I would highly recommend. It won't work in thirty seconds. It will take about three or four days before it starts to build up enough in the system, and it will help the pain and discomfort in the joints. I would take the path of researching the alternatives for arthritis. I don't know what they are, but I'm feeling—are her joints swollen? Have you noticed the front pastern?

BARB: Well, we notice that sometimes her whole body—the skin gets red, on the whole body. I wouldn't say I know what a swollen joint looks like, and we don't see that.

BARBARA: Okay. Well it would just look like a larger joint, that's all.

TIM: Yes. You know, she had some injuries in her legs from running. She's had a couple of breaks down in her legs that were not in her upper body. There's one joint that was broken bad, that looks bigger than the rest. She's a typical greyhound, where her feet are pretty big.

BARBARA: Okay.

BARB: We haven't seen her limping, either.

TIM: Right.

BARBARA: Okay. Okay. Is the leg that was broken—was that the front leg?

TIM: No. She has a couple of toes broken on her front leg. I've been told that it's pretty typical for greyhounds to have breaks.

BARBARA: Yes. They can. I've had whippets for about thirty years, and they're a little bit smaller, but I understand these things. They can break and jam toes. They can mend.

TIM: But you're not getting anything in the shoulder area?

BARBARA: It's funny—I'm not. I'm not getting anything at this particular point. I'm not being directed there as much as I'm being directed to these different joints, and I'm being told that it's heat, a lot of heat, almost as if she wore leggings to keep her legs warm.

BARB: She feels heat to the point of being painful?

TIM: No—that heat would help her.

BARBARA: Heat would help her to keep warm, to keep heat in to help the arthritis. I feel like that's what would be really good for her at this point.

BARB: Do you feel this heat would help, that this pain is so unbearable for her?

BARBARA: I'm not feeling unbearable pain, but I'm feeling discomfort. I'm feeling that when she starts to move, it starts to feel really stiff and aching. And when she starts to move after not moving for a while, whether it's midday or morning, this is a real problem for her. At this time you've done a lot of alternative medicines, so it sounds like you could go out and search the Internet or your resources of books, pick up things that would work for arthritis. That's what I feel it is. You had mentioned that the vet said it was the scar tissue on the shoulder.

BARB: Yes, I see scar tissue there, but I couldn't understand why this happened now, instead of a few years later.

BARBARA: For some reason I'm not being directed to that shoulder. I'm being directed to all the joints.

BARB: Mostly in her legs?

BARBARA: Yes. I'm getting a lot of it in her front legs, actually.

TIM: Okay, and what about her neck? Do you feel anything coming from her neck?

BARBARA: Well, I feel like it's pretty stiff. I feel like it's arthritis in there, and it's calcified. There's calcification in there. Can you hear her neck move? When it moves can you hear it kind of crack or something?

TIM: No. She's been going through chiropractic work, so she's much more flexible in her neck than she had been, and she's getting better. She was very tight at one point. Now—you're saying joints in the legs, and you were saying the wrists. Are you getting nothing from the upper joints in the front legs?

BARBARA: No, I'm not. I'm getting more pastern joint in there. I'm feeling that if she had little socks or something she could put on, they would be helpful to keep heat in. I'm feeling like it's arthritis. I really am, and I think the neck stiffening up is because it was uncomfortable, so she didn't move a lot.

TIM: Is she happy with us?

BARBARA: She's very happy with you. I feel like she's very loving. She loves where she's living. She likes her surroundings. She loves the nurturing that she gets and the attention she gets. Something that she'd longed for and didn't have for a long time, and now she has it. She's really basking in the nurturing that you're providing for her, and the devotion that you've given to her.

TIM: When we walk is she in pain, can you tell?

BARBARA: I feel like when she starts off it's uncomfortable. You know, as you start off with stiff joints and you move them, they're sore. I don't know if you've ever had that. I had it. And I did a quest for a whole year to see what I could do, and vitamin B-6 was the answer, I happened upon a chiropractor who is a good friend, and she said vitamin B-6. And I started to take it and the pain was gone.

TIM: Wow. Because when she walks with us when we go for a walk, and the chiropractor has recommended exercise, she goes very slowly.

BARBARA: Yes—because it's not comfortable for her to move.

BARB: But she needs it.

BARBARA: Of course. It's healthy for her to move, but it's not comfortable. There is that glucosamine—

BARB: Yes, I know what you're talking about.

TIM: We have that.

BARBARA: Do you have that?

TIM: Yes.

BARBARA: I haven't experienced it personally. I always do these alternatives on myself, and then I know if they work or don't work.

BARB: The vet gave her a shot of Atequine today. I guess they use it for horses, for arthritis, and she got it today, and now they're giving her medicine and she seems to be doing much better.

BARBARA: Oh, good.

TIM: We were giving her that glucoflex, or whatever, and she was also on Chinese herbs. But she started to get very bad diarrhea so we stopped all supplements. And we haven't started back on them.

BARBARA: Chinese herbs can be pretty potent after they build up in the system.

TIM: She was getting Chinese herbs for trauma and whiplash.

BARBARA: What's really good for trauma would be the flower essences.

BARB: Back Rescue, or Healing Herbs Five Flowers?

BARBARA: And Rescue Remedy, absolutely. Just put about six drops in about half a cup of spring water and mist her. Mist the aura. Mist the whole body. Wait five, ten minutes, and then mist her again. Five or ten minutes about three times.

TIM: She'll be wondering what's going on. We'll be running after her through the house.

BARBARA: It even works great on people, too.

TIM: I had to take a urine sample for her today and I had a plate underneath her and she almost had a heart attack. She was looking at me like, "What are you doing?"

BARBARA: How funny.

TIM: Oh yes. But she's very loving and very gentle.

BARBARA: Oh yes. She's a wonderful soul. She really is. B-6 won't hurt anything. It is water-soluble so that's not a problem.

TIM: So you're not seeing anything from the shoulder or the scar tissue?

BARBARA: No, I'm really not. I'm not being directed there at all. And that would have been what I thought from your e-mail. But I'm not getting that's a big deal. If there is anything, it's minor compared to the arthritis. Find out about the side effect of the arthritic medicines. As much as they do work really well, they might have their down sides.

TIM: Right.

BARBARA: So do check to see. It does make them comfortable. Sometimes it's not an option. When you get big dogs with hip dysplasia, it's maybe easier to do an injection to make them comfortable.

TIM: Do you feel with the neck, and the arthritis in the neck, that surgery would help it all?

BARBARA: No. I do not feel that. I feel like it's calcification between the joints that's built up.

TIM: So it's just basically pain management for her?

BARBARA: Yes that's what I feel, and to maybe find a supplement that would work.

TIM: The only thing that seemed to be working for a while was Prednisone and traditional medication, but we're trying to take her off that because of the downsides of taking steroids.

BARBARA: Oh yes.

TIM: They can cause heart problems.

BARBARA: Oh yes, there maybe be some downsides.

BARB: Maybe the Atequine will help. That is specifically for arthritis.

BARBARA: And again, find out what the downsides are. You know, sometimes the downsides don't make that much difference—it's the comfort of the animal. If you can't find any other alternatives. It feels like it's advanced. Heat works good. Penetrating heat of some kind. Something like *Tiger Balm* on the neck and spine—you could put a coat on her, and that heat would go right into the joints and help her. Especially in the wintertime, as I feel it's going to be harder for her when it gets cold.

TIM: Maybe we have to live Arizona. Yes, we'll just move because of our dogs.

BARBARA: There you go.

TIM: Not too humid.

BARBARA: Wouldn't be too bad.

TIM: That's when everybody would think we were nuts, because we move because of our dogs.

BARBARA: Well, we do a lot of things for our animals, because they bring us so much joy and pleasure and they balance out our lives. They do a lot of emotional and mental-physical healing. Sometimes they take on our ailments and they can't seem to get rid of them, but they do it with love.

TIM: I'm surprised my dachshund didn't get in there some way. He's kind of overbearing in the house.

BARBARA: You have a dachshund, and he's overbearing?

TIM: Yes.

BARB: A Napoleonic counselor.

BARBARA: Yes. He's actually quite bossy isn't he?

TIM: Yes. Very bossy.

BARBARA: Yes. He's got an attitude problem.

BARB: Don't all dachshunds?

BARBARA: I don't know. I've not been that close to them. But this particular guy rules the roost. He's kind of the king of the mountain, isn't he?

BARB: We call him the mayor.

BARBARA: What's his name?

BARB: Mason.

BARBARA: Mason, of course.

TIM: Every once in a while, a greyhound will go by and nip in the air above him, just to let him know that it wouldn't take much.

BARBARA: But he just holds his ground. He directs traffic. Yes. He's a fun animal. This little guy that feels he must weigh about three hundred pounds and he pushes that kind of weight around, doesn't he?

TIM: He has no idea that he's small.

BARBARA: Well, he's been a lot bigger in other lifetimes and so this was to gear him down a bit. But it hasn't worked yet.

TIM: That's 'cause we're softies.

BARBARA: He has a strong opinion about how he wants things done, how he wants the house run.

BARB: And which bed he wants to sleep in.

TIM: Yes, which is usually our bed!

BARBARA: Oh yes. Of course. In the middle between the two of you, no doubt. "I get the best spot. I'm king. Nobody can push me out." He's wonderful.

TIM: Yes. He's a great dog. He's a lot of fun. He's a challenge but a lot of fun.

BARBARA: Yes. Well, you have to get up pretty early to beat him.

TIM: Exactly. So what we'll do is, we'll try the B-6.

BARBARA: Yes. I would do the B-6 and go on a quest of alternative medicines for arthritis. Get a few books. Try Adelle Davis. *Let's Get Well* is my bible, actually. But you could probably just go to a library and look at it. Check some references and look for alternative things. They have some things that have to do with diet that might be helpful. It's not going to make the arthritis go away. What it's going to do is make her more comfortable, which is what you're looking for.

BARB: Right. Well, I have your e-mail address. We'll let you know how she's doing.

BARBARA: That would be great. I love to have feedback.

BARB: You have a gift, that's for sure.

BARBARA: Thank you.

* * *

Sometimes minor medical situations are causing what seems like an attitude or behavior problem. In this reading it took quite a while to zone in on the minor detail that made a big difference:

ANA: Sammy is the name of the animal. And my question is, "Is he happy?"

BARBARA: He is content. That's maybe a better word for the energy that I am feeling.

ANA: Right, right. Is there nothing that he is unhappy about? He is sort of hanging out.

BARBARA: He is. And that is who he is, actually. He is a kind of guy that just goes along with the program. I get an energy that is willing to do whatever you ask. He doesn't say, "No I don't think I'll do that, today!" But he will just respond, because he is that steady kind of guy.

ANA: That sounds like him!

BARBARA: Okay, good!

ANA: Certainly he is easygoing.

BARBARA: Kind of a nice horse to have.

ANA: I have been having some problems with his feet. With him picking them up. When you pick them up he likes to jerks them away again.

BARBARA: When you go to clean his feet?

ANA: Yes, or when the farrier goes to trim them.

BARBARA: The message I get is, that he has a foot fetish. And how that interprets to me is that there are those animals that have feet and fingernails that are like hands. And they are real touchy about who touches them. And they don't want them messed with. Because they are concerned that they will they not be handled appropriately, and it would be uncomfortable for them. Some people have beautiful fingernails. And they spend their whole life picking up things a certain way. Well, that's what I'm getting as an interpretation for a foot fetish. He is very particular about his feet.

ANA: Right.

BARBARA: He doesn't particularly like people handling his feet. I know that with horses you should clean their hooves often, maybe every time you ride them. Or when they are removed from their stall. But, he just has this—concern for how his feet are. He feels—he has a knowingness—that they are very important to him. And if something is not right it could be a problem for him. That is the energy that I am getting. So when someone messes with them, he is concerned. As layed back as he is, that is a big concern of his. I am not getting where it comes from. Sometimes we have a tendency to say, "Give me your foot," and not talk to them about what we are doing. And so maybe you might try by saying, "I need your foot. I am going to clean it out. I will be very careful as not to hurt you in any way. But this is important so you feet stay pretty and nice." Or, however you would like to communicate. I know it sounds very strange—

ANA: I talk to him all the time. It is not strange to me.

BARBARA: Sometimes we do things because we know in our head what needs to be done. But the animal is not sure. It's like when you are a child, a doctor comes at you with the shot. You don't know what he is going to do, if it is going to hurt, where he is going to poke it. The doctor knows that he needs to give it to you. Rather then saying, "This is what I am going to do. Yes it will hurt." Or, "No, it won't hurt." And, "This is why it is happening—" So you aren't taken by surprise. I guess that is what I want to say. The farrier needs to do it the same way. I know they are understanding and very loving, because that is what they have to be to work with animals. It will never be easy for him to do, as the horse has a big concern about his feet. That is who he is

ANA: He is a bit of a fuss-budget!

BARBARA: He is. Not to go off the subject of your horse, but I have a dog who will not let me touch his feet because he grooms his own feet, as the wolves do. He chews on the nails and keeps them groomed beautifully. And he does not want anybody touching his feet. So I do not challenge that because everything is fine as it is. With your horse, I am feeling a similar foot thing.

ANA: He gets spookie. But, it sort comes and goes. Is he really afraid, or is it sort of a resistance?

BARBARA: Actually what I get is, he is catching a shadow

in his eyes. He thinks he sees something, a shadow that crosses his eyes in some way. I am getting that what is spooking him is the way the light or the shadow or the sun or something hits his eye. And it flashes there and he doesn't know what it is, and so he becomes startled by the not knowing. What I am feeling is, that if he were out in the wild and something would catch his eye, and he did not know what it was, he would turn and run. Out of harm's way. What I am getting—it is the light that hits on his eye, or the way the light refracts in his eye. Hits him as perhaps too bright. But, what I feel is darkness that comes across. Like the side of his eye. He sees this dark spot and it frightens him for a minute. "I can't see what that is. What is that over there?" And he gets a little tense. Does he tense up a little bit? Do his muscles get a little tense?

ANA: He tenses up and he will scoot, he sort of jumps to the side.

BARBARA: I am feeling like when he scoots, he is actually trying to get another view of what it was that he thought he saw. He wants to come at it head on. To face it!

ANA: Yes, he will turn around to face it. He will run away, then face it.

BARBARA: So it is not going to surprise him. In his maleness, he will stand and face it.

ANA: Right!

BARBARA: It is kind of interesting how they will do that. It seems whether they are gelded or a stallion, they still have that maleness in them that for a moment, "I will not run. I will face this to see if it really is a threat. And if I need to deal with this, then I will make my choice."

ANA: Right.

BARBARA: You might want to see how the light hits his eyes. Or if he is facing into the sun. It could be that the tree limbs or leaves may wave and strike him funny. That type of thing.

ANA: It is real to him.

BARBARA: Yes it is real to him.

ANA: That is all that counts.

BARBARA: I don't feel like he will buck or anything. Or rear. He is just turning to face it.

ANA: Yes. Is he getting confused when I am riding him, when I am working him? Does he understand what I am trying to get him to do?

BARBARA: What I am getting is, not always, but sometimes, he gets confused as to what you want him to do.

ANA: Right!

BARBARA: The message I get is, he requires a little bit more lead in. Whatever that means. I don't know if it is that you give the command a while before you actually want him to do it. I am not sure how that works. But, he needs—because he is a little laid back and more relaxed and maybe a little lethargic at times. He tends to think more relaxed rather then, snap, snap, snap. So sometimes it takes him a little bit longer to react.

ANA: Actually, he is only three years old, and I have only been on him for a month. I am just trying to get across some of the basics to him. "Go! Turn!"

BARBARA: And that's maybe what the message was, for "more lead in." Because I didn't know how long you have been riding him or anything. So he needs a little more—actually what I am getting is he needs more ground work. If you could walk him through what you are asking him to do. And then get on him and ride him. And tell him what you want him to do. Then he would understand it better. Interesting.

ANA: I have done a lot of that with him. I haven't done it for a couple of months. I have been focusing on just getting on him. It is only the last month that I have been doing anything more than just sit on him.

BARBARA: Okay.

ANA: He may need a refresher!

BARBARA: Yes. What I am getting is, if you walk him. Spend

a little time. Put the saddle on him, and walk him through the words. And then get on and give him the words again. Not a lot of commands all at once. But, a few exercises is the message that I am getting here. He will do very well if he understands what you want him to do, such as Go and Stop. Then get on him and do those two modalities. So that he feels comfortable and clear as to what you want. Then move on to a couple more.

ANA: Right.

BARBARA: I do not know about training horses.

ANA: Is there any way that you can get across to him to move away from my leg? I can't figure out a way to get him to understand it.

BARBARA: To move away from your leg?

ANA: If I squeeze with my leg, he just he moves away from it instead of pushing into it.

BARBARA: Oh, he is going in the direction that your leg is squeezing!

ANA: That's right!

BARBARA: If you do two things at the same time squeeze your legs and move the reins. Then say, "That's it! That's what I want. Good." Something like that.

ANA: Yes.

BARBARA: Have you tried that?

ANA: Yes I have. He has one spot in the arena that he insists on moving away from. And it is only the one direction. He goes against my leg, and will not come off it. I know he is a baby!

BARBARA: How about on the ground exercises? If you could press on that side and turn him the other way? Interesting! What I am hearing, is to use what they use for dogs. That thing they throw in the water, like dumbbells. Something that has weight! Something that you could put down there that would be like your leg, but not your leg. And maybe there would be two people. And one would press on this so that he would feel it, as if it were a leg. And the other one would direct him in the directions that it goes. So that he would understand he isn't to lean against it. Actually, so he does this leaning in a loving way. Interesting! It is almost like a loving thing. But he needs to go through it with you on the ground, guiding him.

ANA: Where he already understands.

BARBARA: Use something round, that would be like a leg. Someone could press on that side. Walk along. Get him used to that. And then press on that side and give the command. "Turn right!" And maybe you should say the word out loud for a while. So when you get on you, could press and say turn right. What he is doing is leaning into your leg because he loves you.

ANA: Oh, that is nice to know.

BARBARA: It is kind of a loving, "Hey, I like you!" Kind of a nuzzling.

ANA: He is my baby. I knew he was mine when I looked at him. Are his legs uncomfortable?

BARBARA: What I am hearing—it is something about the shape of the way the hoof is shaped. I am not sure if it is too high or too long. It is a little bit at the wrong angle.

ANA: We do change the angle of their feet.

BARBARA: I feel like it is high and straight. It forces him to walk a certain way. Again, I don't feel discomfort, but I do feel it. Is he picking up his feet like in the front, almost like a knuckling over gait?

ANA: He has a lot of action. Yes.

BARBARA: I feel as if the hoof is causing him to lean forward. When he picks up his feet it is like picking up a heavy shoe. Like it is heavy at the end. If that makes any sense to you. That is what I am getting. I don't know if it is too much hoof. In the dog world it would be called knuckling over. Does he have any bend to his pastern?

ANA: Actually, he is built very upright. He has quite a lot

of slope in his pastern. He has a new farrier doing his feet. And he had a very bad farrier before that. Which is probably the cause of the problem! Well, that is something we can correct! Thank you for your help.

BARBARA: You are very welcome.

* * *

It is my feeling that when owners know what the behavior is, or have a better understand of the problem, they can cope and work towards positive results.

4: Animal Attitudes And Behavior

SOME ANIMALS HAVE PROBLEM SITUATIONS that are hard to define. The owner is not sure what is at the root of the situation, or even if it is a problem that can be solved. This is the letter from a horse owner about such a situation:

Dear Barbara,

Here's a picture of the horse I told you about. He is Monty, a five-year-old quarterhorse gelding I've owned since November 1997. Enclosed is a picture of Monty with my daughter, as well as a lock of his hair.

There seems to be a lot of negative energy coming from this horse but to my knowledge he has no health problems. Sometimes he seems to be sulking. I wonder whether he's been abused, but he's only had one other owner besides me. My paint filly, Margo, doesn't like him very much because she senses the negative vibes. My other horse, Burt, has tried to play with him, but Monty doesn't want to buddy up with him either. Hopefully, we can figure out why Monty is such an "unhappy camper."

Karen

* * *

The reading did not disclose any magic bullet to change things, but did give the owner some guidance about what might improve things gradually.

BARBARA: I know you said that he was a puzzle in your little note, but I get that he is a grump. There isn't much that is going to please him. He is going to be unhappy with everything that you do.

KAREN: Okay. Does he like my paint filly, Margo?

BARBARA: It is not a big deal for him. We are not into a buddy system here.

KAREN: Ask him if he likes the baby, Burt.

BARBARA: He likes Burt more! He didn't seem to like him at all. Now it seems he is starting to warm up. Burt doesn't demand a whole lot. Burt is self-sufficient and that is what Monty likes. He doesn't want to be molly-coddled. He is kind of a guy that says, "Just leave me alone." He is not happy. Does he walk around a lot with his head hanging down?

KAREN: Yes, I don't understand it. Sometimes he will come in, I'll go to feed him, and sometimes he will stand there with his butt towards me. To me it not normal horse behavior. It is time to eat, he comes in to eat. He turns around and faces south with his butt towards me. What is that saying? You don't want to eat—you don't want to deal with me? What is going on?

BARBARA: He has a problem dealing with things. He is not being difficult, he just doesn't want to get involved. If you can think of the grouch of the month, that is the type of energy I am picking up. He is just not happy, and the more you try to make him happy the less he is. The more you work at it the less he gets happy.

KAREN: Ask him if anything hurts.

BARBARA: I don't feel anything, as I go through the body, I don't get anything in the upper body, legs, feet, neck, head.

KAREN: Ask him if the previous owner was mean to him or if there was some abuse.

BARBARA: There was something that they did that he didn't like! But, I don't get abuse.

KAREN: Ask him why he is so afraid of the electric clippers. He is terrified of them.

BARBARA: What I get, the message from him is, he was acting up one day and the clippers were in someone's hand and they got upset, and just threw them at him. And he takes it as something that could come at him and hurt him. My feel is that they just lost their temper, they were not abusive people, they were nice people. Just short tempered.

KAREN: He is the kind of horse, I hate to say it, that makes you lose your temper. You try to get along. He has spells where he just does not want to cooperate. I can see how anybody, myself included, could loose their temper. You say "Push" and Monty will say, "Pull."

BARBARA: Yes, exactly. There seems to be a contrary thing there, just for the sake of being contrary. He is contrary! That is who he is.

KAREN: Ask him if he accepts me as the herd leader.

BARBARA: Yes he does, but he doesn't like it.

KAREN: Reluctantly. First, he would not play along at all. But now it is like, "Yeah, okay."

BARBARA: Actually, that is a good way to go with him. To get him to do what you call bonding. Sort of on your terms. Where you do some exercise where you chase them away and make them come back to you. That would work better for him because he needs to do it on his terms. And when you say, "Okay, come here. We are going to put the bridle and bit on, we are going for a ride," it is like he is saying, "Do I have to?" He just doesn't want to be bothered.

KAREN: But most horses do that to a degree. There are some rare occasions that horses really enjoy a trail ride, but most horses don't want to work. Once they get into it, they kind of come around.

BARBARA: Sometimes they do like it, though. They look forward to a change of routine, like going out on the trail. Especially because it is relaxing. "Okay, this is a relaxed trail ride; lets have fun."

KAREN: And he doesn't do too badly with that. Where I am having problems is in a group situation, where he stops listening to me at all. It is like he is so focused on what all the other horses are doing, that I am not there. It is like it becomes a free-for-all. He gets very headstrong, and he wants to buck, and he wants to rear, sometimes. It is just a little half-rear thing. But annoying. I can see how people can loose their tempers, because he very bull-headed.

BARBARA: If you wanted to say an attitude that he has, he is a martyr.

KAREN: It is not because anyone has done anything to him?

BARBARA: Not really, no. It is just kind of his personality. He doesn't choose to be happy about anything.

KAREN: If there is no silver bullet that would make him happy, can we get along?

BARBARA: I feel you should work with this technique of joining up. Once you do that, he is going to feel a little more connected with you and a bit more willing to work. Because he is going to feel like he chose to join up. So it is his choice that he is going to work with you, not your choice you are going to work with him. And when it gets turned that way, I think he is going to be happier about working. He needs to come to those terms, that you are the leader. If he wants to. He doesn't require a lot of love either. He is not a lovey horse.

KAREN: No he is not! He has this cute little innocent face, everybody says he is so cute. But there is this deviousness thing behind this cute face, that always seems to be there—sort of an undercurrent. Here is this cute little face, what a sweet horse, but not that lovey.

BARBARA: I feel as if once you get him to join up, that he feels he is part of the group, rather than that he is being drug off to do something. Being part of something, he will respond better. He will become easier for you to work. I don't think he is going to be simple at any time. Do you know what I mean? Some are just easy. I think that his is going to probably help you incorporate new techniques for working with horses.

KAREN: I had a couple of them already. I don't need another one. I had an appaloosa filly that taught me some new tricks. She and I were bucking heads. "Okay, you are going to do this." "No I'm not!"

BARBARA: Sometimes it is interesting how the animals that come into our lives actually create a path for us.

KAREN: Obviously you learn something.

BARBARA: I think that is part of who you are. That you enjoy challenge, because you pick up a horse that is a bit challenging. And you enjoy trying out new techniques to see how well they work. You can tell your friends that this is really good, and how it worked for you. I really feel that is the type of person who you are. You don't get the easy ones.

KAREN: I don't seem to have gotten too many easy ones lately.

BARBARA: I feel that for you it would be a bit boring—just to go out there and the horse would do everything you said. For you, you would say, "So now what?" So this guy came along and he says, "I am not going to join up, I'll do as I please. Leave me alone. Grump, grump." It might look like a black cloud over him, as you had mentioned in your note. But, the black energy that I feel is just martyr. He is just feeling sorry for himself.

KAREN: Is there any reason why? Did something happen? Some trauma of some sort?

BARBARA: All I can get is, I am looking down trying to look at this linearly. As a colt he was with other horses that when he went up to them, they said, "Don't bother me." And so it became something like, don't pay attention to him. And they became antisocial to him. And he started to sulk.

KAREN: He does tend to sulk. There is no doubt about it.

BARBARA: And that is because, at the beginning he felt like he was rejected. He really did want to be part of it then.

KAREN: I do not know how much you know about horse and herd behavior, but juveniles are always treated like that. They act like—you are not even worth us picking on you, because you are not even considered to be even a full social member until you are a certain age. They ignore the babies. That is somewhat normal. At least when they are real small. Kind of—the older horses do kind of ignore them.

BARBARA: And he took it personally. He took it straight

to heart. So they just go off and they run and play and have a good time and chew and munch. Whatever they do is no big deal. Well, to him it was a big deal. He is a little bit more sensitive.

KAREN: He doesn't come across that way. Maybe he is covering it up.

BARBARA: No—because he is now being reclusive. Because he was sensitive. He is sensitive still. It doesn't go away.

KAREN: If I try to put him on a trailer he—even though he doesn't act all that friendly towards my other two horses—he acts like he doesn't care. But if I am leaving, then he will whinny, "I don't want you to leave." When I take him out into a group, he pays attention to the other horses, he gets into that herd thing and is not paying attention to me.

BARBARA: He is now picking up on the different energies. He is trying to interplay with these energies. I think it would be helpful if there is someway you could have more animals around him, and just walk him by them. Not actually having to perform, but getting more used to a lot of different things going on, so it now becomes secondary rather than primary. I feel like he hasn't had a lot of large groups of horses around him, so when he gets into one it is distracting.

KAREN: He was raised on a big farm but I don't know what his situation was there. I don't know if they kept him in a stall.

BARBARA: I don't feel that he was confined in any way. I feel that he was out in the open, but left off by himself and that hurt his feelings. He just got rejected by some of the others and he went into a shell. That is what I feel. As people, when you are outgoing and then you are totally rejected, you stop trying. And so you go into your own world. He has not gone totally into his own world, but kind of holds back. Not too much makes him happy. Then when he gets out with the group, he tries to pick up all the different energies and play with them, to interact with them in certain ways. His memory goes, "Oh—when they do that, I am suppose to do this," so he is busy doing that and ignoring you, distracted knowing that there are other animals around him. He is always going to have that when he gets into group activities, but he needs to pay attention to you. That's why I thought that getting used to walking through a lot of different horses now and again would help. So the distraction would become secondary, and what you say becomes primary. He needs slower integration, because of what he felt from the rejection. And so I think that when you do this, joining up—and when he starts he is willing to do the joining up with you—that he will become more responsive to you, and have more of a bond. Not a tight bond, you know what I mean, but he will be listening to you as you go through your activities. Right now he gets too busy with all the other energies going, and the interaction.

KAREN: What do you get about my filly?

BARBARA: I get that she is kind of lighthearted, kind of a fun little horse. Lots of energy, energetic. She thinks he is a grump and she does not want to be bothered with grumps. And he doesn't want to play, and she would like to play and she has given up trying to make him play. She just got the message from him, "Just leave me alone, go away, just leave me alone, do what you want, I won't bother you, but just leave me alone. I just want to be off on my own." I feel like she has allowed him to do that, just given him his space.

KAREN: She would try to get him to play—grab his halter try to get him to do things. He would not be mean about it. But he would not respond.

BARBARA: I don't get meanness in him. I really don't get Monty as being mean.

KAREN: Burt can get him to play.

BARBARA: That is because Burt is youthful and he doesn't take no for an answer.

KAREN: Correct. He will keep coming back. He will grab the halter and come back and grab it again.

BARBARA: Burt will just continue to do that.

KAREN: Do you think it will help get him out of the shell?

BARBARA: It might! It might help him. Because he needs someone to continue to interact with him. And as you work with him joining up, I think he will be a little more open to, "Maybe he does want to play with me, maybe that would be okay." He might open up a little bit here. I see the young one, he just wants to play, "I am not taking no for an answer. You are someone I can play with. Lets go!"

KAREN: He didn't seem to like him at first, now he seems to be warming up a little. He will tolerate it.

BARBARA: It takes a lot of coaxing and they might join up, as they would join up, to a little bonding. It will take a little while. It will help him to come out of it.

KAREN: I guess I'm hoping for a magic bullet, but I am not sure I am going to get one on this guy.

BARBARA: No, I don't see a magic bullet. There might be one, but he is not showing me any. But he is showing me that with time he can be happier. I see you working with him and he becomes lighter.

KAREN: You get out there, he is leaning on the bit, he is fighting, trying to rear. It is not just passive. Sometimes it is sort of passive-aggressive, but sometimes it is quite a bit more, like you can't control him at all. It is kind of frustrating. There is a point where I ask, "Is this going to be worth it? Am I going to get past this?"

BARBARA: I feel that you will, with the joining up. I feel that will be very helpful for you. I don't know if it is as far as you want to go. He might not get to where you want him to be. Because that is who he is. It will take him a while. It may take more time and energy than you want to spend and you could gain more spending with someone else. That might be your bottom line on it.

KAREN: Then it's just the wrong task. Maybe a different line of work might be better.

BARBARA: Yes.

KAREN: I am not sure what that might be. Something that he likes to do.

BARBARA: He would like the trail rides. I see him on trail rides.

KAREN: Yes, one-on-one he is not too bad. With one other horse he is not too bad.

BARBARA: Kind of a slow pace, kind of relaxed.

KAREN: I am wondering if another discipline, where he works by himself, would be better. Some kind of western thing where you are performing alone. Or some event where basically horse and rider are it. Of course, that involves a lot of communication between the horse and the rider. He can't be a grump. You have got to be clicking. You have to know that horse and the horse has to know you. And you are jumping and galloping across country, it is a one-on-one thing, and there are no distractions from other horses. It is just horse and rider. Would something like that be more suited to his personality?

BARBARA: What I get is, the more you work with him, the more you praise him, the more confidence he's going to have in what he is doing. "Oh, you are doing beautifully, I am so pleased with you." He needs more praise. It isn't that you don't do it, I am not saying that you are not doing it. But what I am saying is, he works better with a lot of positive reinforcement.

KAREN: He is the kind of horse that makes you lose your temper. I have the feeling that's what happened in his last place. I think that the lady sold him to a young girl, and he was too much horse for her. Because he can be a handful. And she couldn't handle him, and sent him back. You want to praise him, and every now and again you have these little moments where something works—but it is hard, because he is not willing to give you but so much.

BARBARA: If you can start off with a behavior that he does very well, and praise him to the hilt. "You are doing really good, I am so pleased with you, I like the way you are doing this!" Then give him a little new thing to do, but give it to him in pieces, not the whole thing. Maybe just the first bit, stepping over a log or turning to the left, or changing a gait, whatever. Then each time he does it, slip in something he knows. "Great! You are doing so good!" He needs more of that, to come out of this kind of funk that he is in.

KAREN: I can't even find a treat that he really likes. My filly, I show her an oatmeal cookie and she goes nuts. For him, he spits it out. You can't even find that little thing that is going to make him go, "Wow I'll do anything for that." It is like, "Yes. So what?"

BARBARA: Does he like the pressed alfalfa?

KAREN: The alfalfa cubes?

BARBARA: Yes.

KAREN: No, he doesn't like those. The chopped alfalfa, my other horses eat it like candy. He will hardly eat it.

BARBARA: Carrots?

KAREN: He will eat one. "It's okay. Nothing great." You would hope that there would be something that would just really turn him on. Like, "Oh, wow, I'll do something for that!"

BARBARA: Apples?

KAREN: They are okay.

BARBARA: Apples don't turn him on either?

KAREN: It is not like the cookie thing. I wave a cookie—like, "Flash, you want a cookie?" "Yes!"

BARBARA: I get kind of that he might like apples. The sweetness of the apple. Try and see. A sweet apple, not a tart apple.

KAREN: Not like granny smith.

BARBARA: I get that a sweet apple, he would like. He may not do fruit loops for it, but it might be a little bit more encouraging.

KAREN: He is jumpy about being touched. He really doesn't like it that much. That is why I wonder if he has been smacked. The people just got mad and said, "Stop it," and smacked him. He doesn't enjoy being touched. Most horses enjoy being brushed. He is just funny about being touched. You put a blanket on him, he kind of jumps.

BARBARA: I don't get that he has been abused, or really beaten in any way. I do get that he is sensitive. Except that you wouldn't guess it, because he seems to be so bull-headed.

KAREN: I get it about the touch. He does not like being touched. Did another horse beat him up?

BARBARA: I don't get that. I get that he doesn't like surprises. He needs to know that you are going, and what you are going to do on him. Tell him, "I am going to be doing this." He might not like it. But if he is praised a lot it will help. Tell him how wonderful he is, how well he is doing. More positive talking.

KAREN: He is a tough nut. He's a tough boy. In some way I just wanted to write it off. He is just young, but I feel that there is so much more going on. When they are young they will outgrow this. The attitude thing will change. It is more going on than just juvenile behavior.

BARBARA: It might be the challenge you want at this particular moment. That might be what happens for you. If you remember that he is sensitive, even though he is hiding it. That he needs a lot of positive reinforcement. The joining up will help. The young one that you have, Burt, will help to give him this joining up feeling. I think he will lighten up with that.

KAREN: He is not going to go out there and play and kick up his heels and run around!

BARBARA: I don't get that.

KAREN: I have had a number of horses that loved to play and I don't get that for Monty. I don't see him out there playing.

BARBARA: He said, "I did that once and it didn't work out."

KAREN: He is only five years old and like a grumpy old man.

BARBARA: Yes. That is what I get. And it is because he

doesn't know how to communicate and mingle. He doesn't know how to join back up. He doesn't know how to be part of something. He wants to be—yet not enough that he's going to try. He needs someone else trying for him, like yourself.

KAREN: Ask him about his teeth.

BARBARA: Are there sharp edges?

KAREN: Well, we had them done yesterday, and we actually pulled out a little wolf tooth, too. And I am sure they are probably sore now. I am hoping that might help. Whatever we did yesterday, if the bit was bothering him, I am hoping that might take care of it.

BARBARA: I really don't feel that the bit was bothering him.

KAREN: Again I am looking for a problem. I guess you have told me what I need to know even if it is not what I wanted to hear!

BARBARA: Well, let me know how it goes.

* * *

Here is a letter from an owner who believed that a new animal had a behavior problem that was causing another animal distress.

Hi Barbara,

We are having trouble with one of our four cats, Luke, not using his litter box. I took him to the vet to rule out medical problems and found that he does have a low-grade kidney infection and blocked bowel. The vet gave me medicine to give him, and for a few days, he was not using our throw rugs as his litter box, but this morning we discovered another wet rug. I have only caught Luke in the act once, and we wonder if one of our other cats (Casey, Polly, Annie) may have been the culprit also.

We are wondering whether the cats are trying to tell us that they are angry or worried about the dog we added to our family in January. This is the only thing we can think of that may be causing the cats stress.

The dog, Buddy, is a shelter dog of approximately forty pounds—a two-year-old shepherd-beagle cross. He does not hurt the cats, but he does bother them, chasing them in the house or yard or poking his nose at them. Luke and Casey will rear up and swat at Buddy, but Annie runs from him. Polly will sometimes swat him in the nose, or she may run away. All the cats are declawed in the front. Otherwise, Buddy would be pretty bloody by now.

Can you help us find out if it is the presence of the dog that is causing the cats' problem (perhaps Luke is not the only one marking). We would like to know, too, how Buddy is feeling.

We will be going on vacation in August, and we planned on putting Buddy in our vet's brand new kennel. The cats usually stay at home when we travel, but now with the cats messing the house, we feel that we will have to put them in the boarding kennel, too.

Luke and Polly are half-brother/sister and are now ten years old. We got them from friends who had a nearby farm. Casey is about seven. We found him in the train yard near where my husband works. Annie is about three. She was a shelter kitty. We adopted Annie about a year after my white cat, Harvey, died. Harvey was also a half-brother to Luke and Polly.

We've thought that we may have to return Buddy to the shelter if his very presence is what is causing the cats' behavioral problems. The cats were here first, and do deserve a safe, stress-free home. But if we could convince Buddy to stop bothering the cats, maybe everyone could live together in harmony. Please let us know if you think you can help.

Kathy

* * *

The reading showed a very different problem:

KATHY: Buddy is the dog that has been not exactly terrorizing, but I think causing a stressed atmosphere in the house. I want to know why he keeps chasing the cats.

BARBARA: I get Buddy as very active, wanting to play a lot, and he overplays. It's a game, and he doesn't know when to stop. I get him as energetic, creative, as an opportunist. He chooses many opportunities to play, to be creative. He's very creative, and I don't know if somewhere you told me what his breed was.

KATHY: He's a German shepherd, beagle cross. They told me at the shelter. He's certainly been creative with my garden lately. He's got favorite places that he's been digging.

BARBARA: Yes. If it's warm, they will do that. It's not uncommon that they are going to dig for cooler places to lie.

KATHY: So it's not that he's just being destructive.

BARBARA: No, it isn't. You told me German shepherd-beagle, but what I was feeling was a border collie or something like that. He might have a little bit of that in him because I really do get a dog that needs to be kept active, and if not active, will be active on his own. He's very creative in what he does. German shepherds are also very smart, but you can't typecast the breed. You need to pick up the personal energy of this particular animal, and as I pick up that personal energy, I pick up this creativity—as you mentioned, the digging in the yard. I don't know if it's as warm where you are as where I am.

KATHY: Yes. It's kind of hot today.

BARBARA: That's a nice way to cool off—into the soft, cool earth, and it's a natural thing for a lot of animals to do. In the wintertime, you won't find that at all. So he keeps chasing the cats. He needs things to do. He needs things to keep his mind busy.

KATHY: I know he enjoyed the dog training class that I took him to. He was just so alert and even when some of the pets in the class snarled, I always got the impression that he was happy.

BARBARA: That's exactly the impression I get. That he's happy. His happiness, his over-exuding happiness, into where it can almost be pushy, you know. Like, turn it off! It is great you've started with obedience, because he has to keep busy. He has so much energy to burn that if you don't direct the burning he will direct the burning. I don't feel like he's tormenting the cats, intending to be bad to them. He just wants them to interact with him and play. Cats usually have more dignity by saying, "Excuse me—I don't want to play." Maybe a young one might find it fun, but as they get older they get a bit more reserved, a bit more sedentary. And they just want to be quiet.

KATHY: Yes. It seems that every time he sticks his nose in, he wants to play. But they don't and then he crowds them, and they just back up and get into a corner and then they fight.

BARBARA: Right. 'Cause he's insisting, so he needs to burn some of that energy off. And your obedience class was really great for that. If you like to do agility, if you like to teach him things to do at home so that he can be doing something—and that's why I get this border collie because if you don't give them things to do, they're going to find things to do. And it can be destructive.

KATHY: Well, I've noticed sometimes around the house he'll herd them around. He'll follow them closely, and sometimes they turn. Oh, one of them just walked in, and she's the one that usually doesn't hang out with him. This is Annie. Little gray cat. She's a shelter kitty too. Same shelter. I don't know if they were there at the same time or not, but she's the one that seems so scared of everything. She hid most of yesterday, when we had company over.

BARBARA: She's very sensitive, and she picks up vibrations very well. Annie does, and so she stays away because of her sensitivity, she just kind of hides out and stays away from what goes on. She's not as brave as the others. It's best, if they can't handle all your company's vibrations, that they be off in their own area.

KATHY: Right. Yes. We don't insist she join the crowd.

BARBARA: Now she's feeling comfortable. She picked up the energy from our conversation.

KATHY: Yes. I'm sure she did.

BARBARA: Yes. And it feels safe. Sometimes they like to come in and bask in the energy. It's always an experience for them, and they do enjoy it.

KATHY: I know. When I would practice my Raike, I'd open my eyes, and they'd all be sitting around me looking at me, so they picked up on that, too.

BARBARA: Oh totally—especially the cats. Cats hang out between the third and fourth dimension. We people are in the third dimension. Cats hang out in a higher dimension between the two. And so, you know, if you do a meditation group, they'll come and they'll sometimes lie in the middle and just go to sleep because they're actually helping you. They provide help, to help you move into higher levels. They're great for emotional healing. That's their job, and they do enjoy it. They do perform it very well. But I don't believe that Buddy's a disruption to your household as much as that he just has a lot of creative energy. And you know herding, that could also be the border collie, herding sheep, keeping the group together where the group does not want to be that kind of together.

KATHY: Yes. Right.

BARBARA: So they'll protest. It isn't so bad—even though they fight, it's giving them exercise. It's having them move around. It's kind of healthy for animals to be active in some way, even if it is, "Back off buddy, you're annoying me."

KATHY: Right.

BARBARA: They're not vulnerable. He's not killing them. He's not ripping them apart. He's just annoying them, and when they're annoyed, they'll do that. Same with another dog. You know, if another dog wants to lie down and someone says I want to play, and they say back off, and they growl. It isn't because they are going to cut the other's throat out in that particular type of growl. It's their way of communicating.

And I don't feel like he's hurting your family in any way. I feel like he's actually helping. In his own way, he protects them. He watches over them. He loves them.

KATHY: I'm glad. Does he worry at all about his previous family?

BARBARA: I don't feel that at all.

KATHY: Oh good. I wouldn't want him to be pining for them.

BARBARA: No. You know, it's very interesting. Animals don't do things like that. It's not the norm where they would pine away.

KATHY: You hear about the dog dying on his master's grave or something.

BARBARA: Oh you mean like Grayshire's Bobby?

KATHY: Yes.

BARBARA: Yes. Well—that was a very devoted little animal, but the whole town took care of him, so he actually had a life that was a wonderful experience in a way. He had his freedom. He could come and go and he was cared for and he was part of a tradition. He became history. He became a legend, so he was more than just a dog even though it sounds as though, "Oh my God, what if that was me, and I had no home?"

KATHY: We put our feelings on them.

BARBARA: Exactly. And it's not the same at all.

KATHY: Was he abused in any way? Do you get any impression of that? Because I understand that they had dozens of animals where he came from.

BARBARA: He didn't learn that total people attachment, where he's absolutely needy. He's learned to be creative with the other animals, and to make his fun with animals. It's a new experience for him to have a one-on-one with people, like when you took him to obedience class. You're doing something with him. He's getting to experience things with you, with people. So with you, he's learning a lot more about people, and no, he's not pining away.

KATHY: Oh good.

BARBARA: And I don't feel any connection whatsoever to his old owners. He was just part of a group. What did they have, a large area or something, where they ran a lot of dogs? That's what I'm feeling.

KATHY: The shelter told us that they had many puppies, and I guess he was the last of a particular litter they were getting rid of. There were other dogs, other cats that remained at the home, and I don't know whether they had any livestock at all. But I drove by there recently, and it's an awful place and I'm so glad he's happy here because I'd hate to think of any animal over there. It's really an awful, dumpy place.

BARBARA: They kind of suspend themselves above all of that. You know—they just make the best of a situation.

KATHY: They live more in today than we do.

BARBARA: They really do. And so it wasn't an agenda with him, and it wasn't traumatic for him. There was nothing that happened that imprinted him in any terrible way.

KATHY: Can we move on to Luke, who is the one that has been messing up the house? We have put a door back up that we had taken down before, between the kitchen and the stairs to the basement. The cats have been down in the last two nights, we've put them all downstairs and closed the door. I hate to do it because I like having them up on the bed with us. They usually all sleep with us, but it was in the middle of the night, and in the morning, that Luke was caught going on the bathroom rug. And I'm wondering what's going on with that. Is he just totally stressed?

BARBARA: I'm getting an impression. I'm not sure what this is yet. Let me see what's going on with Luke. Luke's personality is someone independent. Let me see. He's pulled back, too. He's kind of—I have to dig deeper for him, to pick him up. He's not just like Buddy. He's not right there.

KATHY: Would it help to bring him in the room?

BARBARA: No. He might not be feeling real well, and he's

pulled back because of that. That's more of what I think I'm picking up here. When they pull that far back, there's a reason for it.

KATHY: Well, the vet found a minor kidney infection that we're treating him for, and his bowel was really blocked up, so we've, poor thing, had a laxative for that.

BARBARA: Is that recent?

KATHY: Yes. Just in the last week.

BARBARA: Okay. Maybe that's what I'm feeling. He's still not feeling well.

KATHY: Well, he was really passive at the vet, which is very different for him. He usually yells like a mountain lion, and they have to subdue him with two lab techs. They can't even handle it. But this time he laid still for x-rays.

BARBARA: Oh—okay. He's a real sick kitty. When they do that, they're real sick. And it can happen very quickly. It isn't something that you know. All of a sudden—it's happened to me, and I know my animals real well—and all of a sudden one day, it just hits and it shocks you. Sometimes you think you can see it coming, but they're so good at camouflage. But that's why he's pulled back. That's why I'm having to dig for his energy, because he's pulled back quite a ways. When I was reading your e-mail, I was wondering if you feed them a lot of fish.

KATHY: Most of the canned food that I feed them is fish.

BARBARA: Yes, because I would, just as a metaphysician, recommend that you pull away from fish, because I find with a lot of my clients that the people who are using a lot of fish create a lot of problems in the animal. It's too much for them. Now and again as a treat is really how fish should be given. And it creates a lot of physical problems. You always think that cats need fish, but the fish nowadays isn't as healthy as maybe it could have been before. It's processed and so on.

KATHY: Right.

BARBARA: I would recommend that until he's well, he not have any fish products whatsoever.

KATHY: Oh, okay. Good.

BARBARA: A different kibble as well—but because I feel there's some real health issues here, and I feel like the urinating on the carpet is not because he chose to do that in a belligerent fashion. It's an issue of health. Animals will, because they're used to being in the wild, all of a sudden they need to urinate or defecate. It's so pressing all of a sudden, they might just do it right there without going to the appropriate place. For us in a household, certainly that's not appropriate, but it isn't because he chose to do that purposely. It's a health issue for him right now.

KATHY: Okay. My mother was watching him yesterday. We had put the litter boxes up on a shelf to make it easier to clean. Not a tall shelf—only about six or eight inches above the floor. She said he was sitting there on the floor looking up, like he was thinking, "God, that's a long way to go." He finally did hop up. But he's been having trouble in the last year or so, jumping up on the counter. He tires and aborts the jump halfway, like he didn't get the right angle. Well, he's ten years old now and could be slowing down. And if you say he's really sick, then he's not feeling like doing much of anything.

BARBARA: No, he isn't, and just to jump up six inches might seem like nothing to you, and to a healthy cat it's no big deal, but to one who's not feeling well, it is a big deal. And so, if you can, I would put something back down to his level.

KATHY: Yes. I have already. I put two of the three litter boxes down.

BARBARA: He's just not well. I feel like the doctor who had pointed out kidneys and intestinal problems here, and when you're blocked it creates a toxic—it backs up, and then what happens is the intestines re-absorb the material which is already toxic, and puts more toxins back into the system. It can work the same for people.

KATHY: Almost like toxic shock.

BARBARA: Well, I'm not sure if it's toxic shock, but it actually puts the poisonous materials that we eliminate, back into our system. It draws the moisture out, which is toxic, and then reuses the mosture. I'm also feeling that he's not consuming a lot of liquids.

KATHY: I haven't noticed him changing. He still hops up on the bathroom sink to demand the faucet be opened, so he can drink from the faucet.

BARBARA: He likes fresh water.

KATHY: Yes.

BARBARA: He's not drinking appropriately. He's not getting enough of the appropriate fluids through his system, and changing the diet will help. He's quite compromised at this point. I feel that he's a lot sicker than you realize. They're pretty good at camouflaging. They don't voice how they feel, or what hurts.

KATHY: I know if they were out in the wild, a sick animal wouldn't want to be that noticeable to others, because they would probably kill it.

BARBARA: Exactly. That's exactly right. And birds are like that. A bird, all of a sudden, they're healthy one day, and they can be lying dead on the ground the next day—because they've been sick all along, but they're pretending they are well, because if they show any vulnerability they're done. Absolutely right. And it's the same with the other animals, and that's sometimes why you don't notice progressively that they're not feeling well, until something shows up. I'm not sure what he's got in the bowels here. It's almost like—I don't know—I'm feeling like little lumps in his intestines somewhere.

KATHY: Yes. They took x-rays. It showed the large intestine. It looked like it was blocked with marbles.

BARBARA: Okay.

KATHY: Very dry.

BARBARA: Those are the lumps I see. And what did they say it was?

KATHY: That he was just constipated. So I've got a laxative to give him, and an antibiotic for the infection. Neither of which he enjoys receiving.

BARBARA: Yes. I can well appreciate—you know—cats are tough to work with, 'cause they've got needle sharp teeth, so anything that's a liquid is helpful.

KATHY: Oh yes. I've made that point of getting their medicine in liquid form. They do not like pills.

BARBARA: That's interesting. Beause that's what I see—these little round things in the intestines.

KATHY: Oh. So they're still there, then? I thought maybe he had gotten rid of them by now. I'll continue giving him his laxative.

BARBARA: Yes. I'm not sure if there's something that's attached. It could be an illness, rather than an infection. They seem pretty solid. Actually, I feel like he got those round things first, and that's what caused the intestines to slow down and be blocked. It wasn't that they formed due to the block. I feel like it was actually in reverse. He got this, as they're telling me, and then because of this, it's like trying to eliminate through a maze. Do you see what I mean?

KATHY: Oh, like maybe polyps or something?

BARBARA: Yes. Something. And so, do whatever you can to keep his system moving. That will be very helpful in keeping the toxins down.

KATHY: They didn't tell me that at the vet's office. They were kind of treating it like, "Here's enough to get him free of it," and that they didn't expect it was going to continue. So I'll have to keep it up and then take him in and have them do another x-ray to see if it really cleared it up or not.

BARBARA: Yes. I'm feeling like the antibiotic is not the solution to the lumps.

KATHY: Well, when they showed me the x-ray, all the

interior organs were kind of displaced, because of the large bowel, so things were scrunched and off-balance. He's always had kind of a very sensitive waist area on his back, where if you hold him he flinches if you touch that area. We even took him to a chiropractor once, and he's the one who said he didn't think it was structural, he thought it was an infection in his kidney, and I took him to the vet and that was it. So, that's been an on and off condition for several years now. Maybe it's just finally got to such a point that it's really become serious.

BARBARA: Yes. And I feel that jumping up with all his organs in different places, nothing's really feeling comfortable inside, so he's always feeling a bit uncomfortable, a bit cantankerous.

KATHY: Yes. He jumps from the counter up to the top of an armoire in the kitchen—which has got to be about four feet—and he makes it. He's never missed.

BARBARA: He still does that?

KATHY: Yes. He did it today and yesterday.

BARBARA: How interesting. I don't get that it's comfortable for him.

KATHY: Maybe that's just a good place to go to get away from everything.

BARBARA: Yes. It might be. Is that his hiding out place?

KATHY: Yes. It has one of these old fashioned bowls that used to have pitchers in them in the old hotels, and he—

BARBARA: —lies in the bowl.

KATHY: Right. He loves that bowl.

BARBARA: That is interesting. And he's just not feeling well. I would definitely follow through with your veterinarian, and recommend that you do another x-ray to see. I'm feeling like it's something a lot—

KATHY: —more than just constipation.

BARBARA: Yes. Yes—something that's been coming on for the last few years. The organs don't get misplaced very easily.

KATHY: Can't take it very well.

BARBARA: Well, as things come back into shape and move, they can come back. That's okay, but it changes the energy of the organs, and so some don't get enough energy. Some get too much. Anyway, I would definitely follow through with that again. Make sure the kidneys are okay, because I don't see the antibiotic doing much for those lumps. I'm feeling like that's happening here, and those lumps have been progressing over time. It's interesting. It's always interesting as you see things, and then people go to the vets, or they've already been to the vets, and it kind of confirms what you see. Okay, is there another animal you want to ask about?

KATHY: Well, Polly is the other female, and she's as old as Luke. She's ten, and lately she's been very lethargic. She seems to have made her peace with Buddy sooner than the others did. At first she was very on guard. You could hardly pet her, and you wouldn't have her attention at all. She'd be looking over her shoulder constantly. But then it kind of settled down, so I think they came to an understanding quicker. I hope she's not ill too, because she's been just lying around lately, too.

BARBARA: As I feel her personality, she is more tolerant. The maleness makes them a little less tolerant, and the females, if they don't have young ones, they can be pretty tolerant. Can also be pretty cantankerous too, but I feel in her case, she's pretty tolerant. As to her lethargicness, again, my guides are telling me, "Food." The diet needs to be shifted.

KATHY: Okay.

BARBARA: I'm assuming that everybody gets about the same thing.

KATHY: Yes. I split one can between the four of them, twice a day.

BARBARA: I'm really not seeing anything that has to do with health, as much as they're telling me it's the heat. Did she quiet down with the heat?

KATHY: Well, she doesn't like to go outside anymore, even with plants to hide under.

BARBARA: I'm feeling like the heat is affecting her more, this year. Is it exceptionally warm there where you are?

KATHY: No—it's been in the eighties or so, but it's been humid. And she hasn't wanted to go out with everybody. We usually let them out before we got our fenced yard for the dog. We just let them roam the garden, and they all stuck around. And you could always find Polly underneath a bush or underneath some of the day lilies.

BARBARA: She doesn't do the heat real well.

KATHY: She's always the first one in.

BARBARA: Yes, and that's what I'm feeling. I'm not feeling any health issue as much as it's just hot, and she would be a kind of cat that would do better in the winter. She likes it when it's cool. Does she have a heavier coat?

KATHY: Yes. She's got a double coat. She's a brown tabby.

BARBARA: Okay. I'm feeling a heavier coat so I'm feeling like she's warmer. She can't seem to cool down as easily. She doesn't like the heat at all.

KATHY: She has been plucking out pieces of fur lately. Almost like she's trying to shed faster.

BARBARA: You mean if you brush her, she's still pulling out her fur?

KATHY: Yes. Not to where she's bald in patches, or anything, but she's grooming more. She'll have little tufts of fur in her mouth, which we pull out for her. But she's always had the plushest coat of everybody.

BARBARA: Yes. I feel a very thick heavy coat, and it keeps her a lot warmer in the summer than she would care to be to begin with. She's just wherever she can be cool—she's trying to be cool.

KATHY: Okay.

BARBARA: Since you brush her a lot that does help, and if you can get a stripping comb to strip out that undercoat to lighten her up for the summer—because when it comes winter she'll get that back again. She's probably trying to do it in her own way. It's a lot more difficult, but I feel that's what her problem is at this time.

KATHY: Is she bothered much by the fact that she's got such allergies? Because she's always sneezing great gobs of mucus all over the place, and we've just about gone through the vet's battery of medicines for animal allergies, and nothing's working.

BARBARA: I would change all her foods. It can very much be a food allergy, and I would find another variety of dry food as well. I'm feeling food allergy, which is interesting. You know, lots of times animals will chew on their feet or chew on their legs, and we think, well, they have an allergy to grass or something, when actually it's an internal allergy to the food they're eating. So there's nothing you can treat it with, because they're consuming this food that makes their skin itch. It's as if you get hives from something you eat. That's what it is.

KATHY: Oh, okay.

BARBARA: What food, what dry food, are you using now?

KATHY: The latest was *Deli Cat*. It's just kind of a mixture of different flavors, probably some fish in there too.

BARBARA: Is there a brand on that?

KATHY: I'm not sure who makes *Deli Cat*.

BARBARA: Okay. I would try to find one that's about as natural as you can. No additives. It's going to take a week or two before you notice any difference, but you might get a small quantity of one to see how they all react and get used to it. Sometimes they eat it with fervor, and other times they'll just walk away from it.

KATHY: Yes, like, "You want me to eat *this*?"

BARBARA: Yes. Exactly. Because they're not used to it. But if given the choice, if this is it, they will consume it. Lots of foods with—what they do for animals, in order to tantalize them to eat food, is to put burnt sugar on it, and it's sweet and they'll eat it. Or they put a lot of oil on it—and it can be a rancid oil—and they would eat it because of the oil, so sometimes you notice they're eating something and they just love it. But in fact they're consuming ice cream and candy all day long, and it really doesn't have the nutrients in it that the animal needs. We have no way of knowing that, unless we read the labels and check on the highest ingredients.

KATHY: Right.

BARBARA: If you can avoid anything with byproducts. Something all-natural would be very helpful.

KATHY: Well, Polly has had—we always assumed it was respiratory allergies. When we got her, she and Luke and another cat, Harvey—who has since passed on—they all came from the same farm that our friends have, and her eyes were gunked up, and her poor little nose, she was sneezing all the time. We assumed it was because she was sitting there on a hay bale. I have allergies, so I assumed that she's probably allergic to the farm. But since she's been away from the farm for ten years and still sneezing with her poor little nose—

BARBARA: So it could be an allergy which could be a weak immune system, and without the proper nutrition to support the immune system, it could be just that. There are nutritional things for people with allergies, as well.

KATHY: Right.

BARBARA: There's different herbs or vitamins or minerals or things they are finding all the time, that will help support the system. It's like asthma. Asthma is just a lack of immunity to different things, so you're always under attack.

KATHY: Yes, I know. I have asthma.

BARBARA: Do you?

KATHY: Yes.

BARBARA: I used to have it myself for years, so I know what that's like. It's an immune system that's always under attack because you have such sensitivities, you don't have the strength to fight that off. It takes a bit of searching to know for you particularly, which nutrient would be best, and again, for the animal, you can go on searching. Have you always just used the same food for the animals?

KATHY: Yes. Or the same brands. They've all eaten the same thing.

BARBARA: If you can do it, I would try something like *Iams*, because they have the lining on the inside of the can, so that the food doesn't get contaminated while it's in there.

KATHY: Yes. I've gotten *Iams* for them sometimes as treats. *Iams* doesn't have that many different flavors. I figure, well, give them a little more variety, so I think they only have four flavors.

BARBARA: Yes, and I understand that, but what I do is buy a number of them, and I just stack them in alternate flavors so every day they get a new flavor. And it's we who think that we couldn't be eating the same thing every day. Do you see? It's not really them. If they were in the wild, they'd eat mouse every day because that's what there was.

KATHY: Right. Sure.

BARBARA: You may want to buy the cans and alternate what you feed each day, and that gives them the variety.

KATHY: You have to be a detective to figure it all out.

BARBARA: Yes you do. And sometimes we look for runny nose and sneezing and we think, "Oh that's an allergy from the air," or something—when in fact it could very well be a food allergy. And because we have the same thing for breakfast, we're always eating oatmeal for breakfast, we think oatmeal's so healthy. Well, for some people oatmeal every day builds up a toxic problem, and so if you eat something once every four days, the body has three days to rest. And so if we can vary our diets by not eating the same thing every day, the same as the animals, then it really helps the immune system.

KATHY: Yes. I've noticed that when I've had too much sugar I have trouble with the asthma.

BARBARA: That's what it does. If you look at holidays like

Halloween. Right after Halloween comes flu season. Everybody gets sick with colds, because all that sugar drops the immune system and lets everything in. That's what I've observed over the years.

KATHY: Well, pet owners have to pool our knowledge.

BARBARA: Exactly. And you know, sometimes the animals teach us a lot by us making us look for different ways to treat their health for them. We think maybe there's something for us in this as well, and it can help us by shifting our diets accordingly. So, they're great helpers.

KATHY: Great company.

BARBARA: Oh, aren't they? They really are a gift, but if you like to do things with your dog, I would definitely look into agility and other competition for Buddy. Get involved with him because he would love it.

KATHY: Yes. We'll see if I can get back into another class. The dog trainer I had for the obedience class seemed to think that it would be quite a ways before he would be ready for an agility class.

BARBARA: Well, go and observe. Maybe go to another teacher and ask. Everybody teaches differently, and everybody has different baselines for it, and because Buddy is very active and doesn't listen as well as you would want him to. Sometimes that's an advantage, because you're starting to harness that energy. He'll be more eager to work for you and he'll work a lot faster than most. It's just not a slam-dunk thing to work with him, but you can do it.

KATHY: It was fun for me too. I enjoyed the class.

BARBARA: Yes. And you're with people who have other animals, and you have common interests. It can be a real outlet for a lot of fun, and agility is wonderful—to watch them perform, whether they do it well or they do it poorly. They're doing something they enjoy doing, with a smile.

KATHY: Right.

BARBARA: And that's worth all of it. Who cares if they do

it perfectly? Life isn't about doing things perfectly. It's just about enjoying it with a smile.

KATHY: We're going to be going on vacation in about three weeks. But now I think we may have to board all the animals, in order to get Luke some definite health care during the time we're gone. I can't depend on the pet sitter being able to handle him, and the boarding kennel is run by my vet.

BARBARA: Oh, perfect!

KATHY: So that should be really good. It's a wonderful place. Buddy likes it. We've visited a couple times and they've got really wonderful facilities. Clean, and not the wire-bottom cages. It's all the molded plastic, which is really comfortable. The cats can be two to a cage and have a pass-through second room. It's like a two-room cage for the litter box to be in. We were worried about leaving them at home, and coming home to piles and piles of poop on the carpet.

BARBARA: I can imagine.

KATHY: So we'll go that route and see how everybody fares.

BARBARA: And then with Luke not feeling as well as he should, that's kind of nice for him to be right there. If he looks a bit piqued, they could look at him for you if need be.

KATHY: Right. And the way Polly has been just lying about, I'll probably put those two in the same cage and Annie and Casey in the other cage. The people there are very nice, so I wouldn't hesitate.

BARBARA: Oh, that's wonderful. It's always nice to have a reliable place for our special people.

KATHY: Right. Yes. They even have a person who lives above the kennel, so there's someone there all the time. Well, you've been a big help. Thank you.

BARBARA: Well, thank you. Thank you, Kathy. It's been an absolute pleasure working with you. I hope you will let me know how it's going.

* * *

Later, I received an e-mail from Kathy as feedback that her reading had been correct:

Hi Barbara,

A few months ago you did a reading for my dog Buddy and my cat Luke. At that time, you saw that Luke was ill with bowel problems, but you also said there was something more serious. We have found recently that he was suddenly acting very aggressively towards the dog, chasing him around and hitting and snarling at him for no reason. When I took Luke to the vet, thinking I may have to have him put to sleep, the vet instead said that he may have an adrenal problem that is making him aggressive and prescribed mild tranquilizers. These have worked well for the last month, and there have been no more fights, just a little hissing, which we can all live with.

Thank you for alerting us to a deeper problem, which saved us from making a very painful decision and causing us to lose our dear Luke too soon.

Your friend,
Kathy.

* * *

Bernard had rescued a number of cats, but was afraid that some of them were making life difficult for others:

BERNARD: Do my cats have to be right with me for the reading?

BARBARA: No, they don't. They don't even have to be in the room. Lots of times they disappear, or they might come and lie down close to you.

BERNARD: The first one is Binkey. Blinka Buns—but her call name is Binkey. I worry about Binkey because she is my oldest cat—she is twenty years old. I just adore her. I am in great fear of loosing her, but I am slowly getting to the point of self- acceptance that she will go. My biggest question about Binkey is, she is always hungry. I wind up getting mad at her. She has a Siamese voice even thought she is not Siamese, and it just drives me crazy sometimes. She had a thyroid problem and I give her Tapazole every day. It's the last six months that she is constantly hungry. I wonder if there is anything that is wrong, or if I just created a bad habit with her? I want her to know that when I get a little impatient with her, it is not that I don't love her.

BARBARA: What I am getting with her is a bottomless pit. Does she have an active digestive system where—I feel she is thinner rather than overweight.

BERNARD: Yes, Yes.

BARBARA: And she gets these hunger pains. She is constantly hungry. It isn't to be annoying. What I get is, her metabolism is working faster than normal.

BERNARD: They have her on the Tapazole* for the thyroid, which could be part of it. Maybe I should have the doc increased the dose. Because that does have something to do with hunger. I have just been feeding her, sometimes a lot, and then she seems better. I didn't want to overfeed her. She is feeling hunger and since she is hungry I'll just feed her. No problem.

BARBARA: Her only way to ask for food is to cry, to meow, to alert you that she is hungry.

BERNARD: But it is legitimate hunger?

BARBARA: Yes it is.

BERNARD: That is something that I can live with. I thought I created a monster by feeding her when she cries, and creating a bad habit.

BARBARA: No, No. I don't feel like that. I don't think that she does it when she is not hungry.

BERNARD: Let me ask you this. I feel really guilty, because

---

* I learned a few weeks later that Tapazole is a very toxic drug. It is used for hyperthyroidism in older cats, and it causes them to want to eat everything in sight. Unfortunately, the only alternative treatment is radioactive iodine, which suppresses the thyroid at a cost of $1,000 per treatment, which requires that the cat be in quarantine for three weeks after treatment.

Binkey and her daughter Olivia are my two original cats. I have taken in these other cats who were strays, and they have had to accept them, and now I am up to six cats. I feel like I have hurt the quality of their lives. Olivia does not get to go outside at all anymore, because she is afraid of one of the other cats. Are they really upset with me?

BARBARA: I don't feel that at all. I feel that going outside was fun for Olivia, but she has accepted that it is okay not to. Does she sit by the window a lot and look out?

BERNARD: Yes. She sits on the couch a lot. She wants to go out in the front yard and I let her out there as much as I can. There she feels safe. She does not have to worry about the other cat that bothers her so much. But I get worried because when I let them out there, I have to keep an eye on them because it is by a street and there are stray dogs occasionally. It isn't really unsafe—I didn't used to have the yard fenced, and they could go where they wanted. And they were really smart and they would never go across the street, Binkey or Olivia. I really felt like I have hemmed them in when I got these other cats, and I built a big fence in the backyard, so Squeaky, who is sitting in my lap right now, wouldn't get hit. Because she goes across the street. I feel guilty!

BARBARA: You shouldn't. There is nothing to feel guilty about. Olivia does like to go outside, but it is not something she can't live without. If she can just sit where she can look outside, she is okay, too. That is still outside to her. She doesn't have to be outside. Both Olivia and Binkey have adjusted to the new animals coming into their surroundings. Animals do that. There are a few animals who take a hard stance on things, but I don't feel like these two have.

BERNARD: Binkey is my darling and I love her dearly. Olivia, Binkey's daughter, is my little savior cat, because I was really sick when she came into the world. She was with me as my companion, when my back was out due to a dislocated disk. She used to love to go out into the backyard and sit by these wild tree rats. I had to hose the bush to finally get her to give it up. One time she brought me in six babies, which I raised and then let go out in the wild.

BARBARA: Baby rats?

BERNARD: Baby tree rats, yes. It was a group effort, actually. First I saw that she got something, and I took it away from her. It was a little mouse and it was still alive, so I put it in a box. Eventually I had six of them—I guess she got the whole litter. I put them in a cage, fed them and got them big enough, and took them out to the foothills and let them go.

BARBARA: When she was younger she did enjoy going outside. Now she is up in age and she is more sedentary, quieter.

BERNARD: What is her health? She worries me sometimes. I guess she is okay—she is not as old as her mother; she is sixteen years old. Is she feeling okay, physically?

BARBARA: They are showing me that her liver may not be as healthy as it could be.

BERNARD: I got in touch with a lady who sells organic foods. I have been feeding them, when I could afford it, the raw organic wild-ranged foods. Except Olivia. I have the hardest time getting her to eat it. I have tried with blue-green algae and all this other stuff. And now I am back to the canned food for seniors. They really like the dry food, but I know it not the best food.

BARBARA: I don't believe that is much of a problem.

BERNARD: You don't?

BARBARA: No. There are some dry foods out there that are totally natural. I have four cats, myself. I have found some dry all-natural foods they really do like.

BERNARD: What is the brand name?

BARBARA: I'll mail you the name of these foods. These are speciality items. All natural and very palatable. The liver also sorts things through the blood. It is the body's sieve.

BERNARD: The major organ of detoxication.

BARBARA: Yes. When it is not working well, sometimes

they get sluggish, sometimes they fail to get rid of the toxins. But I don't see anything seriously wrong—it looks healthy. I don't know why they are showing that organ to me. Sometimes I get a little bit more information, but right now I am only getting that.

BERNARD: Olivia is sitting at the window right now, looking outside.

BARBARA: Yes. I feel that is what she loves to do. If she can't go out and catch, at least she can be watching.

BERNARD: Yes, she does. Now the other question. I will leave these two here for the moment, after I ask you another question. Why is Olivia so healthy and living so long? I am certainly not complaining, I am absolutely thrilled, but people can't believe she is twenty years old, and I can't either. She is just this wonderful creature that has this wonderful long life and energy. Is she just an exceptional spirit? I know they all are, but is there anything you get about her that explains why she likes hanging around?

BARBARA: She has a quicker metabolism, and maybe that is the medication. Again, the thyroid is the balancing act of the body. And I can understand, at her age might be a bit slow.

BERNARD: Can you talk to her?

BARBARA: Yes.

BERNARD: Will you tell her that I am so happy she has picked me to come to live with?

BARBARA: She is happy as well and that is why she is with you. She really does adore you. She loves her time with you, and your intuitiveness about her. She really does. She feels that the two of you are very, very connected. This is an unwritten communication between the two of you.

BERNARD: Oh yes, I love her! She is my girl! Now I have a question about little Whiskers. She can't jump up on the bed much anymore. It seems like she is getting weak in the rear. Does she feel like she is have trouble jumping up now? I want to build a little step. Will that help her?

BARBARA: Whiskers?

BERNARD: No Binkey. Whiskers is my nickname for her!

BARBARA: I will just jot these names down so I can keep track of them—there are a lot of energies to sort out here. It is the spring in the back of the legs. She has lost her spring. They lose some of the muscle tone as they get older. I feel that it is in the thighs that the muscle tone is gone. And yes, if you have a little step that she could climb, that would help her.

BERNARD: I should get her a kitty's exercise tape! I saw them in a cat magazine once. Cat calisthenics! No—it is a joke. Bad joke, sorry. Moving right along.

BARBARA: That is cute. I hadn't thought of that! Someone will think of it, you know. I have seen Yoga for Dogs!

BERNARD: Have you!

BARBARA: Yes, there is a book that has been published on Yoga for Dogs.

BERNARD: Seriously, I saw an advertisement for a video for cats in Cat Magazine. Does Olivia tell me anything? Does she have anything to say?

BARBARA: Olivia, okay.

BERNARD: Is there anything that I am not giving her that she would like, or does she feel safe when she goes out front?

BARBARA: Yes, she is fine. Does she like little round things to roll around and play with?

BERNARD: Yes. She used to love it! Yes. I haven't done too much with her lately.

BARBARA: It seems like little balls or small little things she can roll and kick with her back legs.

BERNARD: Okay. I used to do that with her a lot.

BARBARA: I am feeling that she would like something that has catnip in it, as this is something she likes. She is showing me that is what she used to like to do.

BERNARD: Okay. And one question with Olivia. Why is she so afraid of Sparkie? Sparkie is the next to the newest cat.

She is a black cat, and was a stray, and Olivia is terrified of her. Has Sparkie really been abusive to her? Can you tell?

BARBARA: As I feel Sparkie's energy, I am feeling devilish! I want to say devilish—hell on wheels—if you want to use a strong word. And this one—Sparkie—doesn't let up!

BERNARD: No, she doesn't! She is getting better. Because, at first she knew that I didn't want her here. I just didn't want another cat and she wasn't getting along with them very well. But she got sick here about a year and a half ago, and I finally fell in love with her. Now she is better. She is minding me better because she knows that I love her. I still want to find her another home. Would Sparkie be okay with that, do you think?

BARBARA: She would be okay with that, but she is a hard personality to deal with!

BERNARD: That is the problem! I took her to the *Petco* adoption and she did not show well.

BARBARA: She is like a spitfire!

BERNARD: Yes, she is! She is just a little hellion!

BARBARA: That is what I get, and she will growl and dare anyone to touch her! It makes people shy away from her. They are looking for the soft gentle energy, and not this terrifying wild cat!

BERNARD: Do you know where she came from? Is that possible, that you can get some images of where she is from? Is there any possible way of knowing where she came from? Was she lost? Did she run away?

BARBARA: I do not get family. What I see is woods. Did you get her close to the woods?

BERNARD: I am in a neighborhood close to the river, but it is a tract. I just saw her in my backyard. I thought that she was someone's pet, because she was staring at the bird feeder in my neighbor's back yard. I didn't want another cat, so I didn't feed her. But after awhile I thought, "Well, maybe she is hungry," so I put some food out so she could eat. I have this rescue mentality. So I took her and brought her in. Tried to get her a home in other places, but it didn't work because of her personality.

BARBARA: Yes, she has a really tenacious personality!

BERNARD: For example, she will climb up on my bed and get on my stomach and be happy just to be there. I'll pet her and then all of a sudden she will bite me. She will not bite me to draw blood, but she just freaks out and bites me, and then jumps down.

BARBARA: The biting is, "Stop doing that, it is annoying to me." She doesn't mind a little of it, but what the bite is, is to hold your hand and say, "Stop doing this." Then she leaves. She is saying, "Now I have to clean up this area, again." She is a very meticulous housekeeper, as it were. What I get is that she will have to clean all that fur again, because you have overdone the petting. She does not want to have any other scents on her, for her hunting. She is a hunter. She is not like Binkey or Olivia. She is not a loveable, sweet kind of a personality.

BERNARD: Yes, you are right. She is more wild than the other cats I have. But I was thinking that she is not feral, because if she were feral I could not even get near her. She was always pretty much the same personality. That is why I was wondering. I live in a middle-class neighborhood, and my neighbors treat pets a little bit different here. When they get bored with them, some of them just let them run free. I was just assuming that someone got a cat on a whim and then dumped her! But I was trying to figure out where she came from.

BARBARA: I feel she had some contact with people when she was very young. And then she just went off on her own.

BERNARD: She just wandered around?

BARBARA: Yes. Yes—that is who she is! She is out for experiences, and she has become a hunter. That is an instinct that is built into her.

BERNARD: I know there is a place down by Hemet—a pound—where there is a non-destroy policy. They keep them as long as they can. Do you think that she would have any chance at all of getting adopted? Or can you give me any suggestions on how to place her? She is really creating havoc with Olivia! I'd keep her, but six cats is an awful lot.

BARBARA: Yes, I understand. I well appreciate. I don't see her mellowing out real soon. If you placed her in a special place where they would care for her for the rest of her life, I feel she would be a loner. She would be off in the corner somewhere, away from the others.

BERNARD: Does she crave human attention very much?

BARBARA: No. No, she doesn't! Maybe on a whim!

BERNARD: She comes to me more often now. She will come and hang out with me sometimes. Her place is up on top of the refrigerator, and that is where she hangs out. Or in the back yard. The problem is that she will get on the back step and no one else can get out or in. She acts like a roadblock, because she is just such a snarly little turkey! That is why I want to find another home for her. She is the major stumbling block in my having harmony here.

BARBARA: You could put out a thought pattern for a friend who has lots of property where she could hunt. She would be great on a property that has horse barns or cattle, where they need a cat that is semi-friendly. She doesn't demand much.

BERNARD: I have been trying to place her with friends that have homes and kids. That would not work.

BARBARA: No, she would not work out in that kind of home at all. She would end up turning and swatting at one of the children, because she becomes territorial.

BERNARD: There was an opportunity to adopt her with a family with children, and I knew it would not work. She would bite the children.

BARBARA: You are absolutely right! I feel that if you go to

a riding stable where they need a mouser—but I am not sure if you have any close to you.

BERNARD: There are quite a few riding stables close to where I live.

BARBARA: See if someone would be interested in taking her, if you donated some food for her to eat. There may be other half-wild cats there. She would like that type of situation, where she could provide a service for them, catching mice.

BERNARD: It is her personality, because physically she is not much of a fighter. She is not real strong! But, she is very intimidating to everyone.

BARBARA: Yes, it is the growling.

BERNARD: Screaming!

BARBARA: The other cats will not test the waters to see if it is a bluff.

BERNARD: No kidding! Nobody does! Okay, lets move on to Squeaky. Squeaky is a cat that I rescued out of a home. She was abandoned. Squeaky is a doll, but she is terrified by my only male cat, Moose. It didn't use to be like that, and I can't figure out what has happened. Squeaky hides under the bed. She is better than she used to be. But her life has been terribly impacted by Moose's presence. Squeaky is the only one Moose harasses. Squeaky is sitting here right in front of me. Poor Squeaky. She wants to go out, and I let her out, and she is the one I built the fence for. She wants to go out in the front, but she would cross the street. I know she is street-wise, but this street is busy.

BARBARA: It is tempting fate.

BERNARD: I know that when it is her time to go, it will be her time to go. But, I worry about her.

BARBARA: I get that Squeaky has been in season and had a litter.

BERNARD: Not that I know of. To make a long story short, I do construction. I was doing this job in this really nice high rent neighborhood. I saw this little cat, and I thought she lived with someone. I asked this little neighbor girl and she gave me the cat's name, but I can't remember right now. Then I went back a year later and did a house a couple houses down and she was there. I saw her and she was starving to death. The lady I was working for was not very pleasant, and she said, "This cat comes in, and jumps up on the table, and steals my children's bacon." I was thinking, "You would too, if you were starving." So I started to feed her, and I asked the lady if I could have her. She said, "Sure." I tried to take her to *Concerned Animal Lovers,* but they were closed, so I didn't have any place to adopt her out. I kept her. The lady thought Squeaky had come from a family, and she used to fight with the children because they used to abuse her, and she had gotten dumped or left. What do you get from her past?

BARBARA: I get a lot of feelings that she went back and forth, back and forth. I wouldn't discount what this lady was saying. What I feel with this cat is that the males used to harangue her. They would not leave her alone. And they can be very deadly, the male cats. Her fear of him is that he is a male cat and they just don't let up. If you are a female and you had kittens, and a tom comes by, he may kill the whole litter. Her fear is the fear of men! It is in the form of cats.

BERNARD: With Moose, he does it because it is entertaining and he can get away with it.

BARBARA: Right! Right! He is just testing the water. He is just having fun. He is not going to hurt her, but he knows that when he roars, Squeaky runs and she is scared and it makes him feel really important.

BERNARD: Can you ask her if it is doing any good for me to change her name from Squeaky to Scarlet? I think Scarlet is a more powerful name. I have been calling her Squeaky, because she has this real cute Squeaky voice. I have been trying to talk to her and trying some T-touch on her a little bit with Moose around. She is getting a little better.

BARBARA: I am not sure about Scarlet, either.

BERNARD: Like Scarlet O'Hara!

BARBARA: I am thinking that the name Scarlet, is a put-upon type of energy. It would be helpful if you choose a name that would have a softer Goddess type of strength. The Goddess is not confrontational, but she is so powerful that she does not have to be confrontational.

BERNARD: That is the thing about it. Squeaky is a survivor! She is powerful. I can't understand how she lets Moose, who backs down from everybody, intimidate her so much.

BARBARA: Because that is the energy of the Goddess. The energy of the Goddess—and the Goddess is returning—is that she is more powerful than God. She needed a mate, and she choose God. God took over the earth for the last 5,000 years. God is the warrior! Because that is what God does. God overpowers everything, as it were. It is the male testosterone type of energy. Not bad, wrong or terrible. That is just what it is. The Goddess is very powerful, and much more powerful. And we say, "Well, why didn't the Goddess say, 'Stop it!'?" That is because she does not interfere, but she is so powerful that just by her presence exudes power, and yet she yields. You are correct, when you get that Squeaky has inner strength. It's the Goddess type of energy. She is not going to go and beat him up, that is not who she is. She will yield to Moose's being a bully, because it doesn't make any sense to confront him, to beat up on him.

BERNARD: She just jumped down off the couch, and now Moose just jumped up on the couch. She just ran under the chair and hissed and jumped in another chair.

BARBARA: She will yield to him. And he knows that. That is the way it is. She is not unhappy with it. She just knows that it is a better posture.

BERNARD: It kept her alive out in the wild.

BARBARA: Exactly! Exactly! I get that she has been many places. She has had many experiences. In order to be living today with all the experiences she's had, she had to know when to yield and when to back up and disappear. That is what she does. But it isn't because she is trembling in fear. It is just that she is moving out of the way.

BERNARD: When I first got her, I decided to keep her. I had her spayed. The vet could not find a uterus, so it looked like she had already been spayed.

BARBARA: I get that she's had a litter somewhere along the way.

BERNARD: I still let her out occasionally—out front. Is she suffering terribly, that she does not get to go out front?

BARBARA: No! No!

BERNARD: Are you sure?

BARBARA: Yes! I am sure. It is more about you feeling bad about it, than her.

BERNARD: Yes.

BARBARA: You are the kind of guy that likes to be outdoors. If they locked you up in the house, you would not like it a lot. So what you have done is projected this onto the cats, thinking, "If it were me!"

BERNARD: She loves it so much! The neighborhood she was in was this wonderful neighborhood in Fullerton, that was very hilly, and it was like a paradise for a cat. Unfortunately, she was starving to death. But I am sure that at one point in time it was a great place to live. I thought, "Well, I brought her to this little neighborhood and she can't go into the back yard." What I do is take shifts with them. I put Sparkie, Moose and Scooter in the back yard. Then I let the other three go outside in the back. I try to trade them off with different days, to equal it out some. That is the best I can do.

BARBARA: I think it is just fine. There are some cats, in my opinion, that don't ever need to go out. If they sit by the screen and sniff the fresh air, it is good enough. But, that is my belief. You can't project how you would feel in that situation.

BERNARD: She's not terribly unhappy!

BARBARA: No. She is very happy. She has a secure home. She has nice surroundings. She gets fed on a regular basis. And yes, there are those times when you have to zig when you could zag. But she has adjusted. If someone comes up to her she will hiss, "Don't bother me. I am leaving!" and just go away.

BERNARD: I thought about finding a home for her. Because Moose and she do not get along. Would she be okay? Would she take it well?

BARBARA: She would be fine in another home. She is a very soft type of energy, as I feel it. She would adjust just fine.

BERNARD: She may be happier to have someone care just for her. Because here she feels stifled with so many cats to interrupt her energy. She just wants to play.

BARBARA: I feel like she would do very well with an older retired couple.

BERNARD: Half the problem is me. It just kills me to give some of them up. I get selfish sometimes. But, by the same token, I have to think of what is best for them. I occasionally ask people if they want a cat. But I have not had much luck.

BARBARA: That's okay. The cats find us. And they choose to be with those they've found.

BERNARD: Is that right?

BARBARA: Oh yes! Absolutely. All those cats found you. And they choose to be with you. So if at some juncture you find another home for them—you come across someone and you say, "I have this wonderful cat, would you be interested?"—they'll say, "Yes!" You aren't abandoning them. You are just expanding their experiences. I understand we all have some kind of issues that we are working through in our lives. It is never ending. So it is okay if you find another home for them. It is okay to bring them in your house. And if you feel like you have too many, then adjust accordingly. Do what is comfortable for you. I don't feel that any of your animals are feeling as if they are being put upon. Or they can't move around. Because when you let them out, they could leave!

BERNARD: That is true.

BARBARA: They have the option of saying, "I choose not to leave. I choose to stay here."

BERNARD: I didn't realize that. I just figured, from what I have read, that cats are much more attached to their surroundings than their owners. They love you, but they are more stressed when you change their physical location.

BARBARA: You have nothing to feel bad about. You have saved a lot of cats and given them good lives.

* * *

As you can see, this is a person with a big heart and one who really does care about the animals around him. Sometimes when we rescue animals we a crying out to be rescued ourselves.

5: Animals That Are Ready To Die

IT IS DIFFICULT FOR HUMANS TO REMEMBER that the pets we love do not have the same life span that we do. No matter how long an animal lives, we think it should live longer, and stay with us. We also may feel that the condition which releases the animal could have been helped if we had only known it existed, had only obtained more or better veterinarian care, or had prayed harder.

In some cases when an owner requests a reading about an animal's health problems, we must try to make the owner understand that the issue may be that it is soon time for the animal to die. We need to understand that animals do not feel the same about death that we do, and do not blame the humans for not being able to make their lives last longer. If an animal is in pain, it may transition without any stress or difficulty at all.

Some owners know that the end is near for a beloved pet, but are not sure if it is right to help the animal end its life when it is in pain, or if they should keep trying to make its quality of life better with medical care.

* * *

CINDY: My first question is, are there are other things I should be doing to make him feel better?

BARBARA: I am getting the feeling he is not sure about that, does not know what could help him. I was getting something about the spine. Is there something about his spine? From the base of his skull all the way down his back?

CINDY: Yes, there is.

BARBARA: I am feeling that there is some rigidity. There are things you might do to make him more comfortable. That is what they are showing me.

CINDY: Is he in a lot of pain?

BARBARA: He does notice it a lot. I don't know if it is like a headache or an ache all the way through. I am getting that moist heat would be helpful. It is arthritis or something that is like arthritis. What they are showing me is that something warm would help him. A heating pad with a damp cloth over it, so that there is moisture along with heat, and the warmth can penetrate deeper. But when this is done, he shouldn't go out into the cold air. He is more vulnerable to the cold penetrating. Cold makes him more uncomfortable.

CINDY: Is there a time of day when it is worse for him?

BARBARA: What I am seeing and what they are telling me is, it's in the evening when it gets colder. During the day does he like to lie in the sun? Does he like the heat?

CINDY: He stays inside all the time. He has a wool blanket that he lies on, on top of a pad.

BARBARA: Okay. I was feeling whether he would like to go out and lie in the sun. But, it is the heat. Probably it is not warm enough now, anyway.

CINDY: And the ground would be cool.

BARBARA: The sun is warm but the air is cold. I get that too much heat is not good—it will affect his resistance. He should be warm, a little above room temperature. Animals have a little hotter body temperature than humans. He should be warmed to what his body temperature is. He is a pretty heavily coated dog isn't he?

CINDY: Yes he is.

BARBARA: When we first spoke, you told me he was a chow-lab mix. I am feeling like he has more of a chow type of coat.

CINDY: Yes, he does.

BARBARA: So it is pretty dense. It is hard to get heat through the coat when his body is cold. If he gets warm the coat density does help to hold the heat in.

CINDY: He gets restless in the middle of the night and

wants to go out a couple of times during the night. I am curious what that is all about.

BARBARA: There is some kind of discomfort within the body. It is a sensation that makes him feel like he has to go to the bathroom. So he wants out.

CINDY: He has his own dog door.

BARBARA: So he goes out the dog door. Okay. He feels uncomfortable. It is not quite having to go the bathroom, but it is similar to that, so he thinks that must be what it is. I am getting a sensation in the body, I think around the kidneys. So he interprets that as, "I need to go to the bathroom." Rather than now knowing what it is, I am not sure what is causing that irritation.

CINDY: We can work with the acupuncturist on that.

BARBARA: Does he drink a lot of water?

CINDY: Yes.

BARBARA: I can hear lap, lap in the background and I get that he drinks a lot of water.

CINDY: Yes.

BARBARA: Almost too much. I would not stop him from drinking the water. What I am getting—

CINDY: Is it coming from a thirst? Like, he feels thirsty, so he is drinking?

BARBARA: Yes. But, it is overtaxing the kidneys.

CINDY: We can work with the acupuncturist on all of this.

BARBARA: Sometimes people with diabetes drink a lot more fluids. For him it could be some kind of kidney stone. You could have the acupuncturist check through the meridians.

CINDY: Does he want to stay here for a while yet? He is seventeen years old. Or is he ready to go?

BARBARA: He is getting closer to his transition. I am not saying it is tomorrow. It is hard for me to know. It may be that his kidneys give out.

CINDY: With my last dog. I took her to the vet when she was ready to go. I working with a local veterinarian, and she said that the dog was communicating that she was ready. I do a lot of things to try and keep him healthy, and extend his life. But, if he is getting ready to go, I am going to make it harder if I continue all the things that I am doing. I am putting a lot of effort into taking care of him. I am wondering if he would rather I didn't do so much, if he is ready to pass on.

BARBARA: Right now he is not saying, "Let me out." I am not getting the message that, "I'm done, I'm finished, I'm tired of this."

CINDY: Okay, okay.

BARBARA: He does give the feeling that he has let go of a lot of the things that connect him with this life. But he is not focusing on the end. He does seem to feel that you will know very clearly when the time is very close. And it will happen quickly. Something is going to give out—I keep getting the kidneys. When it happens it will be clear to you and the vet that there is nothing that can be done, or should be done.

CINDY: When he is standing, his whole hindquarters slowly starts to buckle at the knees. He will start to lower down and then he will move and it seems to be okay. And when he eats, he can only eat for a short amount of time. Then he has to walk around and come back and eat again. Because his hindquarters just start giving way, and don't support him.

BARBARA: He is having trouble with his hip joint.

CINDY: Is that where the moist heat is needed?

BARBARA: I am seeing that the heat should be applied to the spine. Actually the base of the skull all the way down the whole spine. At the base of the skull I am feeling a lot of stiffness.

CINDY: He had a bad fall a couple years ago, and injured that area. I don't think it may have healed completely.

BARBARA: It is kind of uncomfortable for him. All they are showing me is a weak muscle. The leg goes into the socket and I get that the muscle that holds the leg in the socket is losing strength.

CINDY: Like some tendons?

BARBARA: They are saying that something in that area, maybe a muscle or tendon, get tired real easily. Then he starts to go down. I don't get that there is any problem with the knees or the back legs. I get the hip joint. Does he roll his foot around as he walks, or does he walk a little funny at the hip?

CINDY: When he walks, his legs roll out—almost in a circle.

BARBARA: That is what I see, a circle.

CINDY: Is he uncomfortable being touched?

BARBARA: He likes to be petted! Do you mean massaging?

CINDY: Would he like massaging?

BARBARA: I am not getting that would help a lot. Actually, I am feeling that it would irritate him.

CINDY: He does not tolerate much touching to begin with. Never has!

BARBARA: I am getting that some touching gives him a little more pain and discomfort. The petting is comfortable for him. As long as you don't get too near the joints. But no massage.

CINDY: This coming weekend my husband and I need to go to San Diego. We would be leaving Sunday morning and coming back early Monday evening. He is very uncomfortable riding in the car these days. Would it be all right to leave him at home alone? He has his own dog door. He would be alone for about thirty-six hours. He has full run of the house.

BARBARA: What I am getting is that he is going to miss you. He would rather not have you go away.

CINDY: The only other option is to take him with us in the car. But it is a two-hour drive each way.

BARBARA: And he is uncomfortable riding?

CINDY: Yes, I think it is with the vibration of the car on the road. We have tried different things to make it as comfortable as possible for him. But he whines as if he is hurting. I think he still likes a short ride around town with me.

BARBARA: His body needs to be very, very still in order to

be comfortable. Any kind of motion aggravates the places that already hurt. He has always loved to ride with you, was delighted to be taken along, and that love makes a short trip bearable.

CINDY: Yes.

BARBARA: The time in the car on the trip to San Diego would be a bit too much for him. His age doesn't let him recuperate as quickly. He gets tired. He rests more these days, stays still longer than he used to—sleeps a little bit more, because normal activity has become very taxing, very strenuous for him.

CINDY: I could make arrangements for someone to look in on him while we are gone.

BARBARA: It feel it is better to leave him home. But it would be good if someone can come in and see that he is okay. Have a little talk to him before you go and tell him what you are going to do. You can say, "We are going to leave, and will be away a while. The sun is going to go down. And when the sun comes up again we will be home." That is how they know the time passing, by the light and the dark.

CINDY: Another question. He had another sort of seizure. Although the vet doesn't call it that. I don't know how else to refer to it. After about three to four months of not having had any. I was surprised, because of all the things that we have been doing. I want to know what that was about. It just came on all of a sudden. He seemed to be in a great deal of pain.

BARBARA: He totally freezes up?

CINDY: Yes.

BARBARA: And when he freezes up that way he is very uncomfortable. It is because of his body and the way it's functioning now. Vitamin B-6 has helped me with a dog who had seizures. B-6 is one of the deficiencies for what causes seizures even in young babies, according to the Adelle Davis book, *Let's Get Well*. B complex is good, along with B-6. His seizures come with being a senior. The body gets out of balance. And the more it gets out of balance, the more new things will start to pop up, here, here, and here. The energy is weakening in the organs, and one thing triggers something else. Age starts to weaken the whole system. The animals seem to know when it is getting close, then things just start to shut down, bit by bit. That is their way of doing it. The energy is starting not to be in the places it used to be. The deficiencies will start to pop up a bit more.

CINDY: Is there anything else in his living environment that he would like different, or wants more of? Anything I could do to make him more comfortable, and know he is loved?

BARBARA: He is pretty comfortable, and he knows he is loved, that you are doing everything you can for him. It didn't sink in when you mentioned to me yesterday that he is seventeen years old. This morning, I realized it—he has had a long and good life, living seventeen years! That is incredible. It is a compliment to you—all that you done to make this longevity possible. You have helped heal a lot of the stuff that he went through in his life, and made it possible for him to get through his life in this animal kingdom, and move on to other kingdoms with an evolved energy. He is very evolved, because he has come to you for your help in developing further than he could have without you. To help him move on.

CINDY: Yes, he is very self-realized.

BARBARA: Very sure of who he is. Very self-assured. I don't feel like he has ever been frightened or cowered from anything in his life. And yet I don't feel he has been out there biting at ankles, either. He didn't have to go through extremes of dog behavior in this life. He was past a lot of things other dogs still need to learn from.

CINDY: Yes.

BARBARA: And it has been good for you. He has contributed a lot to your life as well. You feel like you still need him with you for a while. To continue the special relationship you have together. Sundance, you named him, and it has been a dance between the two of you! There is a lot in that name. You picked that very carefully!

CINDY: Yes, I did!

BARBARA: Yes you did. You did a beautiful job with that, because that is really who he is. It has just been a dance in the sun between the two of you. What a wonderful, beautiful energy the two of you have shared. It has been as comfortable as possible for both of you for seventeen years. And you don't want it to stop.

CINDY: Is there anything else he wants to tell me?

BARBARA: Something about the dog door. The dog door at the bottom. He has to step a little high.

CINDY: It is a standard dog door, in a panel for a sliding glass door. He has to step over the frame.

BARBARA: I just get that he steps over something that is a little bit high. Lately it has become a little more uncomfortable.

CINDY: Yes. In the evening when he goes out. He tends to bump the edge now.

BARBARA: With his back legs.

CINDY: He clears it during the daytime, but at night, and in the middle of the night, he hits it with his back legs.

BARBARA: They keep showing me it is high.

CINDY: We will see what we can do.

BARBARA: It might not be possible to change it. It isn't making his life miserable. But everything is very comfortable and that one thing bothers him lately. It is a minor thing. I feel like he is very comfortable. And is he eating a little less?

CINDY: Yes. Quality wise? Yes.

BARBARA: He has lost his sense of taste. The taste buds are shutting down, so he just eats a little bit. The food doesn't seem to have much flavor any more.

CINDY: The last couple of evenings, when we are in the living room, he will come in and kind of whimper. I think that he wanted to be with us, but his bed was not in the room. So I have been bringing his pad in for the evening. He seems to be real happy now. He can lie comfortably on his bed, and be with us.

BARBARA: He wants to be part of everything that is going on. He likes to lie in his bed but he doesn't like to be in a room by himself. Even when he is sleeping, he still likes the family energy. He feels the company.

CINDY: What about during the daytime? Would he like it if I brought his bed into whatever room I am working in? Because during the daytime he's practically always on his bed.

BARBARA: It doesn't seem like the day is as important to him as is the evening.

CINDY: Okay.

BARBARA: During the day he knows that you are there, and that is fine. It seems at nighttime he wants to be closer to the family energy. He feels a little insecure at night. It gets dark. It gets cold, and then he starts to feel a little lonely. During the day he feels fuller and more protected. It feels like the night pulls him back from his aura, away from his energy.

CINDY: What about his sight and his hearing? We have been clapping to get his attention. Is that working okay for him?

BARBARA: He sometime picks it up and sometimes doesn't, even when you clap. I am getting that there is not much hearing left. My guides are showing me a bell. They say ring a bell. They say that vibration will be picked up through all of his body. Try that and see.

CINDY: And his sight?

BARBARA: I feel it is kind of cloudy.

CINDY: It is getting cloudy.

BARBARA: Yes. But it is not real important to him, though. His routines are so set that it is not a big problem for him.

CINDY: He manages well with his other senses. On our walk today there was a dog on the other side of the park. It was a considerable distance. He immediately perked up and wanted to go in that direction. Like a dog perks up when there is another dog to play with.

BARBARA: He scented it a lot more than he saw it. His taste buds aren't really there, and his eyesight is not super-keen. But, his nose is still pretty sensitive. And he picked up the scent in the air. It was like, "Oh, that could be fun! I'll have to go see what that is all about." It was an animal smell that he thought was interesting. And maybe he saw the dog move, after that. But he picked up the scent in the air long before he ever saw. It may have looked to you like he saw it, but his nose went right to the scent and where it was coming from. The breeze was coming his way, so it was easy to pick up a very fresh scent. But he is no longer real interested in a lot of things. Just the creature comforts. Be comfortable, sleep a lot, be warm. That type of thing.

CINDY: I think that is it! That helped me to get clarity on some things we've been doing. Fine-tuned some others. I'll talk to the vet about the kidneys tomorrow when we go see him. Thank you so much.

BARBARA: You are very welcome.

* * *

About four months later his owners assisted Sundance in his transition. They created a Medicine Wheel and took him outside and told him they were going to assist him in his transition. They placed him in an Indian Blanket complete with the Four Elements and placed him into the Medicine Wheel, then called in the Spirit guides. They did drumming, played a Native American Flute, and burned sage in a complete ceremony. They took him over to the vet's in his shroud. They were also were directed to a book call, *The American Book of the Dead*. It was actually written by a Native American but adapted from the *Tibetan Book of the Dead*. It directs you to do a specific reading with bell ringing before and after the reading, twice a day for 40 days. It is all about moving the Soul through the various stages of transition. The owners felt the experience was wonderful. They also felt that the readings did help them through the transition of letting go, while assisting Sundance and themselves in experiencing tremendous internal growth. So there wasn't the deeper grieving for them, because they were part of the process.

* * *

We learned a bit about McDuff and Jan before. Here is the complete story:

BARBARA: And you wanted to know why he suddenly died.

JAN: I had read in some book about cats, that said cats do not let you know. They hide the fact of their death coming. I didn't know until two months before he died what was happening. It was just so unexpected and sudden, because he was always so healthy. Never was sick in all those years, and then suddenly he wasn't eating right, and it looked like he had a little bit more trouble breathing. His stomach would go up and down in a way that didn't look right. And that's when I began to think that I needed to get this checked out, and that was it. Within five weeks he was gone. And sometimes I thank him for that, because it was such a suffering for me that, had I had to suffer any longer, I don't think I could have done it. You know—maybe it's a gift that they can give you.

BARBARA: I feel like there was some kind of growth in this throat or in his lung area.

JAN: Yes. That's what it was. It was a growth.

BARBARA: Oh, okay. It was cutting off the wind and sapping up the oxygen, so he was getting less and less oxygen.

JAN: Right. Yes, it was a tumor in the lung cavity. In the chest cavity. It was near his lung or on his lung, something like that. And they said that it had spread down to another part, and so at that point it was inoperable.

BARBARA: It came on quickly. It wasn't as if you weren't paying attention. It came on quickly and it grew—doubled all the time. It kept doubling and growing and very, very quickly. Very rapid.

JAN: And I had so been conscious of tumors. I felt his body all the time, and of course, it was up in the chest cavity behind the ribcage, and I could not feel that.

BARBARA: Interesting. You knew.

JAN: I didn't spend a lot of time on guilt, but you can't help but have some. You feel you should have seen the signs sooner. You should have realized that he wasn't quite right, and he just acted always so healthy and so chipper, even until probably about two weeks before he died. He still was acting like McDuff. He was a great actor. He really was, and that was, of course, the shock of it. It was quite unbelievable.

BARBARA: Well, it's like the owners know on another level. But there was nothing you could do. Like you said, you felt for tumors all the time, thinking that something was there. But it wasn't something that you could ever feel.

JAN: No, I just never worried about it.

BARBARA: Yes, but you sensed it.

JAN: I couldn't. I felt that I was keeping on top of that with him, and I would watch him. I was very conscious of his mortality. So conscious of it, that I was constantly telling him how much I absolutely adored him and how wonderful and special, and how I thanked God for him. I don't want to cry because then I'll—. There's been a lot of pain.

BARBARA: Oh, that's okay. It's part of the process.

JAN: There's been a lot of tears down the drain with this one, I can tell you.

BARBARA: They're not down the drain, you know. The tears are wonderful because they are an expression of how we feel. It's good to let it out.

JAN: Yes. Oh believe me, I've cried a lot of tears. It's been over two months now, but you know, at night, it's harder when I'm going to bed. That was our ritual time. That is when he wanted his love. And so, of course, that's when you miss all the things. During the day when you're busy, you're not missing because he's doing his thing—he's sleeping on the bed or whatever, and you're out here at the computer doing your thing. So, it's just been very hard, but I'm noticing it's not as bad as it was. I'm balancing it out now. You know, I adjust. You have to.

BARBARA: Absolutely, and have you thought about maybe looking and getting him back?

JAN: Yes. And I think he's coming back, and that's the other question I wanted to ask you. I think he has found his way back. I will tell you what happened about three days before he died. I kept getting this image in my mind of an apricot toy poodle. I had a miniature poodle about twenty years ago, which died very suddenly under the wheels of my ex-husband's truck. It was an accident. He backed over her. She was still pretty young—maybe about a year and a half old, perhaps. And she was an apricot miniature poodle. And it was an odd thing to be getting this image because I really didn't know what I was going to do after he left. I couldn't retrain another cat in this apartment with the wheelchair. It would have been very difficult to keep it in the apartment. And so I really had thought, "I just can't do a cat again." And I do adore cats, but I thought, "I just can't." So anyway, I had gotten this image, and I kept thinking, "What in the heck is this about?" You can't be telling me this, you really can't, because you know I have a very firm belief in rebirth. And in animals coming back, and I do believe he really was Methuselah, and he still likes that name with the M's. He likes the sound of the M's, and I had a cat named Max—that was the last time we were in California way, way back—and five months later was when I found him, McDuff, and I knew at that point that he was a reincarnation. He was born in the same month as Max died, and he had the same coloration, and I had the same intense love for him. He was really not a cat. He was beyond cat, but in a lovely disguise and a beautiful disguise. But anyway, I realize now I had an image of him the other day, of the red Irish setter that I had so bonded to—way, way back, maybe thirty years ago. And I began to realize that this being has followed me for practically all my life, and it is in a way part of myself. A part of myself, probably the very best part of myself, this being. So what happened was, I thought after he left, I thought that, apparently, what is to come is, that I was to look for this apricot poodle. And I searched for a month on the web and the whole number and whatever, and finally found this AKC breeder. She's an AKC judge, as a matter of fact, and she of many up here is the only one that I felt I could trust. And I thought, "Well, I don't know." She doesn't breed apricots, but she has browns. She had a female that was brown and her mate was black. All he ever had was black pups and not even brown, so she said, "I don't even know if he has a recessive brown gene." So this breeding that was going to be happening around the first of July, she had no idea what would come of it, but it would have been a fluke even if it was a brown. So, I had been looking out, and she was going to call someone else who had apricot poodles because she didn't, and I so would have loved to have gotten something from her. What happened was that on July third her female had one pup, and it was golden.

BARBARA: I'll be darned.

JAN: And she said, "I have no idea where this color came from. It's not in the bloodline. There's no way." And she knew that I had finally said to her, "Not even a brown." I had just decided it had to be an apricot poodle. It had to be what he said. Because I was doing all this, trying to compromise in a way, because it is so hard to find good breeders and good toy poodles, and I was going to have a healthy good dog. And so, it took her eight minutes to get to the computer to tell me that this had happened. And she gave me the birth information and the whole thing, and I could match it up, and I could see that the door that he came through was the Gemini-Jupiter, and I knew that he left with a Gemini moon. It was just so uncanny. So I thought "This is so much. This is more than a sign." This was like big neon lights and all that sort of thing going off, and it was just one. This is very much like McDuff. He was going to have the womb to himself. You know, it is rare that they have less than two. And he was going to have his mom to himself, and you know he was a chow cat; he loved food and was always very interested in what was going on when it came to food. I thought, "Isn't this amazing! a Cancer cat who loves to eat!" Of course you have to be so careful—a Cancer dog actually. McDuff was just so incredibly beautiful that you couldn't catch your breath, and when you looked at him, he had this aura about him. So of course she said, "This pup is so beautiful." So of course—now that is one of the things that I did want to ask, because I know this can be what I would like it to be. I know that he—his spirits, too—will hover about it to be sure that it's going to work. But the pup is strong as a horse, and he's not going anywhere. He's three weeks old now, and I just wanted to see if you got any feeling about that.

BARBARA: I feel this puppy is very lively, very active. It's going to be very agile. I really don't get strong masculine, which is interesting—that the energy I'm feeling is more feminine than masculine. So there's more of a balance here, which is very nice. And the color is very magical. It almost feels, I want to say, like a gold brick. Something that has a lot of value to you.

JAN: Yes, because I think it's going to have a lot of what his coat looked like. I think that it is going to be very close to that, and his coat was magical. It was so gorgeous.

BARBARA: Yes. This one feels magical by itself, and it's like a golden puppy. It's almost like something from Egypt. And I don't even know why I want to say that, but that's the energy I'm feeling here. It's almost like an Egyptian guardian dog, or something like that.

JAN: You know—that is so interesting because he has zero degrees of Scorpio rising, and that is Egypt. That is definitely Egypt.

BARBARA: Oh, isn't that interesting? Isn't that interesting.

JAN: Yes. I've had lots of lives there, and they have certain things in the temple there, and it is Goddess energy. And it's a Cancer. He's got about four planets in Cancer because all of the planets are kind of bunched together now, for a time, as they move on into the signs. And he happened to be born with a lot of these, and Cancer, and that is the feminine, and I knew because of that he would have, as I said to her, he will not be aggressive but he will be fearless. And there is a difference, and he is going to have that feminine energy about him, which is what he—he was the sweetest male. He was unbelievably gentle and sweet. Everybody who walked in the door absolutely loved him no matter what. He just was so—it just exuded from him—this love that he has.

BARBARA: But there's a solidness there. There's a security there. There's a stability there and maybe that's the gold brick, how solid, how strong it is, how strong gold is in intrinsic value. It's just like, that's what I saw first thing and the value here—

JAN: There's a lot of value in the color. A lot of value in the color to me, because it is color that I have always related to, in cats particularly, and I just knew—I just made up my mind I wasn't going to settle for another color. That it had to be what he told me, and it was to be.

BARBARA: This one is more, I want to say, more gold than apricot. I don't know if that's how it is now.

JAN: Yes. It is gold, and that is part of it—he's going to be very beautiful, and it's important to me to have that beauty. This cat had something about him that I venerated. It was like, he was so special that I could only thank God for his presence. This cat had evolved himself to the point of being so much more, I felt like he was superior to me. I felt that. I really did, and I'm not just saying it. It just is the way it was. He had something that being around him was such a comfort and a peace and a joy. The joy is what I felt the most. And I miss the joy.

BARBARA: This one feels like a homebody. Not a dog that wants to be out in the backyard playing all the time. This one will want to be in the house.

JAN: I wanted a female dog, but I finally said, "Okay God, if it's an apricot, then I don't care if it's male or female." So I finally let go of that concept that I had. And, of course, he was going to come out as a boy just to spite me. No—but I think he felt it was his energy.

BARBARA: Actually not to spite you, but males are more wanting to please. They are more wanting to be with you and do for you and be your buddy.

JAN: Yes, it's good to have a guy around the house, you know. That's what I thought. I think that this is going to be a very happy thing, because I can take him places now and he won't be so housebound. I think that was an appealing thing for him because he was such a curious cat and he loved to look out over the patio fence and see whatever he could see. When it was dark and I opened up the drapes to the patio door, he would just lie up there and look out for hours, but he didn't particularly want to go out. I think in his new persona, I think he really wants new adventures. I think that is a part of what's happening here. He wants to go. I think he's going to like to travel, but I think he's going to enjoy being at home.

BARBARA: Right. You can travel with him and he'll be quiet and he'll enjoy it because he'll be with you. He's going to be a homebody and that's kind of what you want. Where the cat, McDuff, would watch at night, because it was his job to do that, to be observant about what was going on, and he could see very well at night, and it made you feel comfortable and secure.

JAN: I had another thing I wanted to ask you. When I left New Mexico I had to put his friend to sleep. Mr. McMerlin. He was an old cat. He was really having a problem with his back legs and I knew that I couldn't manage two cats here. Then this gal that was going to drive me said she just couldn't do it and I had to go by plane, and I could take only one cat, and so, of course, it was going to be McDuff who was still pretty strong and healthy. I had to put Merlin to sleep, which I felt was all right with him. In fact, the vet more or less was indicating that he thought I should, and I said, "I don't know." So I waited, and a couple of times, I called him and was going to have him come over and each time I canceled, and of course the second time I decided if I cancel this time I'm going to have to just go the course here. And so, he was just lying around underneath the desk a lot and that was kind of how he found his little place, the little cave he was in, and stayed there. And didn't make any sounds or noises or carrying on or anything, but he was obviously not eating for the past four or five days before he died. He wasn't eating, barely drinking, but he still would go in once a day and go to the bathroom.

BARBARA: It is like turning a pilot light down and then off, and there is less and less energy. They transition very easily. They just shift right out of the body within seconds. There's no agenda for the animals like there is for people, and so it's very easy for them. When it gets too painful or too uncomfortable or whatever, it's like, "Well I'm outta here." And they just leave the old carcass behind and move on into a lighter realm. And they feel less burdened by that, by the weight of the body that didn't work any longer, and they can just pop into new ones like he's doing. But they don't come back exactly as we knew them. The soul is now needing new experiences, and so it has a new form to suit the need for the new experiences.

JAN: He was a timid cat in some ways. He was extremely sensitive and things scared him. Particularly after we moved here. It was more so because there was a lot more going on all around, and I had the feeling that he wanted to come back as the dog, because he would have a little feistier character. He wouldn't be so intimidated by things. He would have some tools at his disposal. He could bark at something and scare it.

BARBARA: He could be a little more bold.

JAN: Yes. Going forward instead of going under the bed.

BARBARA: Boldness not about attacking or being obnoxious in some way, but an expression of strength, to make you feel more secure. So you can depend on this one more than a cat.

JAN: They have a different role in the animal kingdom.

BARBARA: And they're more emotional healers, where dogs are physical healers.

JAN: Yes. That's interesting, isn't it? Because it's true that I did feel he was. He was an emotional healer, and spiritual. He was like a sponge. He would just be there and you could pour your cares over him. I felt that. I felt that I could just inundate him with that. He could just lie there and sort of— he didn't want to be mauled—but he would just take in everything.

BARBARA: When you held him, you would give him love, but you could feel that love coming right back, and he would just start to purr.

JAN: Yes. He was beautiful when it came to giving love. And he wasn't the usual hang around your neck cat, that's for sure. But I liked the way he was because he was independent, and that's something that I admire in an animal or a person. I like to see them have their own thing going. Have their own space.

BARBARA: Yes. And he gave you strength without having to hang to you and say, "Okay, we're all okay, and I'll be strong for you." He just exuded that strength, a security rock you could hold on to, and it felt secure and loving, and it gave you that strength that you needed.

JAN: Yes. It was very important during these last fourteen years. And it was after I went on disability that I was with him, and so I was home a lot. And that makes a lot of difference, and you bond differently. But I bonded to him in such a deep way that it tore my heart out with the grief.

BARBARA: He filled your heart with love. There was an empty spot there, and he was just pushing that love in there and packing it in, and you would feel full. Then as it started to dissipate, he would know when to come back and do it again.

JAN: Yes. He was definitely able to love. He was just one big thing of love.

BARBARA: And he needed that emotional stability at that time.

JAN: Yes, it's been a lot of changes and a lot of things coming and going and up and down, and he was my comfort and I could come home to him. He has been that one beacon, you know. You came in the door and there he was, and it made everything worthwhile. It lit up your life to have that when you came home, and saw this animal just waiting for you. And it was, "Okay, now the rituals begin." And you know, I thanked God every time I cleaned his litter pan. I always said, "Thank God that he is here—that I have a litter pan to clean." I was always so conscious that he would not always be with me, and it was just like, "Oh thank you for another day with this wonderful being."

BARBARA: You needed your heart filled, and so you still do, but not in the same way. He's left you with some securities there. You were feeling very insecure in those times. You could hold him. You could feel something that was yours, and could keep and it wouldn't run away and it wouldn't hurt you.

JAN: And would never fail me.

BARBARA: Yes. Never fail. Exactly. That's the exact word, and you knew that, and the never fail part was what you really needed.

JAN: So this new baby—it seems like he is pretty healthy.

I feel that she breeds the best bloodlines, and I'm feeling that he's pretty solid. She says he's roly-poly. Of course—he's getting all his mother's milk.

BARBARA: Well, again, that's a good sign. Roly-poly is good. They'll slim up as time goes on.

JAN: You know, he normally takes about five months to come back to me. It's very strange. It's almost about five months. Anywhere from five to six months is what he has done in the past, and he did after Max. He knew exactly what he was going to do, and as soon I made contact with this breeder, I thought,"God, it would be wonderful. But she's not going to have an apricot."

BARBARA: It's like a miracle. Look at the synchronicity of this and the miracle that you performed. She had told you that this was absolutely not going to happen. And yet the universe provides us exactly what we want. So you're a pretty powerful magician.

JAN: Yes, well—that certainly took some magic, but I think it was mostly his magic.

BARBARA: No. No, don't discredit yourself. You had in your mind what you wanted, and he knew what you wanted.

JAN: He knew I wanted her. He knew I wanted my pup to come from this breeder, because I knew that they would be tremendously well cared for and properly raised. He'll stay there until he's probably about three months old, because she feels, when the mother finally decides that she's had it, then he will come. But not before ten weeks. And I know, as a little Cancer, that he will probably take longer. And I told her before that I think this pup will want to be with his mother a little longer than usual. And that's fine by her. She's not trying to get rid of it, you know. It's what is good for the pup and the mother. And I am very, very comfortable with that, even if it takes time, because I need to prepare some things I'm finishing.

BARBARA: By twelve weeks, they are a little more secure

so that when they come to you they don't feel like they have been ripped away from their older surroundings. So that's real smart of you, not to be pushing the eight week mark, but allowing it. And you'll have more personality, too. The personality will mature better, and there'll be better balance with this one.

JAN: Well, Cancer does do well staying with the mother, and also the sucking process is really important to this type. They need to have a lot of that when they're very young, and the nurturing of the mother, so when the mother says it's over, then it's over—for both of them. I think it's always sort of a mutual agreement, whether it looks like it or not. And this breeder's going to make sure he is trained a little before he comes, because he'll be there so long, she's going to have to.

BARBARA: And that'll be good for you, because you won't have to be concerned with it. I feel like this one will be fairly easy to deal with.

JAN: Yes. He's going to be very smart. He's always been that way. He's always been very smart, and I think I'll see it more in the dog than I could see it sometimes in the cat. You don't see what they do, but a dog can do all manner of things because they love to do tricks—and they want to do tricks so then you get to see other parts of their intelligence.

BARBARA: Right. And it'll bring you lots of joy. You'll be smiling and giggling and watching, and that's the part that you need in your life. The cat is more quiet and lazier and yeah, they'll play when they're young, but after a while, they don't play as much. I feel like this one will always play a lot and be interactive with you. Maybe throw the ball and go fetch it and come back and just continue to be interactive with you, so that it distracts you from being concerned or worried or upset about something, but gives you more strength.

JAN: Yes. I think the joy is a real important word at this point. I think I'm looking forward to the joy. I have to have that, because this year has not been the easiest time. I've worked very hard on things that I've been doing, and so much has been taken away from me this year that it seemed as though everything that I valued had been taken away. He was the last straw. It was like, "How could you do this at this time of all times? How could you take my cat? How could you take my cat? Don't take my cat away from me." But I thought, "He knows better than I what His timing is, and what my timing is, and what I need in the future." So I felt that it was just—we cannot read the mind of God.

BARBARA: Well, it's a time of transition for you, washing away the old and bringing in the new. It's not something that you would ever choose it to be time for. You have to be pushed into it.

JAN: I need a sign, because I don't know that it's the right thing to do until you take it away from me?

BARBARA: Right. Right. You don't want to make a mistake here and do something wrong, and yet life is all about making choices. Even what seem like the wrong decisions turn out to be really right and correct. You had to put Merlin to sleep, but the choice was good because Merlin was tired and was old and things were not working so well. So this gave him the gift to be released from what wasn't working, and move on to what is—and to move on to new experiences.

JAN: Yes. Absolutely. Which is so true. I think McDuff was very ready for, and programmed this whole thing, so that he could move on to some new adventures. And I understood that. Of course, that doesn't help your grief a lot—but it helps you understand better. Understanding the esoterics of it doesn't take away the human pain. but it definitely helps a little bit to understand that it's not over.

BARBARA: And being able to see the astrological signs, knowing how magically that was—maybe not exactly for Merlin, and maybe so—but the timing is everything, and so you needed to move and Merlin needed to move. And so you've both moved.

JAN: Yes. Yes.

BARBARA: And so you both moved. Maybe it doesn't look like this would be something that you would have planned quite like that, but you know, it's not something that we let go of very easily anyway. So the universe provides us with the choices of "It's time to let go." And so you made a good choice.

* * *

And the follow up E-mail from Jan:

Dear Barbara,

Thank you so much for the enlightening reading. The poodle guy visit is two weeks away. Can't wait.

Will keep in touch.

Jan

* * *

Tony was an animal who was very close to being ready to go.

BARBARA: Okay. Let me tune into Tony here. Basically, I get Tony is a quiet cat to begin with. Kind of laid back. I feel long hair. Does he have really long hair?

JULIA: Yes.

BARBARA: Almost like a Persian.

JULIA: Yes.

BARBARA: He likes to play now and again. Maybe bat something around. But he's not super active. He's more laid back. So let me go through the body and see what might be going on here, that he's not eating.

JULIA: He's eating a little, but just not as much as he normally does. He normally has a huge appetite, and his appetite now does not seem to be the same.

BARBARA: He's picky.

JULIA: He's not hanging around the house. He normally stays around the house and just lies around. I don't know where he is. He's been gone, and when he comes back, he looks so thin.

BARBARA: Okay. I'm feeling kind of sick to my stomach.

I'm feeling like he's got kind of a sickness there. I'm almost feeling more like a tumor somewhere. Have you felt his undercoat and felt any unusual bumps or anything?

JULIA: No.

BARBARA: They're showing me a growth of some kind. It's like a growth on an organ. It looks like the liver. He's feeling quite punky.

JULIA: Punky? What's that?

BARBARA: It's like he knows he needs to eat but he's not hungry. Part of him knows he needs some food, but the food is not appealing anymore, like it used to be. I feel like he's older. Is he maybe around ten or something like that?

JULIA: Human years?

BARBARA: Yes. Human years.

JULIA: No, he's not that old.

BARBARA: Maybe the rest of him—maybe not numerical years as old—but he feels older in his physicality. Let me see what else is going on here. Nothing with the hips or spine. That all seems fine. It's something in the chest cavity itself, and I feel like it's on his left side, more toward the end of the rib cage. Somewhere in that area.

JULIA: A discomfort or a lump?

BARBARA: Well, I feel like there's a growth there. Whether it can be felt externally, I don't know. I feel like it's pretty good size actually. Good size meaning maybe the size of a half dollar. Not just a dime size. And I feel like it's turned his chemistry around, so his chemistry is not as it was before. It's not normal. They keep telling me it is creating an effect like leukemia or something, where it's affected the red cells. There are too many white cells, so it's compromised his health quite a bit. It would take medical help.

JULIA: Can medical help assist him with this type of condition?

BARBARA: Well—there are so many things out there that are possible, which depend on how far the pocketbook wants to be stretched and how long the quality of the animal's life would continue. I'm feeling like he's pretty far gone.

JULIA: I see.

BARBARA: Yes. It's something that needs attention. I'm not medical—I'm only metaphysical—and my information is as good as what my guides give me. And so it gets sorted down through me. What I feel is that he's a pretty sick kitty.

JULIA: He got sick last year and we took him to the vet. They said he had a urinary tract infection or bladder infection. Something like that.

BARBARA: Sure. They do get those.

JULIA: They said it came because we put him outside, and they said it came from him trying to find water for himself, and the water wasn't clean, and he probably got an infection. Plus I had given him more water, and he did pick his weight back up again. And he looked okay. He had gotten huge, beautiful. And that's when all of a sudden, a week ago, it definitely happened. I didn't see him for two days, and when I did see him he had lost a lot of weight, just that fast. And I said "Gosh, what happened?"

BARBARA: I feel like this is something that has been going on for a while, but it's undetected. Sometimes things happen and it isn't something you can spot immediately. I've experienced that with animals. As intuitive as I am, I didn't realize what was going on until they showed outward signs. Animals need to look as healthy as possible to avoid becoming prey. When they get so sick that they cannot look healthy, you finally notice these outside symptoms.

JULIA: I see.

BARBARA: But there is something going on here.

JULIA: I was going to ask the second question. When we'd just had him fixed—well, actually, it was probably happening before, I guess—he would potty in the house and I had to put him outside. I never could understand the reason why I could not get this cat to stop.

BARBARA: To stop spraying?

JULIA: No. Well—he started with the spraying first, and then we realized he was spraying, so we went ahead and had him fixed. Then after we had him fixed he started dropping his potty in the house. I couldn't put up with that, so I finally put him outside. Maybe if I hadn't put him outside, maybe he wouldn't have got sick. I don't know, but I couldn't let him stay in the house. So there was a brother and sister. I kept the sister in the house and I put him out—and I just let him be an outside cat.

BARBARA: Right. And again, the males—that's their marking, and they do that. That's quite natural for them.

JULIA: The potty? I can see the spraying part, but to potty on the floor? He had a litter box.

BARBARA: Well, sometimes they don't like it. It's also a way of marking. Also it's a form of "Let me out, I want out," and so you did the appropriate thing. You let him be out.

JULIA: Then, when we put him out, he threw a fit. He did not want to be outside.

BARBARA: Well, I understand. But his behavior in the house is absolutely not appropriate. And if you're moving a potty box, changing a potty box, covering a potty box, uncovering a potty box, that type of thing—if you had tried all those things but it didn't work, I can see the problem. Normally when you have a male cat in the house, the best thing to do is to get them neutered way before the spraying starts. If you get another male, that's the best thing to do. They can be neutered at a very early age.

JULIA: Oh, okay.

BARBARA: Then you don't have that tendency. Some will always have more maleness and have a tendency so they would have to be outside.

JULIA: Okay. So basically, he was still marking. Is that what you're saying?

BARBARA: Oh yes. Absolutely. That was just another form

of marking and he had gotten into a pattern of doing that. He's a very macho kind of cat. Very male. He has a lot of maleness to him, so that was what he was doing. Unless you really are on him every minute to change that behavior—and most of us don't have time for that—then outside is more appropriate.

JULIA: Okay. It really hurt me to have to put him outside. I felt so sorry for him, but I didn't have a choice.

BARBARA: Yes. Exactly. Sure, he wants to be in. But again, the behavior's not appropriate for the house. I don't feel like he had an animosity because of that. Yes, he wanted to be in, but he didn't get the message. You have to do what's going to make it pleasant for you as well as the animal. Some people allow these things to happen no matter what, and then they get upset two years later, and it may be too late to change an animal's behavior.

JULIA: You mean, putting him outside didn't cause him to get sick? He would have gotten sick anyway?

BARBARA: It didn't cause the problem. I've had inside cats get urinary tract infections, and they had plenty of water and the best of food.

JULIA: As far as his condition now, with the chemistry changing and stuff, what do you think?

BARBARA: I really think it has nothing to do with being outside. He has some kind of disease in his system that is creating a bigger problem.

JULIA: Oh, okay. I really felt like if I had never put him outside he would not have gotten sick.

BARBARA: No. I don't think that at all, because most animals live outside. And if animals live outside and are away from people, they're a whole lot healthier, believe it or not. Because they take on our ailments, and don't know how to dispel them. They don't know how to get rid of them. It's a healthy environment outside. And so that's where the animals should be as well, with the proper sunlight and the proper air.

He has food and water. He has places to run. He has places to be. So no, I wouldn't feel guilty at all about that. But I feel like his health issue is something that needs to be addressed. It's up to you as to how far you want to take what's going on here.

JULIA: Okay.

BARBARA: Animals do transition very easily. They can move out of the body into another one so easily. They don't have the agendas, like people have.

JULIA: Okay. You're talking about the spirit world?

BARBARA: Yes. Absolutely. It's very simple for them to release out of this body and to move into another one that is maybe working a little bit better and a little bit healthier. So whatever choice you have to make for whatever reason is appropriate for you, you need to know the extent of the financial expense that's involved, versus the quality of his life. A veterinarian will be able to give you some kind of direction on that. But I feel his health is quite compromised at this point. I don't see anything more here that I really could tell you.

JULIA: No. That was it. That was basically the wrap.

BARBARA: I would definitely have him checked out and go from there. Make your decisions from there. Whatever you need to do.

JULIA: Okay. Well—I really appreciate your help.

6: Reincarnation

THOSE OF US WHO BELIEVE THAT SOULS come back to earth in new bodies, often are certain that pets we have now are familiar friends who once were our pets in other bodies—even in our own other lives. Sometimes a person who has lost a beloved pet feels that it should be able to return to them as another pet, and contacts me for reassurance and some idea how this could come to be.

* * *

EDITH: My cat, Madison, died nine months ago. My question is, can he come back to me?

BARBARA: What I am feeling is that this particular cat was a cornerstone in your life, someone you could lean on. Someone you could depend on, felt safe with. Sort of a quiet energy but a solid energy. He made you feel really comfortable. Is that what Madison was like for you?

EDITH: Yes. He was my peace.

BARBARA: What I am getting is real solid, like a building. And now you feel that that part of your life has nothing to lean on. As much as it was an animal, he was an emotional security for you—and now you feel unprotected.

EDITH: That is one way to put it.

BARBARA: Yes, he can return to you! We all evolve and we all go on, to working on more of who we are. And so for him, he was quite evolved. He knew where you were and what was going on with you. He knew when you needed him to be next to you, to make you feel comfortable and secure. And he knew when to just kind of watch. Was that how he was?

EDITH: He didn't really watch. He was always wanting love. We were just real, real bonded. He just wanted to be held. Sometimes it was a nuisance, but he was a real comfort.

BARBARA: Yes. I feel that very much. It feels like the left side of you is totally unprotected.

EDITH: I used to hold him over my heart. He was like my heart connection.

BARBARA: Yes. It was a link you had with him. And you can have that back. He doesn't necessarily have to come back as the same type of cat. Doesn't have to look like the same cat. Because lots of times they don't. If you hunt and hunt and can't find that exact look, and think you haven't found him, that is not true. And he could even be more of a full grown cat—he doesn't have to be a kitten right now. And he might not be a male. Because we as people go male, female, male, female. Not necessarily alternating, but—we sign up for things we need to learn. We alternate within sexes. And so do animals. If he was a calico cat, now he may want to be Siamese. Go out with the intent that you will find him. If you want a kitten, you can look at different litters. Maybe look at two or three litters, and one kitten will come out to meet you. He or she will make it very clear that they are the one.

EDITH: Well, I've been looking for him! He was a lilac. A beautiful, beautiful lilac Oriental. He was declawed when I got him. Apparently he had been very wild, and declawing was the last resort. But when he was mine, he was the gentlest, gentlest soul. So sweet and loving. So I have been looking at Orientals because I didn't know where else to start.

BARBARA: Right! And it may be another Oriental. But don't limit yourself to that type. Or just to kittens. He might be full grown.

EDITH: Actually, you know what? I was thinking maybe not kittens. But—this may sound crazy, but—if I was that bonded to him, I feel he must feel that bonded to me. And he must have come back. And he died nine months ago. He would be seven months old exactly.

BARBARA: Or they can pop right into a new body. They

just pop into the body as it is born. Sometimes, that is approximately when the soul enters the body.

EDITH: I did meet a breeder that I really liked. She seems like she really loves her animals. She raised Orientals. She has a seven-month-old boy that I am going to look at if she doesn't sell him.

BARBARA: Who is the breeder?

EDITH: Her name is Carol.

BARBARA: I have a Javanese that I purchased from an Oriental breeder. But it is the more you start to get connected. You might look at this one and say, "No, no, no. This is not exactly the one I want. No—I am looking for a different type." And yet this one doesn't come out of your mind. This one stays in your mind and you kept thinking about this particular one. And then you think, "How could that be?" But don't question how that could be! Because the universe works in mysterious ways. It is possible for an animal soul to have parallel lives. It might sound very strange. People can do parallel lives, as well. A soul can know that it is going to be leaving this life and it already starts popping into a new one. There are things about how the Universe works that we are not quite aware of. I feel like there will be one that will really stick in your mind. Where you go to visit, do you see one that is—. Do you like gray? I get gray!

EDITH: Well, Carol has a seven-month-old that is a Lynx Seal Point. And she has another one that is solid lavender. The lavender looks kind of gray.

BARBARA: Yes it does. How interesting! The choice is yours, and you will know the energy yourself.

EDITH: That is what I figured. If I pick up the cat I could feel the energy. His energy is like golden love that envelops you.

BARBARA: When you go and find this one, which you connect with, the energy might not be exactly as strong as it was with him. And that is because the new one will come in with extra qualities he didn't have before. It will come in with more things to help you through your life. More things to connect you to another level. He left because it was time for him to leave. He also left because you were becoming stagnated at a certain level. And so, as your new cat, he will have grown and your own growth is going to be more expansive. Does that make any sense to you?

EDITH: Yes. But it sounds like I won't find him again.

BARBARA: Oh, no. They come back with the energy of who they are and what they were. But they come back with more.

EDITH: Okay.

BARBARA: They do not come back like a cookie cutter image of the last time. And you don't cut out the same cookie and have the same cookie again. This is what I am trying to say to you. So you will see that this is the energy, and this is the way he was. But, he is more! Or she. She is more alive and not as needy. Perhaps she will be more independent, like to play more. I am really getting a softer energy. So I'm not sure if—it doesn't necessarily have to be female to be a she in a softer energy. My own male Javanese is a very soft energy. You would almost think he was female rather than male.

EDITH: But that is how Madison was. More like a little girl. Like a little needy girl. He was not like a body. In fact that is how I got him. He wouldn't breed. He wouldn't do any of those things he was suppose to do. But I could see him becoming a less needy animal. I have never seen an animal that was so needy. I'd have to push him off me sometimes, because it felt like I was being smothered.

BARBARA: I think what I am trying to say to you is that, "You will go out. You will find this one. You will see the old traits. You will see some of that neediness, but not at the same level that it was." And so, don't question yourself that maybe you didn't find him. Don't say, "Well, this is not exactly him. "He doesn't do this, and he doesn't do that the same."

EDITH: So I guess my last question is, this breeder in Arizona has a cat about which she said, she would give me the seven-month-old—sell it to me cheap. But she is going to show him on the fourth. I'm wondering if I should drive out there this weekend, and see. So that he doesn't potentially get sold before she returns on the tenth.

BARBARA: If you feel that strongly about this particular one, you should follow your feelings. I don't want to misdirect you. I do feel very strongly toward this one however. But I want you to make the decision. It is important that you follow your own heart. If you have not seen this one and you still feel very drawn, that is significant. You could also just say that he won't be sold at the cat show and he will be mine. Because he belongs to me. We belong each other. That's how it will be. And if he is sold then he isn't the right one. You can stop panicking and just allow the Universe to show you if this is the one. Because if it is, he'll be there. If someone did buy him, then that was close but no cigar. Take the pressure off yourself saying, "They are going to sell my cat. They'll sell Madison and I will never see him again." No, that won't happen. If this is the one that is meant for you, he will come to you. You don't have to ponder or to worry, or to think you have make a mistake. Because you will be guided.

EDITH: Thank you.

* * *

Here is a letter telling me about a pet the owner believes may have come back:

Barbara,

You're very good. I told you that after Moonshine's death I didn't think I wanted another kitty. You affirmed to me that that decision was fine, but you also opened possibilities when you said I also may want another one. You told me that I may have to look over a few litters, but it I looked for the right characteristics, I'd find the right one.

Well, I'd been working under the assumption for weeks

that I was going to have only one dog and one cat. It was so practical, especially when all of us are trying to sleep together. Well, Cathy apparently had other ideas. We went to PetsMart yesterday, and of course the Humane Society was there. I bravely walked past the cages of kittens. But, Cathy came and got me and took me over there. She had picked one out, but it turned out to be a male. So she told me to go in the room and just look. I looked into several cages for kittens, looking over a few litters just like you said, and found nothing. But then I saw this little tortoiseshell baby. She was at the front of the cage. She played with me, and when I held her, she was calm. Well, we had a new cat.

When we went up to the register, Cathy was thinking of names, but she asked me what I wanted, and I said Asia would be a good name. Then I remembered that a few weeks ago, I was just thinking—about God knows what—but the thought came into my mind that I loved little tortoiseshell kitties. I also thought that Asia would be a good name for a kitty.

She's also the perfect cat. She's playful, but she's very, very loving. She's only six weeks old, and she's all cat. She rubs up against your legs. None of my Siamese have done that. She loves to be petted and held, and she purrs a lot.

So there you have it. I just wanted to let you know, and say thanks. I know we made the right decision yesterday, and your enlightenment about how I'd find a kitten was also affirming that we made the right decision.

Thanks,

Blessings, Betsy

P.S. I wouldn't be surprised if this kitty was China coming back to me—sweet disposition and that oriental name connection that just popped into my head a few weeks ago. I think Spirit will let me know if this is true.

* * *

Some pet owners feel as if their new pets may be old pets they'd known.

BARBARA: Dinky was very close to you. Actually she still is very close to you! That is why you are feeling so much sensitivity. I feel her vibration.

OLIVE: I only had a dream about her once. When I was very sick, a little while after she had died. After that I never dreamt about her. I wonder why she never comes to me in a dream?

BARBARA: I can see that she was very gregarious. She was always happy and wanting to play. She would encourage you to have fun with her. Is that how she was?

OLIVE: Yes, she was very close to me.

BARBARA: Was she very playful?

OLIVE: She was the youngest of three dogs at the time. She was only four years old when she died. The other two were seven and nine. She was the baby. She was like my baby. She always had to be near me or wrapped around my neck. Or in my lap. Whereever I went.

BARBARA: That is the interaction that I am feeling. She always wanted to be part of what you were doing, and encouraged you to be part of what she was doing. Kept you happy and amused. She was always fun.

OLIVE: And a comfort.

BARBARA: She didn't want you to feel sad or depressed. I feel that you would have been depressed without her help. Were there things in your life that were not happy then? Was this a time of illness for you?

OLIVE: When she died?

BARBARA: Before she died.

OLIVE: No, but I had lost my sister. The year before. There had been a lot of—

BARBARA: Sadness.

OLIVE: Yes, sadness and worry.

BARBARA: What she did for you was to distract you. By being around you and encouraging you to have fun with her. To suspend your sorrows and your losses just for a moment, to play. To be joyful. If you wanted to give her a middle name, you could call her Joy. She was a joy be around and she was a joy for you to connect with. You miss her so much because she made you forget your worries and your troubles and the constant concerns you have over things. She would bring you a toy or hang around your neck, or sit in your lap or be under your feet. She was saying, "Here I am. Let's play. Let's do something different. Let's not worry any more."

OLIVE: Yes! That is how she was.

BARBARA: She was a wonderful, wonderful little energy. The joy that she had—she was pure love. I feel as if your two hearts connected, they linked. And you could feel her love and she could feel yours. You were never far apart when she was alive, and she is not far away from you now. You don't see her in your dreams because you know that she is around you. Because you can still feel her love. You can still connect with that energy, and feel that warmth and joy that she brought you.

OLIVE: About five months after she died I got another puppy. My dogs are all spaniels, and they were all black and white. The new one is red and white. It was had to find female spaniels in this area, from a reliable breeder. They are usually spoken for way ahead of time. It was a lucky chance that I found this one. A lady had put a deposit on her, but when she came to get her she took a male instead. The breeder had tried for six months to get the woman to consider a male. Then for some reason she just changed her mind and left this little red and white female. The breeder knew about Dinky, and she called me up and wanted to know if I wanted her. And we went out and got her. In a lot of ways she is very much like Dinky. And in a lot of ways she is not! She is entirely different personality, but more of what you described fits her—as far as always wanting to play.

BARBARA: This new puppy? Okay, maybe that is who I am picking up. That why I always ask, because I can be picking up the energy from the people, and more than one of the animals. The one that wants to speak the loudest is always right there. And that is the one which speaks the loudest to me. If we were not getting the information on the right one you want to know about, we can search again to direct, to tune in to the one that one we need to talk about.

OLIVE: Her name is Rosie! And we call her Rotten Rosie. She is a monster! I love her dearly but she is into everything there is to get into. You can't get mad at her, and of course I spoil her terribly. In some ways she reminds me very much of Dinky because she is always—Dinky was—

BARBARA: Always underfoot?

OLIVE: Mainly wrapped around my neck, or in my lap. But always touching me. Dinky was the type that if I walked in and out of a room twenty times, she got up and came with me twenty times. And so does Rosie. She follows me all over, and when she sleeps she has to be touching me. Dinky did that. I get a lot of comfort from that, especially at night. She wraps herself over me very much like Dinky did. But, Dinky— she got the name Dinky because she was dinky. She did dinky things. So we kept saying she is dinky and pretty soon we started calling her Dinky.

BARBARA: Was she more refined?

OLIVE: Yes, she was more refined than this one. This one is a little bit more—

BARBARA: She is more gregarious. This is the gregarious one.

OLIVE: Right, exactly. Dinky was more refined.

BARBARA: She was more feminine than Rosie, more ladylike.

OLIVE: I had people say that Dinky would come back, that her spirit would come back in another pet. I don't quite understand. If that happens, is it the exact personality?

BARBARA: No—it isn't the exact personality that comes back. When you lose a loved-one like this, what you do is go out with the intent of finding them. If you can't find them, they will find you. They could show up as cat. They don't have to be a dog. They don't even have to be the same breed. And they are not like a cookie, cut out with the same cookie cutter. So you will not get the exact Dinky back that Dinky was. As with people, they sign up for certain experiences in a lifetime. And if they have fulfilled that experience, they sign up for a different experience. Maybe a little bit of what they had, but progressed, and ready for new areas of growth. They come back with a lot of traits they had before, but they are more! It is an altered energy. They can keep part of them on the other side and part of them spins off into the new animal. It is hard to explain, because the way we are taught to think, it isn't really logical. But I see many animals as they do come back, partly the old pet you lost, and partly an animal with new facets to develop. I have experienced this myself with my own pets. Wanting one back that I loved so deeply. They come back with similar personality traits, but they have extras that come along with them. So Rosie lies on your neck as Dinky did, and follows you from room to room. Except, that she is more gregarious. She wants to experience more than what Dinky experienced. Dinky was more reserved, and needed more safety and security. She didn't venture out into wild experiences. Part of them can come back to connect with the love that you need, that heart chakra connection. This new one also needs more challenging experiences because that's what she signed up for, for her own spiritual growth. And it is always better that the new one that we have is not exactly like the one it was before. Because life is about expanding and learning and experiencing more.

OLIVE: If there is part of Dinky in Rosie, then—. I am hoping that when I die, Dinky will be there. Then will Rosie be there, too? When she dies?

BARBARA: No. It will be Dinky and Rosie as well. Many books have been written about the tunnel of light and how the energies that were relatives and friends come to welcome us. It is a wonderful and very peaceful experience. There are family, friends, children and animals in wonderful harmony, come to meet you so you can reconnect with their energies. How that happens and how they will look I can't tell you. I don't really know. But I know that we connect with them. It is like being in part of an eternal family of energies that progress in groups which remain together. Have you ever met someone, and felt like you have known then forever? But you just met them? You chat comfortably, as if you have been long-time friends, and yet it has only been a few moments. These are people that you have been with before in other lifetimes.

OLIVE: But if—. Well, my mother died some twenty-five years ago. If she comes back as, say, a neighbor that you feel very close to. Then if I were to die, my mother would not be there on the other side.

BARBARA: That mother would be. The mother that you knew would be.

OLIVE: So Dinky will be there?

BARBARA: If you want her there, she will be there! I feel she will. As the Dinky that you knew, but it will also be Rosie that you knew. It will be that energy.

7: Metaphysical Issues

IN EVERY DISCIPLINE THERE ARE RULES, and New Age thinking is no exception. But like most disciplines, the people involved decide what the rules are, based on what their experience shows to be true. There is only one problem with this. Most people have been trained to believe in a set of rules that at some point have been based on what others have decided is true rather than what has been observed to be true.

Many religions have declared that animals do not have souls. It may be that this belief enables certain cultural behaviors to be allowed, without ethical conflicts with other cultural rules—such as using animals as food.

The fact is that psychic readings have shown conditions to be rather similar for animals and humans who have passed over to the other side. The following reading not only describes 'the meadow' as a place where animals can be with humans and other animals, but suggests that animals come to earth incarnations with a purpose to protect and comfort humans they have known in other lives. This reading is particularly interesting for suggesting the possibility of a soul returning to a body that existed while he was still on this plane.

* * *

CHRISTINE: That's Mattie.

BARBARA: Okay. And as I feel it, Mattie's fine. He transitioned very easily. I see him playing in a meadow with other dogs and cats and birds and this is a wonderful magical meadow that the animals play in when they've transitioned and the soul hasn't moved to another experience yet. And he's very happy, very content.

CHRISTINE: No pain?

BARBARA: Oh no. No—when they leave, they leave all pain

behind. Everything that had to do with that physical body is gone. They're totally released from pain or discomfort of any kind in that experience, to move on to a new experience. And so he's moved into a transitional stage where they kind of wait to come back in—however that is for them.

CHRISTINE: Okay.

BARBARA: And it's a very beautiful place.

CHRISTINE: It's funny I ask. I was feeling so bad, and I started going on the Internet and they had this thing called Rainbow Bridge and that's the way they explained it.

BARBARA: Oh really. Okay.

CHRISTINE: That's the way they explain it.

BARBARA: Well sometimes they transition right back into another body and move on with life. But there is this beautiful meadow. Everything there is very youthful. Everything that's there is very new, is very fresh, is very alive. It's like springtime all the time.

CHRISTINE: Okay. But I feel like he's here.

BARBARA: He can also be with you. When they transition, the spirit moves up into another realm. I can only explain it as I see it, but there's more than I can explain or even understand, because we lose our past knowledge when we go to the other side. We've all been there before many times. And so, as the spirit moves up into the valley and experiences that, the energy that you knew can stay with you, if you choose. And he has. I want to say, "To watch over you," because he feels it is his job, and to comfort you as well, and for you not to worry about him. Do you see what I mean?

CHRISTINE: Yes.

BARBARA: Do you have a special chair that you sit in?

CHRISTINE: I sit on the couch and read.

BARBARA: Okay. I see a chair and I see him on the left side down by your feet.

CHRISTINE: If you were facing the couch that I sit on to read, he would lie on the floor.

BARBARA: On your left side?

CHRISTINE: At the end of that couch. It's not a couch—more like a loveseat.

BARBARA: Oh, okay. Smaller. And that's where I see him. He stays there with you. He's just quiet, and patiently is with you, and you can feel him. It's wonderful that you can do that. A lot of times people have a hard time feeling the energy that stays and lingers with them, to protect them and to guard them and to nurture them.

CHRISTINE: The other thing is my dog, Justin, a puppy that I got right before Mattie died. He mourned Mattie for two days. He was eight weeks when I got him. He was probably here for four or five weeks before Mattie died. I had dreamed Justin's name before I got him. I woke up and I said that I had to call him Justin Illusion.

BARBARA: Justin Illusion?

CHRISTINE: On his papers. This was when Mattie was alive. I dreamed it. I woke up and said to my husband, "My dog's name is going to be Justin, and I have to call him Justin Illusion." So his papers say Bailiff Justin Illusion. It didn't click into my head until two days ago, that Justin has picked up a certain habit of Mattie's. Mattie would take my arm and he would put his mouth on my arm and pull me over, and Justin has picked up that trait. Justin has also picked up another trait. It's almost like Mattie told him how to do it. I don't understand, but he's doing too many things that Mattie used to do. Mattie used to call me into the living room and we used to wrestle. I have another dog. I have an American bulldog. But this dog does things that Mattie did, and people come over and tell me they see Mattie in his eyes. I don't understand it. I really—I'm telling you it might sound crazy—

BARBARA: No.

CHRISTINE: And why did I call this dog, "Justin Illusion"?

BARBARA: Because metaphysically that's what this is. This realm on this side is just an illusion. The real world is on the other side. That's real. This is not real. This is an illusion, so it's a metaphor. It's a very powerful metaphor, if you think about it, because as you said it to me, that's how I picked it up. It's just an illusion.

CHRISTINE: I dreamed that.

BARBARA: You dreamed it. You got the message on another level. You're very intuitive. You're in tune, and so you went with it—which was absolutely wonderful. Because you can ask your animals, "What would you like your name to be?" and they'll tell you. They have an idea of the vibration—there's lots of vibration in the name—it's the soul's vibration for that lifetime. So Justin Illusion is just incredible because Mattie and his personality quirks have come into Justin, but it's just an illusion.

CHRISTINE: Isn't that amazing?

BARBARA: Yes. It's totally amazing. It's quite beautiful, and it's a beautiful metaphor for how it really is here. And most people don't see that. They don't realize that.

CHRISTINE: So I'm right in the way that I'm thinking?

BARBARA: Oh, absolutely. You're right on. Absolutely.

CHRISTINE: That's what I really needed to know.

BARBARA: Yes, absolutely. Because it is an illusion and souls can split off. They can live parallel lives. We do that. We can be living two lives. We can, in our later years, move into a different body and split off. I don't know exactly how that works but I know that it does happen. There are people who have not finished one life, and move into another new one. Do you know? Yet all our memories of this are gone, because if we were to keep all the memories of our other lifetimes, they would so influence this one that we really couldn't live this one as another unique lifetime. That's why we don't have memories from the other lifetimes—but we do have influences. They do bleed through. We do have a sense or feeling about things. At certain times a past life will be very, very dominant in your present life. And so for you to choose this name for this new one is really incredible. And so, as it is, Mattie lives on through Justin Illusion.

CHRISTINE: That's what I thought.

BARBARA: Very magical.

CHRISTINE: That's exactly what I thought. I feel like Mattie didn't just leave me here.

BARBARA: No, he didn't leave. The spirit has moved into a different realm, but the soul part of him is still—the soul is with you, and split off.

CHRISTINE: One more thing I had asked you, is the guilt thing. Mattie had such fight to live, and he was so incredibly sick that I was told around Christmas to put him down. They told me to just get through the holiday, and he could hardly walk, and I would get him up every day and I would get him outside to the bathroom, and I would take him in, and at the end he was urinating all over the floor for two nights. The urine just came out of him. His fur was scaling. His body functions were going, and I had to make the decision to put him to sleep. And even though I made that decision and said yes, part of me feels that I rushed it. It's just a guilt thing I'm going through. When I went there I held Mattie as he waited in the vet's. Usually he would put the chain in his mouth to leave. He never did. He stood there. He waited for my husband to come from Queens. Right before they put him on the table, he put his leash in his mouth. That scared me. And then we put him on the table and he wouldn't lie down—like he was fighting it—and the big thing that really breaks my heart is that I kept turning his head to look at me and not to look at the needle, and it was almost as if when he was dying, I saw the life go out of his eyes. I actually felt my heart drain with his, and it was almost like he said to me, "Okay, Ma, you've won." That's the way I took it, and I can't get that out of my head.

BARBARA: Oh no. No.

CHRISTINE: I just need to know. I just hope that he wasn't upset at me, that I did that to him. That kills me.

BARBARA: No. Absolutely not. In fact, what happened, as you know—the vet should have mentioned it to you—is his kidneys failed. There was no retrieving the function of the kidneys, and it was his time. And he knew it was his time.

CHRISTINE: Yes. And then the doctor had to inject him twice. And I thought that was a sign for me to take him home. I said, "Are you hurting him? If you hurt him, I have to take him home," and he said, "No, I'm not." I'm telling you—as that fluid went into him, something happened to me. I have fluid around my heart right now. I'm going to specialist, and I really feel like I got sick. I really feel like I got sick.

BARBARA: Yes. And again, that could happen because your heart and his heart were so connected. And as he left, you felt like—when the hearts meld and it feels like something is being ripped away, is being ripped out of your heart. And in fact the sensation is there, but it was time for him to leave. The body was not working. He wanted to stay with you through the holidays. The message was to stay with you through the holidays, so that you wouldn't have such real trauma through the holidays. But it was his time.

CHRISTINE: You don't think he was upset at me?

BARBARA: Oh, no.

CHRISTINE: I put him to sleep that day. I put him in the car, and I took him, and had to make that decision.

BARBARA: He was very grateful for that decision because his body was not working, and you released him from something that was not working. You gave him the gift. Death can be a gift—to be released from the pain. We always look at it as something heavy, not a gift. But it is. And so you have allowed him to be released, and that was his gift. And his gift to you was to fill your heart, and so he did not leave. His physical being left because he didn't need that any longer. But his soul is still with you. He's still there with you, and you know he's there, so fill your heart with that which you love so much. You can do that. You can give him back your heart and he can give you his.

CHRISTINE: I feel so much better. I'm so happy I talked to you. You have no idea.

BARBARA: Because your heart does not have to ache any longer. Do you see? Right now you've got deep heartache and you've lost a very wonderful deep friend, but Justin is there. He's in your illusion, and so Mattie lives on.

CHRISTINE: It's so amazing.

BARBARA: It is amazing.

CHRISTINE: This is so amazing.

BARBARA: Every time I talk to someone it totally amazes me, because I learn so very much more about the intricacies of the Universe, and the Universe is so magical, and it has so many magical ways about dealing with, helping people deal with it. But it's like—we feel like we're alone. That if we were to say this to someone, most people wouldn't understand. And they wouldn't know how to work with the material, and that's what we're doing here. We're working with the material that you gave me, the material that I pick up, the material the Universe gives me. And we meld that together to come up with a communication to help you heal your heart.

CHRISTINE: Wow.

BARBARA: Because you don't need to feel guilty. You gave him a gift. It was his time, and I've had those choices under the same kidney failure circumstances too, and I talk to them and explain to them, and when it's their time and they're released from that body, I hear them say, "I'm free! I'm free!" And they can move on.

CHRISTINE: I just keep saying, this is so amazing.

BARBARA: Yes. Because you have picked so much of it up on your own. But it's like you just didn't quite bring the little sound bytes together. And you're starting to now.

CHRISTINA: Yes. This really connected everything I was feeling. So it's kind of like you verified how I was feeling.

BARBARA: Exactly. It's like connecting the dots. And I feel that as you go on in the next few weeks and months, you're going to start to connect more dots. You're going to start to see the synchronization of the Universe and how it really works—and the magic of it all! It is very magical, and the animals bring us so much, and set us on new paths that we had never thought about. They give us direction. They help us with our projects, but in such subtle ways. Sometimes with their passing. Sometimes with their personality. Sometimes with part of their soul that remains in another. And they bring you to play and to wrestle, tell you to lighten up, have fun. It's just an illusion. That's all this is. Don't take it so seriously because we all—all energies come and go. They're born and they die. They're born and they die. They come and they go, and we've done this hundreds and hundreds of times, and the animals do the same thing.

CHRISTINE: I'm telling you, I feel a bond. Like I said, I have a two-year-old American bulldog I love. I'm a real animal lover. They're like my children. And Justin and I have—for two days after Mattingly passed away, I couldn't even look at my dogs. I was so bad, and my best friend called me and she said, "Christine, it's not their fault. They love you. They need you." And it made me kick back and say, "You know what? Yeah, you're right." Because I was so bad. But I have such a bond now with Justin. I'm telling you, I feel like Mattie's there. I keep saying that, but it's so incredible. It's just so incredible. And last night my friend came here and we were talking about Mattie. Justin got up and took my arm as if to say, "You don't have to be so upset."

BARBARA: Right, and we're still here. You might not see Mattingly as you used to see him, but we all take on new forms and we all take on different looks, and become male or female. The message is, "We're fine. You don't have to feel bad about this. We're fine, and we want you to be fine too. So come on, let's play. Let's get up. Lighten up. Let's move from this energy. Let's move from this feeling of not feeling happy and joyous, and let's play!" Do you see? They're really giving you such a wonderful gift of fun and joy and play. It's very magical. Very powerful and very magical. That's really incredible! You know you're in tune, and maybe you need to be looking at your own metaphysical path, whatever that is and however that evolves. Do you see? We all have some metaphysical path in our life. And you could pick up a different book or listen to a tape, or go sit in a workshop for an hour or two—a topic or a title of your choosing—and just play. Just enjoy. See what the Universe—the Universe is so intricate. It has so many things that you could learn about, do and read. We're all just a big family of light, so you know it's about you moving on your path and not being stuck here. Not to have a broken heart. It's not Mattingly's intent for you to feel like that. And he can't say to you, "Lighten up." But he says it to me, to say to you.

CHRISTINE: Right.

BARBARA: Because Justin is here, and so is part of Mattingly. "So let's play. Let's wrestle. Let's have fun. Don't feel bad. Don't feel guilty. You did nothing wrong." See—we go through and look for all the things we could have done wrong, and then we beat ourselves up about it. The Universe has no intent for us to do that, but it's something that's in our belief system. Someone said something to us once and we believed it. It might have been their agenda and not ours, but we believed it. And so we made it part of our agenda. And yet maybe that's one of those beliefs you just need to drop. What you do is Universal timing. What you did was perfectly correct and every movement that you made was co-created, so there aren't any mistakes. There are just experiences. That's all.

CHRISTINE: Okay. I feel so much better.

BARBARA: Oh, I'm so glad. It's really incredible. I've recently had a number of people who have lost animals—or their animals have transitioned—and I've received so much fabulous information from the Universe. Provided to me to pass on to my clients. It's another whole realm that I wish they would give us some memory of.

CHRISTINE: Me too.

BARBARA: Yes. Because then we wouldn't feel so bad about something passing, but know there's joy and a gift in the passing.

CHRISTINE: Yes. Too many things added up the day that I took Mattie. My girlfriend—I haven't seen her in six months—she came over because she thought I needed her.

BARBARA: Isn't that wonderful?

CHRISTINE: And she said to me, "You have to take him. I'm here, I'll watch the girls." She came out of nowhere. It's almost as if everything happened for a reason. Everything. The dream, Justin, her coming here, me calling you.

BARBARA: Exactly. And now, knowing that you don't have to have the heartache. That your heart doesn't have to ache anymore. That you didn't do anything wrong. The Universe provided all this timing, and it was such a gift. Look at all the synchronicity of that and say thank you, because much help was sent to help you get through, but not to get stuck in, that time. To move on from it, to glean the gifts from that and move on with those gifts. Keep the gifts and move on with them, because there are many gifts. You have an ability to hear and communicate with the other realms. You got the name. That's your gift. Maybe animal communication is your gift as well.

CHRISTINE: That's so amazing. I never realized that until talking to you.

BARBARA: Yes. Absolutely. Not everybody gets that kind of information, and normally people who are gifted with animals—who can feel and sense the animals—are a little bit closer to the communication. It doesn't mean that we don't all have the gift, because we do. But most people aren't close enough or quiet enough to tune into it, and you are. I was born with this gift. I've done this in many lifetimes, but I still ignored it for many years. I just moved into this, and it was so easy. So for you, it might be the same. Animals leave us with wonderful legacies.

CHRISTINE: Well—I'll tell you one more thing.

BARBARA: Sure.

CHRISTINE: I wasn't going to say anything, but I will really quick. One night I went to sleep. I'm telling you, it wasn't a dream because I know what a dream is. But I woke up from it almost like I was there. It could have been a dream, I don't know. I saw Mattie. His hair was flowing. He was golden. He was blonde. His hair was so shiny, so beautiful, and the only things around him were blue skies. I saw blue skies and light. It was beautiful light, and he was sitting up straight with his head up—almost proud. And he was just sitting there. And then I woke up.

BARBARA: And see, that's what I said about the light. We're like a family of light. When you go, you go into the light. You go into the tunnel, into the light, into the Universal love and energy. It's hard to explain the light. I'm like a Light worker. I keep my beacon on, so others can find their way.

CHRISTINE: It didn't feel like a dream to me. It just felt like I was there. I can't explain it.

BARBARA: Of course.

CHRISTINE: It didn't feel like a dream because when I woke up it didn't feel like a dream. It just felt like I was there and I saw him.

BARBARA: Well, you can travel. You may want to get a book on astral travel, because you can travel.

CHRISTINE: And I never told anybody that.

BARBARA: Yes. Well, most people would go, "Oh that's different." But if you start to get books on astral travel or just go listen to a speaker for an hour or so you'll go, "Oh that's what I did, and that's what it is." He connected you to travel where he was, to see how beautiful he is, how happy he is—and he's in the light. He's in the love of the Universe and he's being loved. And the shiny, beautiful coat, he's telling you he is being totally cared for.

CHRISTINE: It's so amazing that you've opened me up to this. That I called you—and I'm just amazed by this!

BARBARA: Well—there's no accidents. When a book falls off a shelf and it falls on you, it's like, "Oh that's an interesting book." Yes. Someone hands you a book and says, "I think you need to read this." Someone mentions a book. Someone says, "I'm going to a workshop. Why don't you come along for company?" So there are never any accidents. There are many paths to get there. There's not just one path where, if you miss the path, you've missed it. No. There are many paths to get there. So, just as you're doing, kind of look at the synchronization and ask questions. The next time you get this in a dream, or you see something, you can say to them, "Well how are you? Are you okay? Are you enjoying yourself? Where are you?" You can talk as you do this, and talk to the energy, and you might hear something back. "I'm fine. Can you see? I'm being cared for. My coat is so shiny. I am so healthy and I am in the light. I'm in the Universal love. Everything is fine with me. Not to worry."

CHRISTINE: It's amazing that I saw that.

BARBARA: Yes. Absolutely. You have some great gifts here, and some real abilities.

CHRISTINE: And I didn't even realize until I talked to you.

BARBARA: Yes. Well, sometimes we need to talk to someone who has experienced it. I've experienced a number of these things. When you talk to someone who has this, you learn you're not crazy at all. You're right on the path, and the message is, keep following the light. You are a Light worker. You are a metaphysician. There's a book that may help. There's a book by Barbara Marciniak. It's *Family of Light: Pleiadian Tales and Lessons in Living.* It's channeled material. She channels the Pleiadians. You might find it and thumb through it. See if it relevant to what you need to know.

CHRISTINE: I'm a big reader. I'll go get it.

BARBARA: Any of the metaphysical bookstores or a large bookstore should have it. I found it very, very interesting. And you might find other books there that pique your interest.

I don't want to direct you on which way to go, because that's not appropriate in this case. You have, as I feel it, a very broad path. You can take many avenues, and you can learn about a lot of different things. I feel like you could absorb them very easily and it's going to be like an "Aha!" for you. It's going to be that incredible for you. They're going to confirm things you know, that you might not have thought about as being very important. And the message is, that you have lots of time to do some work.

CHRISTINE: I absolutely do, and I needed something to inspire it.

BARBARA: Yes. See—so there you are. I'm sure there's a metaphysical group, or someone close by that gives talks on many different subjects—so that you don't have to really have to get involved a single subject. You could learn something about a lot of them, and then jump in where it feels right for you. You might get involved in something for a year—maybe two or three years—and might move to something else, thinking, "Why did I do that?" But each time it's like building a dowry basket. You're putting things in your basket, picking up all these bits and pieces, so that when you finally do the end result, it will play on all the things that you've learned through time. Do you see?

CHRISTINE: Yes. I am just—this is just unbelievable. I might call you in a couple months to let you know how I'm doing.

BARBARA: Oh, I would love it! Absolutely. I always love to hear from clients, and how things are going. For me it's so heartwarming. It's very important for me to help people get past that hurdle, to have more understanding, and then move on with life. Because the animals have no intent of having us get stuck. They want us to move on, and that's their gift. They give us many gifts—but they're so subtle that we almost ignore them, thinknig that because they can't talk they don't have a lot of value. But they are invaluable. And Mattingly has given you this wonderful beginning here, and with Justin. And keep a journal of all these little—you know, a journal is always helpful.

CHRISTINE: I'll do that, too. I bought a notebook a couple of weeks ago. I bought a notebook, and I haven't written in it yet. I went to the store and bought a notebook. And maybe that's why.

BARBARA: So that's your preparedness. And what they say is, to keep a journal of all these different thoughts and ideas. Then go back and look to see how much progress you've made, and maybe you'll want to manifest different things. Look at what you've manifested and how you've manifested so beautifully. You just ask and the Universe will provide.

CHRISTINE: Wow.

BARBARA: Yesterday was a very powerful day. I guess there was a large planetary lineup on the 28th. And I'm not an astrologer, but I have some people who are into astrology. So I don't know how the energy will set up after this, but—you know—maybe you just ask, and you'll receive. And it's always, ask for your higher good. It might not be that you'll get it exactly the way you want it, but as long as it's always for your higher good then it will be provided in the form that you need.

CHRISTINE: All right. Great. This is great. I'm so happy that I talked to you.

BARBARA: Oh, thank you, Christine. And me too. You know you inspire me, as well.

CHRISTINE: I'm definitely going to call you again and tell you how I'm doing.

BARBARA: Oh, thank you.

CHRISTINE: I just feel like, I've always felt as if there's something more. I think you've just made me see it.

BARBARA: Right. We're always saying, "This can't be life. There has to be something more to life than just this."

CHRISTINE: I just feel like—I don't know. I don't know. I feel like I'm in such a rut in my life right now.

BARBARA: Exactly. So you just needed a little kick-start to move out of it, and to know exactly what direction. And so the synchronicity of this is incredible. So this is Memorial Day, and this will be a memorable day for you.

CHRISTINE: Absolutely. Absolutely.

BARBARA: And I wish you all the best and thank you for choosing my service, and if I can help you again, please let me know.

CHRISTINE: I will. Thank you so much.

* * *

Here is another example of a feeling that you have known the energy before, yet your current memory has no recollection:

CAROL: It's a cockatoo and his name is Tuxedo. My major question is, I'm trying to figure out why he came to me as this particular bird. I don't know if you can answer, or have a concept or a feeling about something like that.

BARBARA: Sure. Came to you at this particular time?

CAROL: No. Why he came to me in my life at all? It's a real strange story of why he came to me. It's not something typical. I just wanted to see if you saw anything or felt anything different or unusual.

BARBARA: Let me tune into Tuxedo's energy, so that you and I know we're talking about the same bird. Does he toss his head around?

CAROL: Well, he does but I think that's normal.

BARBARA: I feel that he does it a lot.

CAROL: Well maybe he does more than normal. I don't have anything to compare it to.

BARBARA: Okay. He can be a bit noisy at times. He likes your attention. He likes to be with you. I feel that when you're together he's sweet. Okay. So why has he come to you at this time in your life?

CAROL: Well, he's been with me a while, so I'm just wondering if there's a reason.

BARBARA: Sure. That's a good question.

CAROL: I have a story to go with it. A very strange story.

BARBARA: Okay. Let me tune in here and see how he came to you and what the reason is. I'm feeling that—my first impression is something to do with distraction, something to distract you.

CAROL: Could be.

BARBARA: I don't know if you worry a lot.

CAROL: No.

BARBARA: Or you were doing something that—

CAROL: There was stress at that time.

BARBARA: Okay. It feels like what he does is, he suspends that stress, and you get busy just paying attention to him. So it kind of releases that moment in time for your body, where it's like you don't think about it—you are right there with him at that time. It's kind of a loving thing that he does with you. It's kind of an exchange of energy. He's busy doing his antics, and he amuses you.

CAROL: Very much so.

BARBARA: Yes. He makes you laugh and it makes joy in your life. I feel like he brings joy to you.

CAROL: Yes. Very much.

BARBARA: Yes. And what better thing than to have something come into your life that brings you joy. That is such a gift. Absolutely. And so I feel like you two have these little games that you play. You have your fun time.

CAROL: Yes. Lots of fun time.

BARBARA: Yes. And do you play hide-and-seek or something with him?

CAROL: No, but we play games. Tricks and games.

BARBARA: Yes. So he's teaching you joy and you're teaching him tricks.

CAROL: Could be. Anything else regarding why he came to me? Why this particular bird?

BARBARA: Rather than a different bird?

CAROL: In a sense. This one only.

BARBARA: I get a feeling that maybe you had a past connection. I'm not sure if you believe in other lives or past lives.

CAROL: With him—you mean as a bird, or as anything? Could he have been anything?

BARBARA: Yes. It's the energy. Was he a bird? I feel you have a bird connection for some reason that goes back quite a ways.

CAROL: Could be. It's the only one I've ever had.

BARBARA: Now. But you really do have an affinity to him, and it feels as if you are able to teach him things and he picks them up easily, and you wonder, "How am I doing that? How do I do these things with him and I don't know how it's coming to me?" Do you know what I mean? Do you wonder about that?

CAROL: Um-hmm.

BARBARA: Like, "It feels so natural, and yet I don't have any training."

CAROL: Um-hmm.

BARBARA: And so I'm feeling that it comes from other times. Actually in a long time past—hundreds of—

CAROL: Do you believe that he could be with me from before—if there is such a thing?

BARBARA: Oh, yes.

CAROL: This particular bird?

BARBARA: Yes.

CAROL: Or as a bird?

BARBARA: The bird's energy. Not necessarily a cockatoo.

CAROL: Oh. Not a set bird, but a bird's energy—or something with the energy of a bird?

BARBARA: It's his soul.

CAROL: Okay, but it's not the soul of a person.

BARBARA: No.

CAROL: I don't know. I don't necessarily believe one way or another. I'm just asking.

BARBARA: That's good. It's always good to ask. What happens, as we evolve, we all pass through the animal kingdom. Then, as we move out of the animal kingdom into the people kingdom, we don't go back. So we don't go back to being an animal and then being a person, and back and forth. So the animal is evolving into the human set from the animal set. They're evolving to come this way. But as your soul has many life experiences in many times, so does the soul of this animal.

CAROL: So you believe he was a creature of some sort, with the energy of a bird but not necessarily a bird?

BARBARA: I feel a hunting bird actually.

CAROL: A hunting bird? Oh, could be.

BARBARA: Yes. I feel the ones you put the little—

CAROL: Oh. The hawk?

BARBARA: Hawk. Yes. And that you trained hawks in a time past, many times past.

CAROL: Maybe. I never met an animal that didn't like me or that I couldn't reach on some level.

BARBARA: Exactly. You have a way—and it takes a special person to have a way with birds. Because you communicate differently with them than you do with a mammal, because they are an animal hatched from an egg, which is a little bit different vibration than those live-born. Do you see? And so you understand their needs, and so it becomes a beautiful dance between the two of you.

CAROL: Do you feel anything else just about him? Just anything—a general idea about him? Anything else?

BARBARA: He's quite opinionated.

CAROL: Definitely.

BARBARA: Yes. He has his own opinions and he has his own times. There are times where he just goes off babbling, or antics, or doing what he does, and there are other times when he's right with you. And there are times where he's distant. Is that what you mean?

CAROL: Just ideas. If you feel anything. I'm trying to understand him better. I've had him eleven years, but he's still a mystery. I think if he were a person he'd be my soul mate. That's the strangest thing about him.

BARBARA: Right.

CAROL: Of all the animals I've ever had—and I've had many—this is the one. There's just something different.

BARBARA: The reason this feels like a soul mate to you is because animals that we've had at other times—that soul vibration comes back, and it almost feels like a person. "I would have known this. How did I ever know this energy?" And you can feel it. You have such a sense of feeling, and you were so connected with this one. He was big. He wasn't a small hawk. He was almost like an eagle, this one that you trained. And you were buds. Each of you knew each other and he protected you, and he was with you a lot, and so it became a special bond. And so when this soul energy returns, you feel it. But you can't see it in your mind's eye. It's like, "How do I feel this? How do I connect it with something? It must have been a person I knew from before." Because people want to connect with people, but don't realize that they also connect with animal souls.

CAROL: Yes. I just want you to tell me if there is anything else you want to say that you feel about him, or should I go ahead with the question?

BARBARA: Sure. Go ahead with the question.

CAROL: Well—basically my question is, I was wondering about his health. He's always had weak health but he's doing better.

BARBARA: Weak health.

CAROL: Yes. He's doing pretty good. It took four years to get him healthy, when I first got him.

BARBARA: It was his diet, as I feel it. He wasn't on a proper diet.

CAROL: Yes. Well, that's true. I got him sick. He was sold

to me sick but I didn't know it. So he's lucky to be alive. I kept working until I found a way. But I was just wondering if he's going to—

BARBARA: How is his health, now?

CAROL: Yes. In general.

BARBARA: I can feel him at the beginning, where he lacked food qualities, the different foods that he needed. For a bird of his size and character he needs a vast variety of diet, and it took him a while to come back. Was it his liver?

CAROL: I really don't know. Infections—it could have been, but I don't really know. It was a struggle because he kept wanting to leave. I didn't know he was sick when he was sold to me. The lady wanted to get rid of him and—birds hide their sickness.

BARBARA: Oh yes. Exactly.

CAROL: That's what I was told. You can't tell when they're sick. That's their guard.

BARBARA: Well, you know—if they show any signs of weakness, then a prey will take them out. That's why the bird looks healthy all the time even though it could be on the edge of death. So I feel like what you're doing now is good. He needs a wide variety of fruits and vegetables. I'm going to assume that's what you're already doing with him.

CAROL: He's on a special veterinary diet, as well as he is slowly taking on other things. But this has been a long process. We're on the winning side but he still has a weakened immune system. He does one or two times a year go into a problem and then we get him out of it very fast.

BARBARA: Have you tried Harrison's?

CAROL: I think that's what I'm using.

BARBARA: Oh, okay. It's all organic?

CAROL: Yes. It's the best.

BARBARA: All organic?

CAROL: Yes. My vet said, "I don't sell anything I don't believe in." And this is what really—I kept him alive on cereals and corns and things like that. Basic stuff, but that's what really made the difference. He's been on that for years now, but you don't know if he'll talk, do you?

BARBARA: I don't feel that he's a big talker. He hasn't put it together. It's almost, as I feel it—if he had a tape. Have you played a tape?

CAROL: No. I prefer to do my own thing. He's with me a lot, because my office is in my home.

BARBARA: I feel that he needs a lot of time with repetitive words, so that's why I thought of tape. Because once you get the first few words flowing, the rest will come fast.

CAROL: Yes. Yes. He acts like he's starting. I've had him for eleven years and he acts like he wants to say something. I thought maybe there's a maturity level. I don't really know about that with birds. Some birds talk younger, but they're not big talkers. He looks like he's trying to say something. But I was just curious. I never give up, but anyway. You don't feel where he's from, or if he's been abused or any of that kind of stuff?

BARBARA: I don't feel he's been abused as much as neglected.

CAROL: Neglect—or else just ill health.

BARBARA: Well they just didn't pay much attention to him. It was kind of something they bought ,thinking that they would like this, and then they kind of set him aside. He got food and he got water, but they had no interest in him.

CAROL: I was wondering where he's from. From a foreign source?

BARBARA: You mean domestic raised or not?

CAROL: Yes. I don't know if he's domestic. I was told he was not, but I don't have any background at all. Basically he was wild when I got him. Had no handling at all with people.

BARBARA: Usually if you hold onto a bird they totally give up immediately. That's usually a wild bird.

CAROL: What do you mean, "They give up"?

BARBARA: they don't fight you.

CAROL: Oh.

BARBARA: But if you grab them and hold them and they fight you, it's usually a bird that's been hand-raised.

CAROL: Really?

BARBARA: Yes. A vet will tell you that, as well.

CAROL: Oh. Almost the opposite then.

BARBARA: The opposite what?

CAROL: If you hold them and they fight with you, they've been hand raised? If you're a stranger?

BARBARA: Yes.

CAROL: Well isn't that interesting? He didn't fight with me. He just didn't seem to have any connection to a human being at all.

BARBARA: Well, it can be that a bird is hand-raised and if you do nothing with it, he reverts more back to the wild bird. But he will come back to the hand—to being tamer—being he's a hand-raised bird. Do you see?

CAROL: Yes. I do.

BARBARA: Because it started at the beginning and the imprint is there. It's just that nobody has worked with the imprint, so it takes a little a while. But a wild-caught bird tends to be not trustworthy.

CAROL: Yes. Well, he's never been trustworthy. He's very atypical of a cockatoo. He still doesn't like strangers. He basically bonded to me, and then secondly to the family members only. He has no relationships and is very fearful about other outside sources, and the lady told me. She had a pet store and she said he was from the wild. But after I bought him I wondered if he is a black market bird. That's why I've always been curious about his background, because there was just nothing calm or tame about him. But he's also had ill health. Basically she sold me something that was going to go off and die, I think.

BARBARA: Oh. He was from a pet store.

CAROL: I don't know where she got him. I don't have any

background. She didn't say, but that's beside the point. I just mostly was curious about the spiritual bond that I have with him.

BARBARA: Yes. And that's what it is. You worked very hard to bring him through, because you two were so connected that it was like, "If I lose him, I've actually lost my soul mate." That's how it felt to you.

CAROL: That's the way I feel. Yes.

BARBARA: And so most people would say, "Take him back. This is a sick bird. I'll get another one." But for you it was not about doing that.

CAROL: No. There was a bond there, of some sort.

BARBARA: Exactly. There is a bond. There's a very strong bond and it's an unspoken bond.

CAROL: Is there anything else you can feel or think?

BARBARA: I feel the wildness in him. It was the first thing that I felt—the tossing of the head—warding off any strangers from coming close. "Don't bother coming close, because I'm wild!" Yet when you deal with him, he's not a wild person.

CAROL: Oh no. Not at all.

BARBARA: But it's kind of a game that he does. He puts a message out there and he makes it real clear to back off.

CAROL: I think it's his defense, because he's been a weak link.

BARBARA: Right. So if he appears strong and bullies, nobody will come after him. Nobody will bother him, and that's what it feels like. He feels that his immune system still needs food which is very good. I would check with your vet and see if you can add some fresh fruits and vegetables and things like that.

CAROL: Yes. I do. I do.

BARBARA: Peppers. Does he like peppers?

CAROL: He loves hot anything. Hot sauces. He loves them.

BARBARA: Yes. That's what I'm getting. Jalapeno peppers.

CAROL: Oh, he just loves hot things. Yes.

BARBARA: There's a lot of vitamin A in hot peppers. Vitamin A fights disease, so that would be really good.

CAROL: Great. Anything else? Otherwise I'm going to tell you.

BARBARA: Go ahead, tell me.

CAROL: I was going to say that I bought him sight unseen. Through an ad in the newspaper. I watched the newspaper ads and saw the that price kept going down. I knew they were worth well over $400, you know.

BARBARA: Yes.

CAROL: I kept thinking. It went down to $400. Then it went down to $300. Then it went down to $200 and I thought, "I need to get this bird." Because I didn't want to pay a lot of money. I didn't have a lot of money, and I was going to buy something that I could afford, that someone wanted to get rid of. So that's what I was looking for in the pet section—where I could get a deal—and it was a pet store, and the price was so good that I said to the lady, "I want him and I'm going to buy him sight unseen." I remember that it was twenty after six on a Thursday, and this was eleven years ago, and I said "I want to buy it sight unseen. How can I get it? I can't get over there on time. Will you take a Visa?" "Well," she said, "we don't normally take Visa," and "blah, blah, blah." And I said "Well, whatever. I want it on hold. I want this bird." And the next day I ended up going over. I called her. I was running late, and I called her and said. "Okay, I'm coming over to get my bird." She's never seen me. I've never seen the bird. I don't know anything about it. I've never owned a bird before. But the bizarre part of the whole thing, that's so mysterious to me—because I have a very strong type of personality, you know. Very sensitive, though. Feel everything. I have a very strong sense of feeling but I'm not a weeper, crier or that kind of personality.

BARBARA: No. Exactly.

CAROL: And I walk into the store to get my bird, and there

were cockatoos all over. They all look alike, you know, and I remember walking into the store and looking down at this bird—this one—and I started weeping. And the tears came right down my face, off my chin. I had no idea what had overcome me. Don't have a clue to this day. And I finally went over to the lady and said, "I'm here to get my bird." It could have been any one of the birds, and she took me to that bird. Well, the bottom line is, my question—I had lost a friend, my best friend passed away. The closest friend I ever had in my life to this day, and probably ever will have. He always loved to fly. We did a lot of flying together and we just had beautiful, great, wonderful companionship. And he died. And he always said if he could ever be anything, he'd want to be a bird. And I thought maybe he sent it to me.

BARBARA: He did.

CAROL: Well I don't know that, but I'm just saying.

BARBARA: Yes.

CAROL: That he sent that particular bird or his energy came to give me peace and give me happiness, because it took nine years to get through the grieving of this person. And that is very atypical of a grieving situation. Nine years to get through the grieving of the loss of this person. I could not pull my life together. It was that painful. My mother just died. Loved her to death, and I don't have that kind of same grieving. It was a bond we had that I've never had, and I have a bond with this bird like I've never had with any other animal. And I kept thinking, possibly, he sent it from heaven—sent his energy to give me peace and happiness. Beause this bird has brought me more joy than any creature I've ever had and I've had lots that I've loved.

BARBARA: Right.

CAROL: And that's all I have to say about it. It's just bizarre, the weeping. And I don't even know you can feel like this. I don't even know what bird it is. I don't even weep. I'm not that kind of personality.

BARBARA: I understand.

CAROL: Nothing made sense.

BARBARA: And that's why, when I say this is a past life, this is a soul that you met in another life, that is why you wept—because you knew the energy. You didn't know the face. You didn't know the situation. But as soon as you connected with that energy, you knew on another level. And you just—it was just almost like a sobbing—

CAROL: I was sobbing. That's before I even knew it was my bird.

BARBARA: Exactly.

CAROL: That's what was bizarre

BARBARA: Yes. Because we don't experience a lot of that, and because someone didn't tell us when we're young, "This is what's going to happen to you." We always think it is a peculiar way of acting.

CAROL: I call it—I'm very spiritual. I believe in God and everything, but I say it's not of this earth. It's unexplainable.

BARBARA: Right. And it's the soulmate and the energy that you felt of this animal. You were a man in that life. You trained this wonderful, huge bird. It was eagle-size and you were inseparable, the two of you. It was such a love between the two of you.

CAROL: It's the same thing I have with this one.

BARBARA: Yes. Do you see?

CAROL: And I've never been bonded to anything like it.

BARBARA: No. And you just knew right away by just feeling that that was it.

CAROL: But I don't know if he sent it. I'm always wondering if he sent it, because he always wanted to be a bird. If he sent this particular bird back for me, this particular one.

BARBARA: He sent you the experience of joy and the bird is the flight. It's the freedom, and it's bringing you joy. It's suspending the stress for you, and that is a gift.

CAROL: Yes. Well I've always felt that it was given to me

for a reason, and for a gift, and I always like to believe it was from my friend—to bring me peace from the pain I was feeling. That's my belief.

BARBARA: Yes. Exactly.

CAROL: Have you ever heard of anything like this?

BARBARA: Yes. Absolutely.

CAROL: So it's not typical but it's not—

BARBARA: It doesn't happen to everybody, every day, no. But it does happen to special people like yourself, yes.

CAROL: Because I tell this story to everybody. Really. I'm not ashamed of it. I say it's unexplainable to me. I only have my own idea, but I would love to meet another person who could tell me the same concept. You know—of a different story, but an idea—because I've never heard anybody—

BARBARA: It happens to many people. A man meets a woman and you start to feel this connection—as if you've known them forever and you've just met five minutes ago. That is someone, a soul energy, that you have met, coming from another time and space. Another lifetime that you reconnect with.

CAROL: But you're saying that other people have told you about their connection to an animal.

BARBARA: Oh, and I've had this happen to me. I went to England to get a dog that was part of a life that was two or three hundred years before. Same dog energy that I was devoted to, with this animal.

CAROL: Well—basically, my questions are done. I'm just trying to see. I wish I could run into someone who has—. Well, you're saying you had somewhat of the same experience. But I thought, maybe—you talk to a lot of people—that you've heard some kind of concept like this before.

BARBARA: Absolutely. If you go to my website and read the story that's on there now. This was a horse which, when this woman first saw him at a rescue when he was older, she just sobbed. And she's been working with rescues for years—

CAROL: Right, so she found a connection.

BARBARA: Absolutely.

CAROL: Beause it's an instant thing.

BARBARA: Absolutely.

CAROL: It's not something that you create, or you cry when they die. It's instantaneous.

BARBARA: It was totally instant with her. And she was very much a metaphysician, and knew the lifetime it was. She knew where she had seen him and didn't want to lose him again. She'd lost him before. He died in her lap in the pasture then, and he did the same thing now. She just wanted to die with him.

CAROL: When my friend passed away I actually felt I was going to die, because I didn't feel the spirit of life within me. And I feel the same thing with this bird. I dread what might happen if he dies. But fortunately they live about a hundred years, if he gets good and healthy. And he'll pass on to my son and I may not have to experience that, because I feel the same thing. It's like I have this connection and I don't know what I'll feel if he goes. But I have a firm belief that somewhere my friend had interaction with this particular bird to bring me the happiness that I needed to reawaken my mind.

BARBARA: Exactly. It was to say, "Stop grieving, stop feeling sad, be joyful, suspend yourself in joy, laugh, get on with it."

CAROL: Because I'm not a wimp. I'm not a grieving person.

BARBARA: And you were stuck.

CAROL: I was stuck. I don't know how to put it. I thought I was going to have a heart attack.

BARBARA: Exactly.

CAROL: I even actually lost five years of my life. I actually went into such shock that I lost all my ability to speak, and all my ability to do mathematics. A part of my brain died. I had to re-learn how to speak and I had to re-learn mathematics.

I could read, so God told me after a year and a half that I needed to read. I wasn't a big reader. I started reading, and that's what helped re-program my brain.

BARBARA: Wow.

CAROL: To be able to speak again. It's an amazing interconnection. I love this story because it's fascinating to me.

BARBARA: Yes. It is. Absolutely.

CAROL: Yes. And to this day, my short-term memory isn't what it used to be. It affected the short-term memory. It's like I got stuck in this grieving and couldn't get out. I prayed every day. "I want out of this. I want out of this. I don't know why I'm stuck in this." I didn't have a clue. I'm very strong and very organized and a "let's get it done" type of person, so it's not typically me to be stuck somewhere. The whole circle is a really unusual circumstance that most people wouldn't be able to get.

BARBARA: That's right. And see, that's what this is. The bird represents flight — is freedom.

CAROL: Yes. He represented a joy and a peace that just started the upward motion, because finally something happened. I could function. I did my work and I could think but I had to relearn a lot of things. I couldn't go to a 7-11 store because I couldn't remember what I went for, but I made myself sit in the car until I could remember, and I would be there for a half hour because the short-term memory died.

BARBARA: See. So you're such a strong person.

CAROL: Yes. I am. I'm persevering, but this guy has it too.

BARBARA: You must remember that he is mirroring you and you came back from close to leaving, and so did he.

CAROL: I hadn't thought about that.

BARBARA: This is very synchronistic here. Think about the synchronicity of him mirroring your life and now how you're teaching him to talk and to learn as you had taught yourself to talk and learn.

CAROL: Oh yes.

BARBARA: And how it took persistence and time and repetition—and so that will pay off.

CAROL: I hadn't thought about the mirror. I know they mirror but I hadn't thought about it—that it is almost the same sequence of relearning. He looks like, with the way he's moving his tongue—and he's making noises he's never made—like he wants to say something, which I love. He's learned all the tricks but he hasn't learned to talk or say anything now. I sure wish someone would call me and tell me—

BARBARA: There will be some stories on my website that will probably help you with understanding synchronicity. I have a story out right now about the horse.

CAROL: Okay. I'll try to see if my friend can get there on his computer. He's just starting to learn, so we're both trying to teach each other. Thank you.

* * *

Arrow was the very special horse belonging to a woman who believed they had been together for many lives. E-mail from Lisa concerned Arrow:

Hi Barbara,

I enjoyed finding your site and reading your clients' comments and the story of the month. I need your help. I have a wonderful horse named Arrow, who is a strawberry roan, 33 years old and a gelding. He and I have walked together through many lifetimes, I know, and I just found him again in this one several years ago and brought him home immediately.

For the past year he's been having episodes much like astral travel, I think. He will run and move a lot in his stall when he's sleeping, and then he gets himself stuck at a forty-five degree angle from the shoulders up, on the wooden stall walls or in the doorway of the stall. He's injured himself many times, and this morning much to my horror he was in the worst state, wedged up against the wall of his stall. There was a five-foot-long arc of blood where he was trying to get away from the wall. I tearfully screamed out and whimpered out a prayer to God to help him, and by the Divine grace, Arrow was somehow able to pull himself up on the wall by his teeth and turn himself around. He was very weak.

A vet who was new to me came and had to use a cattle prod (oh my GOD) on Arrow's legs to get him up. The vet spent a while urging me to put Arrow down. He has a terrible gash over his right eye, and his legs are badly swollen from all the traumatic flailing and kicking he went through during the night.

I need to know what Arrow wants. I feel strongly he's stayed this long because of his huge guardian spirit he has for me. We have an unexplainable love for each other, and are very telepathic with each other. But I cannot get a glimmer of what he wants me to do for him.

Does he want to die? Can he die without me intervening? I've told him many times, "I'll be all right somehow—I'll get through it." But I can't get the "ah-ha" right-knowing from him. My heart breaks when I see him suffering and hurting, but he seems to be fairly oblivious to the injuries. He goes about the pasture grazing and slowly ambles back to the barn. I don't know what to do and it's breaking my heart to think I'll make the wrong decision.

Please e-mail me some information about your sessions and hopefully I'll be able to afford it.

God Bless you, Lisa

* * *

This is the story as it unfolded:

LISA: Arrow has been down for a day and he can't get up. What is going on with him? Is he sleeping? Is he having seizure or a stroke?

BARBARA: Let me tune into Arrow. The horse that I am getting is big, gentle, very loving, very understanding, a wonderful animal and very solid. Okay. I can see that he is down. Now I will go through why he might be down. I am not getting a seizure or a stroke, but I feel like it is in his muscles. He is weak.

LISA: Yes.

BARBARA: Very weak, and doesn't have the strength to get up. It is like there is no strength there, to get himself up. If he got himself up I feel that he would be weak and unable to walk.

LISA: I went into the barn at 5:30 and he was wedged up against the wall.

BARBARA: That is when you sent me the e-mail.

LISA: He had been struggling to get up, and had smashed his front leg against the wooden wall—probably for hours. His head has a bad gash over his eye, and his lip inside his mouth is sore from rubbing his gums on the wall. He, with the grace of God, managed to turn himself off the wall and lie down across his stall. I called the new vet here in town to help him. The vet said, "First of all we have to get him up," and we tried to get him up with a halter and a rope. But we couldn't. I went into my grain room and when I came back the vet had a four-foot cattle prod and he was shocking Arrows legs. It terrified Arrow and he finally woke up. But he does this thing like astral travels. You look into his eyes and he is gone, and his nose is pulled up like when he is sleeping. And that is what he has been doing all day and all last night. He is lying out there in the barnyard now. His legs are twitching. He will eat. He has eaten a bale of hay and drank three gallons of water, and had two huge brand mashes. He nickers to me. Then he struggles. He got up to a sit and I held him up for a few minutes and I couldn't lean into him any more. I thought that he was going to come down on my leg and maybe break it. I don't know if he is wanting to die or if he wants help. Is he ever—it sounds so melodramatic—is he ever going to be able to get up? We had two rains yesterday afternoon and he laid out in it. But, the ground is damp and I put a bail of straw under him. As he is flaying his legs around trying to get up, he has made a nice little circle that he is lying in. So I covered that with straw, trying to get him away from the moisture, and I have thrown blankets on top of him to keep him warm. I don't feel that he is trying to die or wants to die. But I can't let him lie there.

BARBARA: Yes, I understand. They are showing me the spine. There is something to do with the spine. It is either numb, there is no muscle tone—it is lacking. It is in the back and not in the front, as I feel it. It is in the back legs—where he can't enough strength to get up.

LISA: Yes, that is it!

BARBARA: Something has happened to the spine. Either a vertebra is frozen or snapped. The only thing I could see as a suggestion would be a chiropractor. Someone who would know about the spine and could manipulate him enough to get him on his feet. Because he has been down quite a while now, and that is not good. Do you know of a chiropractor?

LISA: No, no I don't. I—

BARBARA: I know there are a lot of people doing things with horses now. They can identify right where the spot is and what is the prognosis. The cattle prod is not the answer, for if he could get up he would get up. What I am feeling is that he just can't get himself rolled over enough, so his body is lying not on an angle, but up. Do you know what I mean?

LISA: Yes I do.

BARBARA: I feel like he wants to get up and he has the will to get up, but he body is failing him to do this.

LISA: Can you talk with him? Can you find out what he wants me to do? Because I know he is exhausted—he is an old, old horse.

BARBARA: I don't like to make a decision and the horse really doesn't know the options he has. When it really gets unbearable he is out of here. He is just going to lift out. You know he needs help in one way or another. The question is whether or not you should give him the gift to transition? Sometimes the body fails and sometimes it just fails past the point of being able to do anything. And the gift would be to allow him to release out of that—to move into another one that works. That is an option, but there are no absolutes here, because the Universe is much wiser than I in how things need to go for his Soul's path. But he has to get up.

LISA: I know.

BARBARA: You have made him as comfortable as you can, and isn't as if he can't eat or drink. But the rest of the organs need to be moving, and they are not. And that is going to create other problems. This is a very dear, dear friend for you.

LISA: Yes.

BARBARA: I can feel that bond. So it is a hard choice, because he is eating and drinking and he is alert in his own way. If he stays down too long the choice will be made. The other option is to get someone who can do body manipulation. He might be damaged to where it is not an option any longer to make him right.

LISA: I just can't get a feeling from him. I have been with him all day long and I have been asking him, "Do you want me to help you go?" My heart tells me he won't live through the fall. He has been bad before, then he will bounce up and he will be fine. This has been happening for some time. One night I went into the barn and he was stuck sideways in the outdoor sliding door. His legs were bashed and bloody and he was just jammed and I couldn't raise anybody to come and help me. I sat up with him all night and it was snowing and covered him. I would give him hay and just laid there with his head in my lap for ten hours. A vet finally came at seven or eight a.m. We got him up and got him pain medicine. He was very weak and very wobbly. He came out of that, and he wouldn't lie down for a few days, and again on Tuesday it happened and he didn't lie down until yesterday morning. I just can't see him suffer. I don't want him to see him get hurt and die like that.

BARBARA: The closure needs to be more with you than with him. He will go along with however you choose it to be. He is not going to be upset. As you were talking, what I was feeling was, he is disorientated. They regress to childhood. They don't know were they are. They do things that they would normally do, and things that they would never do. Almost like Alzheimer's. That is what is going on here. He is going down and then coming up. What do I want to say? It won't ever be safe for him to be by himself. Do you see? The bouts will come. He doesn't know where he is, and he gets totally disoriented.

LISA: Then he'll come out of it, and he will look around, and nuzzle me and nicker and then he will flail to get up and then he can't. Then he goes off again. God, I just can't, I can't— It is going to break my heart to keep living without him. I feel like I waited all my life to get reunited with him. When I found him I was volunteering at the horse rescue, and I had for years. I worked on every kind of horse and every type of trauma you can have. I loved them! But, I wanted to heal them up and send them on to a good home. I saw Arrow and I remembered, I remembered him from a past life, living on the plains as an Indian woman. At first when I saw him I burst into tears and he whinnied and nickered and just crushed me into his chest. He was saying to me, "Where have you been?" And I need to know all the things that I should ask you. Will he be at peace and alright? Will he need to know if he is here? Or is he ever going to come back in this life? I don't know if you can answer any of that?

BARBARA: Well, he will be at peace when he transitions. He will still be with you when he transitions—I know that. It is very common for the animals to stay with the owners. You will feel him, but you won't be able to see him. You will know he is there but you won't exactly know how you know. Just because you don't see the physical body doesn't mean that they are gone. We are so in tune with what we see as physical, that we think what we can't see is not real But it is, all the same As I read the energy, whether he is in a body or is not in a body, it is the same energy. After he transitions you can get him back.

LISA: How?

BARBARA: You go out looking at horses with the intent to find him. He won't be exactly the same. It won't be exactly as Arrow looks now, but you will know him by the energy. You are going to look at different horses and one will come to you, and you will know that this one is like your Arrow. They will be a little more lively and not be as laid back. I feel that it will be a filly, and it will have the mannerisms, the security, the love, the connection that you have with Arrow. They do transition very easily. When they are released from a body that doesn't work, if you could hear them, what they say is, "I'm free! I'm free!" because they have been trapped in this body that is not working any more. So they need release. Eventually it gets to where they just say, "I'm out of here," and they release themselves—which is when they die. They reach a level of, "I won't do this any more, and I'm out of here." But when you shut your eyes you will be able to feel him. And I can feel this connection. There have been a number of lifetimes where you were so connected with him, and then you two parted. You feel now, "No not again. I just found him and all of a sudden he is going again." That is what feels so tragic for you. But you can find him again. His energy in a newer body, a younger body that is working properly. Then you can each enjoy each other more fully. Do you see?

LISA: How do they—obviously the horse does not incarnate in a baby body.

BARBARA: They can if they want to, but it doesn't necessarily have to be.

LISA: From the way you are talking about this it seems like he would come into an adult body.

BARBARA: He can.

LISA: And how do they do that? Does the horse—

BARBARA: It is a Universal mystery. We incarnate many, many times but our memory is gone about how we do it. Our Soul can do many wonderful things. Our Soul can even split off and live two lifetimes at the same time. It just does that. The Soul in the next body will take on—not an identical path, but a similar path. And you have such a deep connection with this one that this one will reincarnate for you. Will come back. I feel it may be a horse a year or two years old. And again I can't answer exactly how they do it. And how will you know that it is them? Because they will have some mannerism that you will recognize. Did he do something with his foot? Did he kind of paw?

LISA: Yes.

BARBARA: This one—when you meet this one, it will do similar things. It will paw. "Do you remember me? This is me again." And there will be little signs. You will go, "Oh—Arrow used to do cute things with his foot, or throw his head in a certain way. And she does that, too." It might be a male. Could be a gelded male. I feel like a feminine energy, this time. It could be either male or female, but the energy is going to be light. Where Arrow was—I want to say, almost a draft horse. The type of a personality that's strong, sturdy, stable—a cornerstone, personality. This one, as I see it in the next transition, will be lighter, will be more fun, will make you laugh a lot, will make you feel happy and will touch that part of your heart. Will fill that part of your heart. It won't be perfect, perfect, perfect—do you know what I mean? It's not Arrow! But it is that part of Arrow that will lift you. She almost might be a little bit of a challenge, where he was not so challenging. Do you know what I mean? I would get some opinions before deciding what to do. I would get a chiropractor if you can.

LISA: Yes.

BARBARA: Maybe the vet knows of one that could come out and give you an evaluation.

LISA: I have had, over the last two months, four vets. The one who knows him, and treated him at the horse rescue, said, "This isn't a horse wanting to die. This is a horse that's having trouble getting up." The other three said, "He is having neurological problems." My God, if you had seen his face, his eye where he was hurt. There was an arc of blood five feet across, where he was going back and forth with his head.

BARBARA: He got himself into these things, because he losing his ability to reason. Do you see.

LISA: Yes, I do!

BARBARA: I feel it is not going to get better, and he is not going to be brand new. His age is against him with this. It is a gift that you have found each other. That you didn't miss that part.

LISA: I know!

BARBARA: What we are talking now is a gift. And you have a technique to go out and find him again if you want to. You don't have to. It is your choice. But if you want to.

LISA: I can't imagine him not being there.

BARBARA: I know.

LISA: I have always felt old animals' Souls and peoples' Souls and I always had—when I first heard about the horse rescue I thought, "I have to volunteer there. It is going to make his life complete." I didn't know quite what I meant by that. When I saw him again I had flashback of the Plains Indians. I had flashbacks of being with Arrow so many times.

BARBARA: As a warrior, too.

LISA: Yes.

BARBARA: He was your trusted steed!

LISA: Yes. All day long I have been talking to him and telling him how grateful I was that he was back, and how much I am going to miss him.

BARBARA: But you know that was a gift, too. That you have had a chance to be with him. That there is time for closure, and you can talk to him and he understands. How much you remember him, and how much you cherish him, and you can just talk to him like you do talk to him. And he is going to understand. And when you are ready to release him, he can release himself. Then he will be free of this body that is no longer working, and the memory that is failing him. So much of him is not there anymore.

LISA: I have asked him, "Please make it easy for me and just go. Just go out of your body and snap that cord and just go."

BARBARA: If you help him to go, he will be grateful. Because you are going to be able to release him from a prison. His is in prison right now! He is down. He is stuck. So it can be a gift that you give him. Maybe like a final gift. This affects me, because I know what it is like to meet an old friend and then have to release them. But if you talk to Arrow and explain why you are doing it, how you know the body is not working any more, that you will meet again. If you met many, many, many times before, you will meet again. And if you want to meet again in this lifetime, you can do so.

LISA: How long do you feel that would be?

BARBARA: For you to find another?

LISA: For him to come back!

BARBARA: Whenever you are ready. Whenever you are ready to look again, he will be there. It is Universal timing. It is triggered by the intent! You are going out with the intent to find him again. And the timing is yours. For the Universe has a bigger picture with this, and I can't tell you timing. Because on the other side there isn't any timing. Do you see?

LISA: Yes.

BARBARA: It is not like we do it by a calendar, linear, by the clock. It isn't like that. So when I ask them timing I hear, "Soon. He will return soon for you." As you know, you have had a chance to help many horses and they do touch your heart, and this one is very special for this one has touched your heart many times. The timing is yours. When you feel comfortable in knowing that the release is a bigger gift than anything. And it is a gift—allowing him to transition is a gift! And when you are ready and when you feel healed enough, you will go out and you will find this one. You might have to look at five or six different horses. Maybe five or six different places. But you will know. And he will let you know. I feel like his time is soon. He needs—he will move soon. I am not God, and can't tell you exactly. I just get, "Very soon." If he gets up and goes back in his stall, this will happen again. This type of thing.

LISA: I know. That last time he did this in a snow storm, I thought, the next time—

BARBARA: It is very hard on him and exhausting for him. He tries, tries to get up, and the whole thing is exhausting. Yes, he is able eat and drink and that is good. But he needs the rest to go with it. So when you are ready to give him the gift of release, he will be fine with that.

LISA: I don't know what I want to say. I kind of feel that it's—it's easier and better to let him go. Because he'll do what he did Tuesday, when he got up. He was weak and wobbly and the longer he was up walking and grazing, he came right back to his true old self and ate all the buds off my rosebushes. He demanded his brand mash, stood there and pawed, until I handed it over.

BARBARA: He does a lot with that paw, doesn't he?

LISA: Yes. It is just—God! I wish, I just wish, it were within his control to say, "All right. I'm done". And go. To me it is important—who helps him die. My other vet is closer into the city and it is a longer drive for her and I am not sure she could come. And I feel like it should be tomorrow or tonight. I just had a flashback of him from other lifetimes. Every other time I remember him dying with his head in my lap.

BARBARA: Do you draw?

LISA: Yes.

BARBARA: Okay, What I would recommend is that you draw the picture you see, you and him in these lifetimes. I feel like that would be very valuable for you. You would be tapping into his energy with these pictures. You would be with him, and you could see and feel and help to release what feels like it is stuck. But to do pictures of these lifetimes as you see him would be very valuable for you. It would be like, in memory of this wonderful animal who has taken on all these lifetimes with you. It could be like a memorial to him. You could publish it as a book. A lot of people would like to know about that which you see. It is life, and we all have these questions. "How does this work? What does it look like? What did they look like before? How did you know?" You just pick it up on another level. And he is going to go on in this artwork. Do you see? His Soul will go on, in the artwork that you do.

LISA: Yes.

BARBARA: What he gives you is these thoughts and pictures and this beauty that you knew. So that you can do something with it. The animals give us gifts. They always come in many different ways we never thought about. Maybe it is meant for you to do this artwork and publish it. He is going to help you move into something that is going to be more of a life work for you. These animals are kind of like a jumping off point. They get us into things and put us on our path. I feel like that is what he is helping you do. But he is not going to stay here forever to do that. So you are going to move on to what you need to do, and he is going to move on to what he needs to do. Does that sound like something that you could do?

LISA: Yes.

BARBARA: Take a lock of his hair. I really feel that would be important to you. So that you would have it as a memory of him. And it holds the energy of him. You could put it on a picture. Something that would connect you with that Indian lifetime that was so very precious to you. You were very connected to that one. It was a wonderful lifetime for you. One of joy and one of peace and one of creativity, as I feel it.

LISA: Me, too. I have always, all my life, wanted to get back there. And then I meet Arrow at the horse rescue. He came in about three hundred pounds underweight. And his hooves were almost fourteen inches long. He couldn't walk. And we were walking up from the pasture to the big gate to put him in his pen, and he tripped on his long, long feet. He stopped and it was an instant rerun of ... he stumbled and I was beneath him on this grade, with a little hill. He just froze dead solid. He bent his head back and nickkered and talked to me and crushed me into his chest. "Oh, I am sorry. I didn't mean to scare you, I wouldn't fall on you." And I remembered that, walking with him, that very precious time. And it is really, really funny, I had him with me. I just tell him, "Please, when you go this time. just take me with you. Kick me in the head and take me with you when you go."

BARBARA: It wasn't his intent to return and take you with him. He loves you, Lisa, but he didn't come back for you — to stop your life when his stops. He intent was to give you a kick-start on to another road for yourself. To help you move in a little different way than you do with your life now. I really feel it is with your art. Maybe with drawings. I don't know how that is going to work for you. I would recommend that you give him that gift that he gave you. To move into a little different avenue for him! Do pictures of him or him and you. Or however that works. Even if you don't want to make then public, make them pictures for you, and frame them put them in your own home. "As I remember Arrow." And you could write a memorial to him, and how you remember him, and how special he was, how you feel now. You could write down the different things that he did. Then take that group of papers and bring it down into a page or a few paragraphs and frame it. With his picture. So he is not gone.

LISA: That is always the hard thing. Anytime I had past life regression. I had a regression once and what came up was an Indian woman in the southwest in a big pueblo dwelling, kneeling by a creek with a pot that I had made. And I was a potter in this life, also. I remember I was washing my hands in this little creek, surrounded by cottonwood trees. I was looking at my hands, and being so grateful that they were so strong and so large. And in this life I have very tiny hands. But in that life it was the last day, and I was walking with my little pot under my arm. And the wind was blowing a long piece of my hair over my face. And I walked at sunset to this pueblo dwelling, and my dwelling was on the bottom floor because I was an older female and I was alone. And I remember putting the pot by my sleeping mat, and lying down with my arm crossed over my chest, and there was a blanket over the door that was pushed back. I raised my head up and looked at the sunset, knowing that I was going right then. And I remember how that was to go into Spirit. The amazing thing about that was, I was in a group of people. It wasn't a guided regression at all. This was in January, and in November of that same year my mother handed me a box on my birthday. And I started to weep. It was so weird—this uncontrollable crying. I opened the box and there was the exact pot that I had put under my arm in the past life. The pot was carbon-dated at the museum and certified to Casa Grande 1300.

BARBARA: Oh my God!

LISA: I know. And that was so strange. This whole lifetime, it is like things have come back. The pot is there full of feathers by my bed. And my beautiful old horse, Arrow. And it is so sad for me because he is leaving again.

BARBARA: He is leaving again. But he can then return again. You could spend more time, more quality time together that you were not able to spend. Do you see?

LISA: I do.

BARBARA: Yes.

LISA: I know it is just the trusting. It always comes down to that. Do you really believe, do you really trust this?

BARBARA: Trust what?

LISA: That the Soul never dies, and the Soul comes back into a body.

BARBARA: But you would be the one that would know to

trust! Because of all your past-life knowledge. You know about these lifetimes. You can feel them, you can walk in them, you can remember them.

LISA: Yes.

BARBARA: So you of all people would know that the Soul returns again and again and again. Yes! So you can trust that. That is something you know. You think that it is different for the horse, and it is not. It is no different for the horse. In fact, we come in through the animal kingdom. We were maybe a horse, maybe a bear, maybe a deer, maybe a dolphin. Then we come into the human kingdom. So we all come by that path. Every single one of our Souls. We start off in the mineral kingdom, go to the plant kingdom, then to the animal kingdom and then to the human kingdom. That is four. I understand there are three more sets. I don't know what they are. Hah! Trust that. You know that we come and go and we return again, and we come and go and we return again. It doesn't look the same and it doesn't feel quite the same. But we know it is. You know you had that life. You knew when you touched that pot. I feel like you need to connect with that pot. What did that pot hold for you? What's in that pot? What is about that pot? Was it was a gathering pot?

LISA: It was a storage pot. Like a water pot or it held corn meal, probably.

BARBARA: It has much more value to you than just a working pot. Do you see?

LISA: Yes. And I remember, in that last moment of that life, that the last thing I saw was the incredible sunset and that pot. And sometimes when I look at Arrow, he is copper colored. He is absolutely brilliant when the sun shines on him. You can barely look at him. He is brilliant—a brilliant red copper color. I remember being with him in sunsets and seeing the same color. He has a very unusually long head, like a thoroughbred head.

BARBARA: Long nose.

LISA: Big mouth.

BARBARA: Yes. So you know that he has returned to you many different times, and many different ways. If you want him to return again he will! It is easy for animals. It really is. To transition, they just release out. People hang on and struggle. But like you say, "If I can just get kicked in the head," or go into meditation and release out. That would be something to learn. Just to go into meditation, step out of your body, go across the Valley of the Dead, and into the Light. Also, in a meditation, focus on a time past that you would like to explore. You get into the River of Time and float down the river, and when it stops and you get out you're maybe in the past lifetime you were focusing on. There is more detail than just these few words, but this will give you an idea of techniques for tapping into past lives.

LISA: I always—. It's funny, for all the years I have had him, and every time I think about him dying, I fall apart.

BARBARA: Of course.

LISA: He licks my face. He nuzzles my eyes and he will put his lip over my nose. Like, "Just stop it! Just stop it!" I told him—

BARBARA: He wants you to smile. He is not unhappy. His message is, he is not unhappy and he wants you to smile. And he does things to make you smile. And when it is time he will be at peace to go. It will be okay. It is the struggle that he is in now. He is a fighter! But do write about all those things you like about him. All the things that really hit home for you. And write about your pot, too! Because there is more about that pot than a pot that's just holding corn.

LISA: Yes, I know. And it has been with me for ten years and I still—

BARBARA: It is kind of magical, that pot.

LISA: Yes.

BARBARA: There is more magic there than you are aware of. Maybe just writing about what you feel. Just sit down and write. As you start to write you may think, "This sure feels silly. I don't what I am going to say. I don't know what this is all about." Just let the words come, and allow it to be. Even the words might seem funny. But, that's okay. Don't worry about them. Don't worry about spelling or punctuation. Just write. Just let it go. And connect back with that. Feel how that was. What made that life so special? Why is that life more special than this one? What did I do then that I am not doing now?

LISA: Oh, I know that already. I know that. I remember walking through the pueblo and thinking about it, and knowing that I was dying that night. Feeling the gladness that I was getting back to my husband, who had died before. And glad that I had been strong, and able to be widowed and alone in that group, and teach little kids. That is what I did in that setting—making pots for everyone. I feel like I have no idea in the world why I am here in the year 2000, in America. This country is crazy. I live on a little farm, and it is very wonderful. Just—it is like, when I am with Arrow, physically touching him, and smelling his sweet smell, I think I just want to go back to those times when it was Our Country. I have a very strong rage about that. People here discrediting my ground. I know where it comes from. I know where all of it comes from. It is just a gut-ripper. If I chose this lifetime to be here by myself and learn the hardest lessons, I have done them. I learned my stuff. I am stronger and it didn't kill me. I am very tough. And now I want to just be done. I told Arrow, tonight I wished that I could just go, too.

BARBARA: Your work is not done. His work is done. Your work is not done! You have some gifts you can share with others. And you will find those gifts and your ability to—to imagine, by bringing what is real into this illusion. And that is what I would move towards. I would take the gift that he gave you. The gift that you have. And make that your love. People will be drawn to you from there. The right people! And the loneliness will end. Because you will now be with the right people. People who understand. I feel like your work will do that. You will draw those people to you. Even if you just do some work and take it to a small store. I feel like you are a talent that hasn't be discovered yet. And it will bring you where you want to be. Or what you would like to have. But this is kind of a shifting time for you. And it is hard. Shifting is hard.

LISA: Yes. I'm glad every year that I get old. I think, "Thank God, thank God, I am really at peace with a lot of my life." It is just the carry-over from the past lives that I remember.

BARBARA: There is unfinished business. So you can get in touch with that and get the charge off it, is what you need to do. It is not about not remembering it any more, it is not about forgetting it, it is not about walking away. It is about getting into the energy of what does create that charge? That really bring tears to your eyes. That makes your heart ache. What is it about that? Then to take the charge off. So it becomes just a story and not gut-wrenching story. Do you see? Now it is right there for you to look at. And once you go through it you will say, "Wow that was easy! Why didn't I do this long ago?" It is facing fear. That is the toughest. But, when you walk through it, you just think, "Oh my God, that was not hard at all I just had to walk through it." You will be fine. You are very strong. And you are very capable. You are very talented. and it is now time to use your talents. To get what you want. To do what you want. To be who you are. You are a late-bloomer, that's all. Some of us are, and we wait for what feels like forever. I see you going on many, many years. I feel that, as the years move forward, you are going to be connecting with who you are. And you are going to find more peace in that. And Arrow was your start. He was your pivot point.

LISA: I know he was.

BARBARA: And he really has you locked into that energy, that is going to help you catapult into where you want to be. That is his gift. Gut-wrenching as it, it still is his gift to you. Without this kind of trauma going on, you wouldn't feel as deeply as you do. Do you see? You wouldn't be connecting as you do. So that is a gift, too.

LISA: I just feel that, every loss of him—and it is going to sound odd—every tribal loss. I thought about that tonight. I feel losses of him. It is like it's—. I am having trouble trying to explain it, but it is like every Plains Indian tribe, every child who died, every elder who died, every—. It is like, for some reason, with Arrow, that is very clear and I can see them. Sometimes at twilight, out there on the prairie where I live, I feel them. I remember one night being out in my pasture, and I was asking Mother-Father-God for protection and help. There was nothing going on. I lead a very non-stressful life. And it was absolutely incredible! Arrow whinnied, and I turned around to the east, and the moon was coming up. And I saw— as clear as I can see the papers on my desk—I saw, for an instant, a line of warriors on horses with feather headdresses and staffs with feathers hanging on the end. Arrow whinnied to them!

BARBARA: He recognized them, as well.

LISA: Yes, because there was nothing else to whinny at. It was just one of those, bring-you-to-your-knees moments.

BARBARA: Magical moments.

LISA: And I have had so many with him, I just—. I wish if they could just make themselves illuminated in the Spirit Body, so you can tell they are out of their body and they are right here.

BARBARA: You are a powerful woman. You have the power to do anything. I feel in that Indian lifetime that you had something to do with being a Medicine Woman.

LISA: Yes.

BARBARA: That was a powerfully responsible job. You had the knowledge to know to leave when you wanted to leave. When it was your time. That is how you knew that was your night. So you can do it. You can do a lot of things. It is just that people don't talk about these things. People who are non-metaphysical wouldn't believe it. To a Metaphysician, we know! To a Magician, to a Spirit, to a Medicine Man or a Medicine Woman, they know!

LISA: Are you writing a book?

BARBARA: Yes. Someday it will get done.

LISA: I think it would be a wonderful book.

BARBARA: Thank you. It will be something just like you and I talking. Just sharing what I share one-on-one—sharing the process with other people. I am so blessed with so many different Guides to help me through what to do. As I talk to other people I go, "Ah, that sounds pretty good!" Because, I know what is real. But I am like you—human and connected to Earth. And I have doubts, just as does the next person. And when I lose someone very, very cherished to me, I do the same as you. The last time I lost someone close to me was my dog, Allison. I knew it was her time. And I gave her the gift of passing on. But, I walked through the garden with the other dogs, and I talked to her, and told her it was time—and she wagged her tail and smiled. And when she went to the vets, they had never seen her that happy and that relaxed. And they couldn't believe it. I didn't tell them the story, because they wouldn't understand. But the two of us knew. Her kidneys failed and it was time. And when she left I could hear her say, "I'm free!" And she was gone. So that is what we need to know. Your work needs to be shared with others on the American Indian energy. It is a very powerful energy. One people don't really honor the power of.

LISA: They are afraid of it!

BARBARA: Probably so.

LISA: This society is not even a culture—it is just a society. And it doesn't honor anything expect machines.

BARBARA: They do not honor Mother Earth. She is very powerful. I will send you the tape of this reading. You may want to listen to it from time to time. For I know that I am just a conduit, so what I say might trigger things for you, that might help you. Things you might not have heard, or the next time you listen, will be heard differently.

LISA: I'll be glad to get it and listen to it.

BARBARA: Some of my clients say the tape has been helpful to them to tap back into that energy again.

LISA: I think it does. I am already grieving, and Arrow is not dead yet. I have heard everything you said, but I know that I will hear it differently when I listen to the tape.

BARBARA: We are meant to hear things now and learn more when we hear them later. That is how it is. There is a big plan there. When I get my book out, I will let you know.

LISA: I really think it is important—what you have to say about the animal's Soul easily coming and easily leaving. And the gift that the animals give their people. I really think it is important. So many people grieve uncontrollably, unconsoled. It would be an enormous healing tool. At the Rescue I could look at a horse and tell which one would die. And I would always say it the same way as Penny Smith: "She is going to just run right out of her body—you just watch." In a day or two, a mare who was down would all of a sudden get up and run, and fall down dead. I know that to be true. I think that we have so much fear of our own physical pain and own death. We don't connect to the spirit very well in this country, in the society.

BARBARA: Thank you for the feedback. Please let me know what happens with Arrow.

* * *

E-mail from Lisa about Arrow a day later:
Starry Starry Night

It was very quiet here tonight, sitting with Arrow's great head in my lap, with tears splashing on his mane and washing his eyes. I sat for a very long time out in the pasture, while he journeyed on ahead—running now with the Great Horse Nation. He died under the Milky Way just at midnight, with a butter cream in his mouth and a gentle sigh and a kiss on his eyes from me. He told me he was falling, falling, falling into the hands of God.

 Lisa

8: Pigs And Fishes

THERE IS A HEXAGRAM in the Chinese Book of Changes, the *I Ching*, called 'inner truth'. It is said that such dependability comes to those who possess an inner understanding about what is real, that they can affect even pigs and fishes. The people who rescue animals have such dependability, and the animals seem to know it.

* * *

Michelle rescues pigs, and had questions about several of them:

BARBARA: Michelle—how I like to start is to get the name of the animal, and your first question, and from that I'm going to tune into the energy to make sure that we are on-key with the animal that we want to talk about, and then I'll go into your question.

MICHELLE: Okay. His name is Dean, and does he know that I love him?

BARBARA: Okay. The first thing I get is that this is a pig.

MICHELLE: Yes. I'm sitting next to him, too.

BARBARA: Oh are you? He doesn't have to be there, but if he's there, that's fine. The first thing I got was, he loves to root. That's obviously what pigs do, but he's very avid about it. He likes to stick his nose in a lot of wet mud and just almost blaze a trail. Does he do that?

MICHELLE: Actually, he's indoors a lot so he might have done that.

BARBARA: Okay. But he doesn't do that now?

MICHELLE: No, he's blind, and he stays inside.

BARBARA: All right. That's the first thing they showed me. The question was, does he love you, and yes, I feel like he does. He knows that he needs you and he likes to stay close to you. And I mean close to your leg. If he can feel you, then he feels safe. He feels comfortable, and when you move away and he's out and about, he feels a little bit uneasy about it. I feel he's very loving. Let me see if I can get some uniqueness here on that being.

MICHELLE: Can I ask another question?

BARBARA: Sure.

MICHELLE: Does he know what happened to his original owner in Michigan?

BARBARA: What happened?

MICHELLE: She killed herself and then he went from home to home. I don't think he had a good life after she died.

BARBARA: I'm feeling like this was a lady, a pioneer type of spirit, very independent.

MICHELLE: I didn't know her personally.

BARBARA: Yes. I know, but you know, I'm kind of tapping into this energy here, and I'm feeling like she found out or she knew that she was sick, and she was too independent to go to a hospital or to lie around and be sick. It was not an option for her.

MICHELLE: So does he know or does he just know that things changed?

BARBARA: He really doesn't—. I'm feeling the energy, but I'm not really feeling that he felt it a whole lot.

MICHELLE: Oh. That's good.

BARBARA: But I feel like that's what happened to the first owner. She was ill and she was a pioneer spirit and she was much too cantankerous to give in to any kind of disease.

MICHELLE: What about his health? Is he in any pain? Does he have an idea how he feels? He's obviously not doing too well, but they can't figure out what's wrong with him.

BARBARA: Let me see what we can do about going through here. and see what we can pick up in the body. I'm getting a big stomach, but I think that's standard for pigs.

MICHELLE: He could have stomach problems. He vomits.

BARBARA: Actually, what they were showing me was some kind of a blockage in the intestinal tract. Feels heavy. Feels compact and stuck.

MICHELLE: Yes. His feces isn't normal. It's very, very hard. So he could have at least an intestinal problem. His tests when he came in from Michigan, when the vet looked at him, showed a chronic infection, but he hasn't taken to antibiotics. He'll take them, but he doesn't seem to get better. He just has relapses.

BARBARA: It could be that it's built up bacteria.

MICHELLE: When he got here, he was blind. But now his eyes have started to recede. Did someone hit him in the head, was he abused or anything like that?

BARBARA: They're telling me no. They're telling me it's part of this disease that he has.

MICHELLE: Okay.

BARBARA: It's created, as they're saying, a toxic condition through his system. Pigs do not perspire.

MICHELLE: No.

BARBARA: So if something gets in there, they can't get rid of it through the skin like we do. You know—sometimes we can slough off toxins and take a shower, and wash it off the outside of our skin. Pigs can't do that.

MICHELLE: Is he happy?

BARBARA: He's happy. What I'm feeling, what they keep telling me, is that if there is something that could grease the slides. Something your vet would recommend that would loosen the bowels and clear out his intestines, something gentle, I'm feeling like whatever it is, it has been stuck to the wall for a while.

MICHELLE: Okay. I'll write that down. Could it be a parasite?

BARBARA: Well, I'm not feeling a parasite. What I'm feeling is a blocked food substance. Whatever has been consumed has built up in kind of a spot on the intestines, which also can cause a fever, but would create some real intestinal problems.

MICHELLE: Okay. Does he say when he started to feel sick? Oh—He has seizures, too.

BARBARA: Sometimes you'll find that seizures are an imbalance in the nutrients in the system. I've used vitamin B-6 to help alleviate that.

MICHELLE: Yes. I've heard other people use that too.

BARBARA: Right. It can be. There are many epilepsies so there's not just one type of epilepsy, as probably your doctor has told you. You need to record the pattern to identify his type of epilepsy. You will need to document it. Does it happen after a certain stress situation? When does the epilepsy come up?

MICHELLE: It's when he's out in the cold, I think. It is kind of cold-induced. When he came to us, he had lost about 100 pounds in a year, and was having seizures and defecating and urinating and lying in it. And it just kind of felt like he had given up hope. He was just lying there. When he came to us, he was very unfriendly—and I kept him in the house and he had trouble getting up, and he'd cry during the night. I'd go up and help him get up, and as time went by he got stronger and much more friendly. Now, like right now, he just rests his head on me. But he's been kicked off the sofa and now lives in the kitchen or the back room, and I'm hoping that's not making him too depressed, is it?

BARBARA: No. No.

MICHELLE: Okay. And does he like being with the other pig, or would he prefer being by himself?

BARBARA: Let me first stick with the health issue. Let me take that down the line a little bit, and then we will go to other things. You said the stools were dry, and what I'm feeling was—

MICHELLE: It alternates too. When he gets sick, it'll be like diarrhea, just water. That happens and he'll go through a bout of that. I'll give him medication for that and it goes away.

He'll start eating again. He'll only eat stuff like plain white bread, turkey. Occasionally, he'll eat pig food. If I didn't offer him the other food, he would not eat. He would starve. He loves cherry soda as opposed to any other liquid. I can offer him juices and stuff, but he'll take the cherry soda over that. I know that's not the best diet for him, but I'm giving him soy powder mixed with protein powder. I've just started doing that with acidophilus and vitamin E, and he will drink that sometimes. It's just my way of trying to get nutrients into him, to keep his weight up. But even though the vet isn't happy with that diet—if I told her that's what he was eating—he would literally starve otherwise. He would not eat. He gets that way. I've had him almost die once, and after that I was just like forget it, I'm not going to do that. If he's going to eat something, that's what he's going to eat.

BARBARA: Does he like raw vegetables?

MICHELLE: He'll eat—I don't remember if he's tried that. I think he likes lettuce sometimes. It all depends. One day he'll be doing really well and he'll eat. Then I'll get up the next morning and he's thrown up all over the kitchen and he won't want to eat. And he won't drink, and he'll get a little worse and then the next day after that, he'll start eating again. And it just goes through this cycle, and the diarrhea just started a couple of months ago. He would be sick and then be normal the next day, and he had abscesses coming up on the outside of his skin, and the vet said maybe his intestines have abscesses up and down them caused by bacteria, and so she put him on antibiotics. He's so picky, if he tastes the antibiotics he will not eat. If he tastes it in any of the foods he eats, he will not eat for several days—because he doesn't trust that you're not going to put it in his food.

BARBARA: Is there anything you can wrap up in a ball so he'll swallow it—like a ball of cheese or something?

MICHELLE: No, he picks at. What he'll do, he'll eat it for the first couple of days, and it might make him sick or something. Then he'll start dissecting the food you give him. Once he catches you doing that—like being dishonest—he won't eat the food at all.

BARBARA: He's very smart. Is there any kind of pig chow that you can soak?

MICHELLE: No. I've tried that. I've tried soaking it with cherry soda. He'll drink the cherry soda off the top, or if he's in a really bad mood he won't even drink the cherry soda. He'll just spill it and that's it.

BARBARA: I feel like he needs oil in his intestines to help dislodge this mass that's kind of stuck in there. You can imagine having something stuck in there. The food would go down so far, and then it starts to back up and then you throw it up and then you wouldn't feel good.

MICHELLE: I wonder if mineral oil would help?

BARBARA: Ask your vet what would be the best.

MICHELLE: Actually, I know she would say mineral oil. Because one pig that was sick—and she's fine now—but she said, "Get a turkey baster, get mineral oil and go in there."

BARBARA: Yes. That's what he needs, actually. He needs some kind of lubricant in his intestines.

MICHELLE: Is it way up there? Is it his small intestine or his large intestine? If it's his small intestine, I don't know what I can do unless I tube it to him.

BARBARA: Well, it's going to go through all of them to get out the other end. I'm not sure how much oil he can take. I wouldn't consider him a normal pig, and a normal pig amount. I would do it in small doses so it doesn't actually blow him out, as it were. It's gentle.

MICHELLE: Yes. Okay. Okay.

BARBARA: If you can get him to eat food with oil on it, that's fine.

MICHELLE: What about something herbal?

BARBARA: There is something out there in a small tablet that works very well, that people use. An herbal laxative.

MICHELLE: There's a laxative that's just vegetables.

BARBARA: Yes. I can't think of the name of it, but I can see it. There are little tablets. You could open up his mouth and poke it down inside.

MICHELLE: Yes. I can do that. The thing is, when you start something like that he just cries. I feel like I've let him down, like he's thinking "You're not supposed to be hurting me," and then I go and do something like that. Does he know that I'm trying to help him?

BARBARA: It's old programming. He's worried that something else is happening, and he gets scared. He doesn't know, so he cries. It's kind of a defense mechanism. If he's not sure, he cries, but it's very temporary. It's not a begrudging thing. He's just scared. He's just become scared.

MICHELLE: So he does know that I love him?

BARBARA: Yes.

MICHELLE: And does he love me?

BARBARA: Yes he does, and he depends on you. He counts on you and he knows that you are doing the best for him, but he cannot help being picky. See, that's the way he is. Does he like alfalfa? Alfalfa would be dry.

MICHELLE: I think it all depends. He might like it one day and then never eat it again. And then with the diarrhea and stuff—I would hesitate trying new stuff. I haven't noticed anything that instigates the diarrhea.

BARBARA: Well, it could be the intestines. I feel like there's a blockage there. It lets a little bit pass by, but most of it kind of backs up, so he's not assimilating nutrients. So he would be losing weight, he would be withering away. They aren't getting to the stomach appropriately. You see the intestines draw nutrients out of the food and supply the body. I feel the intestines are very sluggish.

MICHELLE: Yes. I've got a zoology degree so I know how important the intestines are. They're very important.

BARBARA: Yes. Yes. So that would be my first priority. If

you can get the tablets that work as a diuretic, I wouldn't overdo it at all. I would do it very gently. Maybe a half tablet the first time for a week, and half a tablet each day for a week, and see how he reacts to that. If you can hide it in different food each day—be creative on a daily basis.

MICHELLE: Yes. I can slip it into his soda.

BARBARA: Maybe you do it in the evening. Well, first thing in the morning, he's gonna have to go. Pick a time that would work for you, that when he needs to clear this out, it's comfortable for you.

MICHELLE: Yes. At this point I'd get up at two o'clock in the morning, so I'm not too worried about the time frame.

BARBARA: This type of thing, something that works gently, that's going to start—. It feels like it's dry and stuck to the intestines, so it needs to move forward with that. If you can get that moving out, his intestines will start to recover a bit, and he'll be able to absorb nutrients. I feel like it's some kind of disease affecting the eyes. I don't know what that is.

MICHELLE: It could be they are kind of cloudy. So I guess it could be glaucoma or something.

BARBARA: Cataracts.

MICHELLE: Cataracts. But the vet—when he was under when he went to the vet—she flashed a light in his eyes. She said, "Oh, he's blind. And that looks like it might be from a disease, or someone hit him very hard in the head, because for his age he shouldn't be having that problem."

BARBARA: I feel like it's a genetic thing for him or a disease. I don't feel like a hit in the head.

MICHELLE: Okay, good, because that would break my heart to think he'd been hit in the head. I'm glad he loves me and knows that he is loved. That would worry me because if anything, when he passes on, I want to be there with him, I don't want him to go alone.

BARBARA: Yes. I understand. You have a deep connection with him, don't you?

MICHELLE: Yes. Very deep. It started after Baxter, a pig I just adored, died. And the other day I walked back there and I called Dean, Baxter. I'm very attached to him. There is another pig I had a medical question on. You said I don't need to be with the animal?

BARBARA: No. If we are going to move from Dean, it's easier for me to focus on one and then focus on moving to the other.

MICHELLE: Okay. I do have a question. What foods make him feel better?

BARBARA: Dean?

MICHELLE: Yes.

BARBARA: Not much at this point, and I think the cherry soda, what I'm feeling is what the cherry soda does—is it sweet? It's carbonated?

MICHELLE: Yes.

BARBARA: Yes. And it helps. Sweet carbonation is great for upset stomachs.

MICHELLE: That's what I thought.

BARBARA: So he knows what he wants. He knows what he needs. It's not necessarily good for him all the time, but I feel that his stomach is upset. Once you get this blockage to move on, and not stick itself somewhere else, but get enough fluids in him, he needs to have—work with your vet—either fluids or oil, so that it makes this mass lubricate or rehydrate, so it moves on rather than getting stuck somewhere else. You see? That's what I want to tell you.

MICHELLE: Okay. He's not in pain, then.

BARBARA: As I feel it, he feels sick to his stomach. He kind of feels like when you are pregnant and have morning sickness—that's kind of how he feels. The intestines need to be cleared and brought back into a healthier condition. Not that you haven't made that healthy for him. But the reason he doesn't eat a lot or he's a picky eater is because—

MICHELLE: He doesn't feel good.

BARBARA: He doesn't feel good. Or when he does feel good, he eats a lot and then pays for it later. Because in a way he's very hungry, but he can't eat in the volume he needs to eat. Do you see? He can't keep it down.

MICHELLE: And the last question for him. Is he happy here?

BARBARA: Oh yes. He feels very happy and very secure and he just really does adore you.

MICHELLE: Oh good.

BARBARA: Yes. He really does. He knows that as much as he's grumpy or he doesn't feel good, he doesn't mean to be a grump, but he just can't help himself. There are times when he feels bad about being like that, but that's how he feels and that's how he expresses it.

MICHELLE: For the most part, he's very sweet.

BARBARA: Yes. He wants you to know that when he's grumpy or he doesn't do things right, it isn't because he doesn't love you or doesn't want to, he just has other things going on. "I don't want to be bothered. Just leave me alone right now." He's just going through a grumpy mood so you know you must say, "Okay, I understand. You're not feeling well, you're feeling grumpy. When you're feeling a little better, come on over."

MICHELLE: I wanted to ask about two animals. Roland is a saddle-bred horse that we've had. He's in the back yard right now, and he's not supposed to be there. I just want to know how he feels about me in particular. If he knows what he's doing is bothering me, or does he like me? Is he just being a pinhead?

BARBARA: I feel that Roland does what Roland wants to do.

MICHELLE: Yes. I'm looking at him right now.

BARBARA: He runs life according to Roland. If Roland wants to do something, that is what he wants to do. It has nothing to do with whether you're pleased with him or displeased with him. That isn't something that comes into the equation.

MICHELLE: One time he got out past the electric fence, and he stood in the kitchen window until I saw him. What are the odds of that horse standing there till I see him? He'll back up into the barn and poop in a bucket—one of the pigs' buckets. He keeps doing it over and over again. So, it's stuff like that. Or he'll stand in my way.

BARBARA: He's got a sense of humor.

MICHELLE: I love the horse. He's just so ornery.

BARBARA: Well, orneriness is that he does life according to Roland. He's stubborn. He makes up his mind to do something, and that's what he decides to do. Is that not Roland?

MICHELLE: Well, yeah, he gets out. He does whatever he wants to. And if he doesn't get to do what he wants to do, that's when you'll find poop in a bucket—something of that sort. Or he'll just walk into a stall and poop right there in front of you. Poop and then walk back out.

BARBARA: He has his own attitude.

MICHELLE: That's what I thought.

BARBARA: Yes. He has a real attitude.

MICHELLE: Okay. Not to move too fast, but I was just pretty much venting on that guy. The other pig—we have thirty pigs here at the sanctuary; we're going for nonprofit. We have pigs coming in all the time. This pig, his name is Black Oscar, and he's rather big. He was emaciated when I got him from the Carolinas. He kind of looks like a moose head. There's something wrong with him. He had testicular cancer. When he got here, the vet removed his testes and there was a tumor. He hasn't been feeling very well. He's put on weight and everything and he just doesn't seem as peppy as he used to be. I'm concerned that he's on his way out. Is he in pain? I brought him into a stall against his own free will, and now he won't leave the stall. He's an extremely sweet animal and I'm just wondering if there's anything I need to know about him—to help him feel more comfortable. Because if he's not in a lot of pain, I'm not going to put him down. I'm willing to pamper him.

BARBARA: I don't feel pain. I feel discomfort. I feel like maybe there is a tumor or tumors actually inside, more toward the hip area. Not in the hips. In the rear intestinal area. Maybe as it came from the testes, it spread in that particular area. In the groin, that's where I want to say. More in that area.

MICHELLE: Does he like the friend he's with? I'm up at the barn now, and he's lying next to Spamela who is fixed on him. I opened up the stall between two of them and now the two in the other stall have become friends. He's sleeping right now. He sleeps a lot.

BARBARA: The uncomfortableness is, you feel like things are big inside. Kind of swelling a little bit.

MICHELLE: He does look a little rounded.

BARBARA: It feels like a growth that sticks. Kind of a cancerous growth that has attached itself well in some areas.

MICHELLE: I know testicular cancer is a slow-killing cancer. I know they removed it, but when the vet saw him she said, "Something's wrong with that guy." Not so much that she knew he had testicular cancer, but because his facial features were so odd. And he's got a very broad moose-like head, as I mentioned. I saw him when I went out to rescue six pigs that were all running loose. I took him right away. I have a little Ford Aspire, but I said, "He's coming with me today. I'm not leaving him here." He's never, ever taken a bite out of me, but about a week ago he swung his head at me. I could tell he was in pain, and he kind of growled at me and tried to bite. So I figured maybe he's having a flare-up of something.

BARBARA: I actually don't feel sharp pain as much as I feel that as something starts to swell inside and then it puts pressure on other things, it's uncomfortable. Do you notice when he's lying down he's trying to get comfortable in some way?

MICHELLE: Yes. Some times lately he has trouble getting back up.

BARBARA: In the rear?

MICHELLE: Like his belly. And I'll go in there and help him up. He's rather big. I'd say he's close to three hundred pounds. We have so many here. You have no idea, the horror stories they have. I'm hoping for the most part that they're happy. Is there a way you can get a sense of whether they're happy here?

BARBARA: The energy feels good. It feels like you're working real hard to keep it pleasant for all of them. I feel like it's a lot of work for you, however.

MICHELLE: Oh, but it's a labor of love. I love it. It makes my heart sing. I can't imagine not having them.

BARBARA: Wonderful!

MICHELLE: When people say a pig needs a home, I'm say, "Oh sure!" I work weekends to supply money for the sanctuary until we become nonprofit. And we've had people donate stuff. For the most part, I've seen animals come in here that were so awful. We've got three farm pigs, Larry, Emma and Yorkenberry. I think they're about three hundred at least, and they couldn't walk. The vet called and they were piglets. They were about three months old, and I would not leave them there. Another vet said no. I took them home. Now they run around. They get out, but now they run around and they're rather big. And they're sweethearts. They run with the horse. If the horse starts to run, they run. They bark a lot like the dogs, and run in crazy-eights.

BARBARA: Isn't that cute?

MICHELLE: So it makes it all worthwhile.

BARBARA: Absolutely.

MICHELLE: So with Oscar, he's not in a lot of pain?

BARBARA: He's uncomfortable. He's getting more uncomfortable. It is getting...

MICHELLE: It's not cruel right now is it?

BARBARA: No, no. But you'll know. If he just can't get up anymore or take care of himself, you might want to let him transition to be a little piglet or whatever. They transition easily.

MICHELLE: So far, he's eating, drinking. He gets picked on a little bit, which breaks my heart, because he just lets them pick on him.

BARBARA: Well, he doesn't have the energy to fight back, as I feel it. It's not a big thing for him. He's kind of on the dwindling end of the scale. That's okay. Animals transition very easily. They just pop right out of their bodies and pop right in somewhere else.

MICHELLE: That's good.

BARBARA: It isn't like people, where we feel this is the end. So you release them from a body that's not working, so they can move on with their Soul's path.

MICHELLE: I really miss them though.

BARBARA: Of course you do. Absolutely. But you can get them back. You can get that energy back, you know. You go out with intent to find them.

MICHELLE: Yes. I think that's what I did with Baxter. I went out looking. That's when I started the sanctuary. I've come across so many animals. And lost so many of them, too. It's been hard but it doesn't stop me.

BARBARA: That's wonderful.

MICHELLE: Walter's probably the last guy I need to know about, unless my husband wants to ask about the dog that died. Walter is a pig. He's neutered now, but when I picked him up in the Carolinas at a vet clinic, he was limping and was on the downside of the kennel so he was being peed on. The people said he was vicious, that he was really scary, that he charged at the woman, and that he was living under the porch. So Animal Control came out and picked him up and said, "If you don't come get him, we're going to put him down or send him to the slaughterhouse, even though we think his meat is probably too tough." He's a pot-bellied pig. Most of them here are. Anyway, I get there and there's this old pig, and he's limping. All I did was, I got licorice and I put it out in a trail, and I opened up the Ford door with the seats removed in the back, and I was like, "Come on, guy." And he went right in. Didn't snap at me, didn't bite. And I said, "Your name's Walter and your luck's just changed for the better." And he's been sweet ever since. He's a sweetheart. He's always had that limp. I can see him out there, and he's put on some weight, and he's grunting, and he's walking with a limp. I'm just wondering if, when I give him medicine, does that help him? Does he feel better? Or would he rather not get the medicine? Because it's Abute. The vet said I could give them.

BARBARA: Oh, like they give horses?

MICHELLE: Yes. It's a very small amount. I've given it to Black Oscar in the past, and it helped him sleep. With Walter I didn't really see a difference in the way he was walking, but he was just not grunting as much. I don't want to give them something if it's hurting them.

BARBARA: I don't feel as if it's hurting him. I feel that the weight is the problem, however. Maybe he's had a break or a sprain or something and he can't support as much weight on that hip. I know pigs normally put on a lot of weight, so it's a Catch-22.

MICHELLE: Especially since he's neutered.

BARBARA: Right, and also, it's cold. I feel that the cold also gets in there. During summer he's probably better than in winter.

MICHELLE: Yes. He is for the most part his heaviest now. We're in Oregon so it is warming up. They did travel across the country in a livestock trailer. I was not leaving them.

BARBARA: I feel that they're able to romp together and play together and they really do like that. They're very social, as I feel it.

MICHELLE: Yes. They are. They can be quite mean to each other, too. When one of them is not feeling well.

BARBARA: Yes. Like people. I feel like they're pretty close to people.

MICHELLE: Oh, they're very. They're the fifth smartest

animal—considered the fifth smartest. And you know, they don't have a thymus gland, which means they're always hungry. So when you say you eat like a pig, it means you're always hungry.

BARBARA: I didn't know they didn't have a thymus gland.

MICHELLE: Dean, why are you crying? I leave the room sometimes, and he'll just start to cry.

BARBARA: Right. Because he feels like he doesn't know where he is, or he feels a bit disoriented.

MICHELLE: Yes. He does act that way sometimes. Disoriented. Poor guy.

BARBARA: Yes. He likes the attention you give him and the security that you help him feel. He feels that from you.

MICHELLE: Oh good. Because I'll always be there for him. Always.

BARBARA: He counts on that.

MICHELLE: I feel that he does. That's why—it's not that I feel like I have to do it, it's that I want to do it. Like with all the animals there, I never feel like I have to do it, I want to. I couldn't understand how others who say things would not want to do it. I don't understand how they could just keep going, walk by and not do anything.

BARBARA: Well, they don't have the love or connection that you do.

MICHELLE: I feel like I do.

BARBARA: You really do. You have a special connection with them.

MICHELLE: I feel like I know how they're feeling.

BARBARA: You do. You absolutely do. It's not if, and, or but. You do. You know. You are very connected with them.

MICHELLE: It does seem like they trust me more than anybody else. They'll come up to me but they won't come up to others. And vice versa, there are some that are really shy with me, but when one pig lady comes over, there's one pig that just adores her and goes up to her and stuff. With me, the best word for it is, the pig is a snot. What did I ever do to you?

BARBARA: It really has nothing to do with that. It's like with people. Some people have an affinity to some people and with others there's nothing wrong with them but you just don't have an affinity to them.

MICHELLE: Yes. That's just the way she is, and I kind of love her for that, so sometimes when I'm walking through the barn or something and I see her eating, I'll say "Hi, baby," and touch her back. She'll do a little annoying noise, like she knows I'm doing it on purpose. One of my favorite stories—not to get off the subject—when I was working at the zoo there was a Kalabus monkey named Sylvia. She was rather fat. They have the long white tails. They're black with a white face and the long white fluffy tails. She was squatty and had no teeth, and if you gave her something hard, she would slap your hand. I'd been there five, six years, and I would sit down with them and feed them. She would be sitting at my feet, and I would hand her a carrot. And I would look like really innocent. She would look at me, at my face, and then look at the carrot. Look at me. Look at the carrot. And then she would pick it up. And if I showed any sign of smirk on my face, she'd slap my hand. If I didn't, she would just pick the carrot up, throw it away and think, "Oh what an idiot." I felt that with those animals, we got into a play type of relationship. Where they'd dangle their tail in my face when I was cleaning, and then I'd pretend that I was going to grab it, and they'd lift it up real quick, and things like that.

BARBARA: Their way of playing. You have a real affinity to animals. You understand animals. You're very connected to them—much more than to people, actually.

MICHELLE: Yes. That's true.

BARBARA: Yes. You understand them totally, where sometimes with people you don't quite understand them, and people don't understand how you can understand the animals as well as you do.

MICHELLE: Well, they've got very good hearts, very good souls, I think.

BARBARA: Yes. And you feel that and connect to it. But not everybody feels and connects as you do.

MICHELLE: And that isn't necessarily a bad thing, is it?

BARBARA: Absolutely not. That's how I've lived my life.

MICHELLE: I've had so many people tell me it's stupid.

BARBARA: Well, it's not what they would call standard operating procedure. But if everybody did standard operating procedure, who would take care of the unwanted—like you are, building a sanctuary?

MICHELLE: The thing is, it's people to blame for why they're out there. The animals that come here abused were abused by people.

BARBARA: Exactly.

MICHELLE: And I'm not going to just walk away. I couldn't walk away from a person, and I'm not going to walk away from an animal. Oh, I guess I should have let him talk to you. We have five minutes.

BARBARA: Oh, you're fine.

MICHELLE: Jeff, did you want to ask about Puffs? His question was, is Puff around him at all, his dog?

BARBARA: Let me get into Puff here. Kind of was his dog. Was very loyal to this dog. Dog was very connected to him, more men than women. Good size dog. Is this Puff? Fairly good sized dog.

MICHELLE: Yes.

BARBARA: He made your husband feel safe and secure. He kind of did his own way of guarding without hurting anybody, but he was very alert.

MICHELLE: Yes.

BARBARA: Yes, he is around.

MICHELLE: Is he happy?

BARBARA: Yes. He's with you guys. He's hanging out.

MICHELLE: Okay.

BARBARA: Yes. He's happy. He just says you don't know I'm here, but I'm here.

MICHELLE: Does he hang around with him most of the time?

BARBARA: Yes. He sits. Your husband sits on a chair?

MICHELLE: He sits on the sofa.

BARBARA: Okay. He spent time at his feet.

MICHELLE: Yes, he always was at his feet.

BARBARA: Yes, well, he's still there. He's still hanging out. They transition, but they transition into a different form. But you can just shut your eyes and kind of feel the energy about. It's kind of right there, and yeah, he's hanging out. He loves it there.

MICHELLE: Oh good, because the UPS truck ran over him. Which was horrible.

BARBARA: It was one of those accidents that happen.

MICHELLE: Yes, it was on our property though. He had gotten off his chain or leash or whatever—and anyway, he just wanted to know about that.

BARBARA: You know, I feel like there was a real love connection between the two of them. They were buddies.

MICHELLE: Yes, they were.

BARBARA: And he doesn't feel that, but if you can shut your eyes and feel as it was, you can tap into that energy again.

MICHELLE: I don't know if he can. He's not a real animal person, but he loved that dog.

BARBARA: Well, he has to be somewhat of an animal person to have all these animals around.

MICHELLE: Yes, I guess so.

BARBARA: He might not have the deep affinity that you do for some of them. Maybe he doesn't understand that because he's a little more earthly, a little more grounded, more logical—

MICHELLE: More sane.

BARBARA: I don't think it's sane. It's just that he looks at things with logic rather than with his heart.

MICHELLE: Yes. Well, that fits his personality type.

BARBARA: It has to be logical. If it's not logical, he doesn't understand why you're doing it. As long as he has no problems with your caring for so many animals, you do what you do and he does what he does, and you come together and share experiences.

MICHELLE: Yes. Here comes Roland. I've actually, I think I've come close to having to go to counseling because of that horse. When I meet up with another animal person, I describe that horse as a living hell. I'll start talking about "He did this, this and this," and they'll look at me and say, "You're crazy. That horse can't be that smart." Oh yes he is. He is smart.

BARBARA: Yes. He is smart. He's very creative with his mind. That's where he poops in a bucket or goes into the stall. He's making a point. You're absolutely right. You've got him pegged.

MICHELLE: Yes. And when I lost my first kid, I was four months pregnant, we were back in North Carolina, and I went out there and it was pouring rain. I stood there next to him and put my arms around his neck and stood out there and cried. I was out there for maybe twenty minutes and he stood right there the whole time. He did not leave. He didn't tease me. He didn't do anything. He was there for me. I'll never forget that. It was a very sweet thing for him to do.

BARBARA: Yes. And it's interesting that he understands how that is. He has a very deep understanding of a lot of things. And one might say it's quite annoying, because he can think outside the box—because he's very creative in his thinking. He really is—he works at it.

MICHELLE: Oh, he is. He does, because if I bring the food out for the one horse, he has to come—and this sounds trivial, but—he has to come out and take a bite out of the food of the other horse, before he will go to his bowl.

BARBARA: That's a power thing.

MICHELLE: And what annoys me is that I used to put all the nutrients and stuff on top, for the other horse, and now I've had to stop doing that. Roland would come and eat all the nutrients off the top of that bowl, and then go and eat his. I'd say, "Roland—don't do it. Don't do it." And even if his food was in his bowl, he would circle around, eat a bite out of that other one and come back. And I couldn't help but think that he knows.

BARBARA: He does know. Right. It's a power thing. He's on a power trip.

MICHELLE: Yes. I think he is a jerk, and I think I love him for that.

BARBARA: Well, he's not a jerk. He's very intelligent and if you can direct that intelligence to riding or tricks or something like that, he would do very well.

MICHELLE: He would, probably.

BARBARA: He's very creative.

MICHELLE: He's a very beautiful horse. He's about sixteen hands, saddle-bred and happy. I can tell he's happy.

BARBARA: Of course.

MICHELLE: So he gets to run around. I don't know how he got down here. He must have broken through one of the wires. There was one time, while I was watching from the kitchen window, he ran through the gate, but the gate wound up around his neck. He ran through the back yard with it, warped and bent the gate permanently, and then it fell off. He just ran around, stopped and ate some grass. That guy had just ripped my gate, and there was no reaction on his face. It was like "Oh—oh well. I guess I kind of expected that would happen if I put my head through the gate."

BARBARA: Well, you know he kind of does things to make a point.

MICHELLE: Yes. That he can do them.

BARBARA: Yes. He's showing you who's the boss, and it's not you. He's got that message real clear.

MICHELLE: I feel like there's mutual respect, though.

BARBARA: There is. But he's messing with you.

MICHELLE: I know when he sees me get angry, he'll stop. There comes a point where, "Okay, you've just pushed my button too much, you just smushed me into the back stall with your butt on purpose when you didn't have to, and now I'm mad." And he'll just kind of move real quick and get out of the way. For the most part, he would never hurt me. I can tell. He wouldn't carry it that far.

BARBARA: No. He's not vindictive, but he is creative and he wants to be in power.

MICHELLE: Yes. He can crawl under electric fences. That's pretty good, isn't it? With sixteen hands.

BARBARA: For a horse, you betcha.

MICHELLE: We only figured he crawled because there was no other possible way he could be getting under the fence. This is in North Carolina. There's no way he could jump this. No one ever saw him do this, and where he would get out there was no way he could jump. It would have to be crawling under the fence.

BARBARA: So your eight acres are fenced in now?

MICHELLE: Yes. Most of it is fenced in where the animals are, but the other part is open so if they get out toward the back, I feel like I can call them back with food. Not the horses but the pigs. But at the same time there are coyotes, and I always worry that if one of them gets hurt, whether they're going to be back in time before it gets dark. And I would go out looking for them until I found them.

BARBARA: Will coyotes eat a pig? With three hundred pounds?

MICHELLE: I think they would attack them. I know one of my cats disappeared.

BARBARA: Well, cats are easy. I hate to say that—it just sounds cruel—but cats are smaller prey. But three hundred pounds of pig is—

MICHELLE: The smaller ones are maybe eighty pounds. Seventy pounds for the babies.

BARBARA: Okay. That's something they probably could—

MICHELLE: And they came into us from two fat pigs that weren't fat, but were pregnant. I thought, "They keep looking fatter and fatter. I'm going to have them on a diet."

BARBARA: Oh! And then they had babies.

MICHELLE: Yes. And I was eight months pregnant and nobody was there to help me. I felt, "Oh my God, I have to stick my head all the way in there." One of them had problems and it was a nightmare. One didn't make it because it was just stuck way in there, and the vet just sent me home and said, "Here's some Oxytocin Good luck." The vets back there weren't very good with pigs, and it took me three hours the next day to get that thing out. She was so swollen—the mom was—but she made it. I couldn't believe it.

BARBARA: Wow. Good for you.

MICHELLE: And what the weird thing was, it was my mistake. In the car she rolled over on her piglets, which was my fault. I should have put them in a box on the way to the vet, and it suffocated. But them I resuscitated it. And the vet tech was standing right there, like, "Oh well, I guess it's dead." Its body was still warm so I put my mouth over its snout and breathed in and pumped its heart. It came back. It's still here. I can't remember which one it is.

BARBARA: Wow. Incredible.

MICHELLE: I couldn't believe it. Oh my God, I never brought an animal back. It was so small. It just made my day, that it lived.

BARBARA: I could just imagine. That's like giving it the gift of life.

MICHELLE: Yes. I couldn't believe it, and then two people wanted to buy them to raise to bred them when they saw them. I said "No way." No. Because a lot of people will breed them and lose sight of where these animals go, and then they suffer.

The father's three hundred pounds, and they're thinking "little pig." Well, anyway, thank you so much.

BARBARA: Well, Michelle, thank you.

MICHELLE: This was fun.

BARBARA: Yes. It was fun for me too. I love it.

MICHELLE: I will probably be in touch again as things progress with the animals, to find out how they're doing. And I will try what you said for Dean. And then in a couple of weeks get back to you to see if he's feeling better.

* * *

Another situation where a rescuer needed help concerned a wild dolphin. And although a dolphin is not a fish, the *IChing* specifically referred to them in the discussion of inner truth, so I think they qualify for this chapter.

ELAINE: It is a dolphin, and we've never seen it before six days ago. I'm not one to name animals, so we haven't been calling it by a name. And we don't know the gender so we haven't really given it a name. I have a sense that it's a female. The question I have, the main thing that we really need to determine, is if she's eating—because that is what is going to tell us whether we need to catch her and find out what's wrong with her. If she's not eating, we're just watching her slowly dehydrate and then starve. We are starting to see her ribs start to show, and the only way they get their water is through eating, so that's pretty much the point we're at now.

BARBARA: Elaine, the first thing I heard from my guides is that she is not eating. And the next thing I got was that there is something stuck in her throat. I guess I can't determine how that is, but it feels like—it doesn't feel comfortable. I don't know why I want to say, "Fins going the wrong way." I'm not sure whether it is like that, or it's something that's ulcerated. I feel she's a bit listless, concerned about her eating. She looks like she's getting thin, and I feel like she's losing her energy. Can you tell me a little bit more about where she might be located?

ELAINE: Where she is, where she's been spending—we've had numerous calls from one person in particular who has been diligent about trying to find her every day—is between Summerless Key and Kudgoe Key on the ocean side of the Atlantic side in about a half mile square area. It's a lot of shallow water with channels cut in there. She spends an unusual amount of time in the shallow water—not swimming just resting on the surface—and she will go in the deeper water, but she doesn't spend a lot of time there, which is typical of a sick animal. They can drown like we can drown.

BARBARA: I feel the water is warmer in the shallows. I feel like her metabolism has—I wouldn't say it's slowed down, but it feels like she is having a problem producing enough heat to keep warm. I'm feeling the shallows are a protection from drowning, and also more warmth there then in the deeper waters where it's cooler.

ELAINE: Well, probably she doesn't have much of a blubber layer. Also, something could swim up beneath you and bite you in the belly when you don't feel well. So it's sometimes for that reason.

BARBARA: Yes. So they pick that up.

ELAINE: She's starting to get signs of being overexposed to the sun. Her top, the part that's out of the water the most, is almost black now. It's not blistered and burned—because they actually will blister like we do—but they start to turn very, very dark. She's starting to get to that point, and this has been going on for a while. Yesterday, the Marine Patrol went up in a plane to look for her, because they couldn't find her with a boat, and they found her and in the near vicinity was another dolphin with a newborn, but they weren't associating at the time. Today she was trying to keep up with five dolphins with newborns, but they weren't assisting her and they weren't bothering with her, they were just ignoring her, and she was trying to keep up with them.

BARBARA: She was trying to use them for protection. She

doesn't feel protected all by herself. I guess they're more vulnerable on their own, rather than in pods.

ELAINE: Yes.

BARBARA: And she doesn't have the energy to keep up with them. I feel like it spent more energy than it was able to accomplish for her.

ELAINE: We've pretty much left them alone today, because we didn't want to disturb the pod with the newborns by trying to observe her. We felt if we left them alone maybe they would assist her, because there were so many adults—probably all female, since generally how this type of dolphin gathers—and if they would assist her, they could catch fish and feed her. We've seen that before, but we have to go and check in the morning. And my gut feeling is that she won't be with them because I don't imagine, you know, with the babies they keep moving—because they need to get the babies moving and they also don't want to be found by anyone. I would imagine, from a biological standpoint, that if someone's sick you're best not to hang around with them when you have a little baby because you will draw in predators too.

BARBARA: And she really doesn't have the energy level that a healthy dolphin would have. She doesn't swim with any spirit, as I see it. She swims but is lethargic.

ELAINE: Right. It is out of necessity because we went out a few times with jet skis, and even though we put it just on idle and we stopped and drifted near her, she would stay on the surface until we got a little close and then it was just out of necessity that she would go underwater and swim. It wasn't like the others, which are long gone before you ever get there.

BARBARA: It's always interesting. If people have some kind of ulceration I would think salt water would be the greatest thing for that.

ELAINE: They really don't have the capacity to drink a lot of salt water, so it wouldn't go down its throat. I don't think that she would do that. It's interesting that you say that be cause I've talked to a few people and this particular dolphin has a very bad dorsal fin. It's been injured in the past. The dorsal is the regular shape but its only half size—as if the trailing edge of it, the back edge, has been completely cut off. And there's been a dolphin in that area for years, between the next two islands up. Several times fishermen, charter boat captains, have told me in the past that a particular dolphin—it may not be this one because I thought that one had even more dorsal fin—but that a particular dolphin they were describing, stole their fishing lures all the time. From the first day, I was feeling that this animal is just old and has come into the shallows to die in a familiar area. Or she's got so many hooks and things in her. We've seen that before. After they die, we open them up and they've got feeder wire and treble hooks and lures stuck inside. They're very smart, but you can't keep them from getting into something that they have no experience with. So until they die from it, they're learning their lesson. They eat them over and over.

BARBARA: Maybe that's what I feel in the throat—the different bits. I thought maybe she swallowed a fish upside down or something, because it feels thorny, prickly—

ELAINE: Right. Right.

BARBARA: It feels like that has created ulcers or abscesses or some kind of sores in the throat.

ELAINE: Okay. So you feel like it's more in the throat than down to the stomach.

BARBARA: Actually, I am. I'm not feeling as much—well again, I don't know the anatomical parts and how they fit in—but I'm feeling closer to the mouth. I'm feeling at the throat area. If it were a person, it would be no farther than the chest bone, up in that area, and I did feel something prickly. But again, they give me these messages and I've got to sort them out in my brain. Like what is it, maybe a fish backwards, rather than lures.

ELAINE: It's not unusual. They have tried to swallow sea

urchins and things they're not supposed to. We don't have a lot of urchins here anymore. Years and years and years ago, there were, but there aren't anymore. My instincts would be that it's a fishhook.

BARBARA: It's small. I don't feel like it's sea urchin because I feel like there are smaller prickly things, smaller points, things like that. And again as to the number, I don't feel ulceration of just one, I feel a few—different sizes, so it makes it uncomfortable to swallow. I don't know how you can resolve that.

ELAINE: Well, we can use an endoscope. Actually, you can reach into a dolphin that size, you can reach—they have chambered stomachs like a cow because they're kind of in that same descendant, same family of animals, but they're not as distinct. You can reach into the stomach with your arm. Because they don't have the same kind of trachea that we do, you don't have to worry that they can't breathe. We can do that. We have a sea turtle hospital here that has an endoscope that we can use and look down in there, because they swallow plastic bags.

BARBARA: Yes. It feels like if it goes through, it could go straight through to the stomach. Like nothing could really stop it.

ELAINE: What do you mean?

BARBARA: From the mouth down to the stomach is just like a slide.

ELAINE: Right. The trachea goes up through the middle of the esophagus, like a tree growing up in the middle of a cave. The food has to go on either side of it, and they do have the ability to pop that out and lay it down if they want to swallow something really large. It's not permanently attached on the top, and it will lie down. It's kind of a really strange apparatus, but you know, someone with a really big arm could push that down and the animal would not be able to breathe. But pretty much anything goes down. They can swallow fairly large things.

BARBARA: That's interesting. Yes. That's what I feel. And again, I'm tuning in through you as to who is in your mind's eye. But that's what I feel. It could be a bunch of hooks and things, too. I feel prickly, and it feels like ulcers. Whatever it is, it's created a problem. I don't how that works. A bit like you had said.

ELAINE: Well, I think that's all today. That's almost all I can tell you about her. It's just such an invasive thing to capture her, when she is still swimming on her own. We've certainly gotten sick ones in shallow water before—many, many times before, and you could walk up to them. She's not to that point yet so that's what we're trying to figure. It's one of those darned if you do, darned if you don't situations. We're waiting for her to get just a little sicker so we can get her without a big rodeo, because they can drown when you try to capture them. There are so many things that can happen. Plus it's a horrible experience to put any wild animal through.

BARBARA: The capture itself?

ELAINE: Yes. It's not something that we take lightly, so that's why we want to explore every avenue rather than wait until she turns up three-quarters dead somewhere.

BARBARA: I understand. I feel, however, that she is dwindling pretty fast. I don't feel like it's a whole lot longer, because I feel her weak, pretty weak.

ELAINE: That was my concern today. That she was going to do herself in by trying to keep up with those other dolphins. I think if they didn't have the babies, they may have helped her. Or if they didn't have babies soon to come.

BARBARA: Yes. It feels like she really wanted to be part of them but like you said, they instinctively have other things that they need to be concerned about, and that's the newborn. And that was their first concern. For her to stay with them was not appropriate and they knew it.

ELAINE: Yes. They didn't try to chase her off, though, so I guess that if she could keep up, they'd let her do her thing.

But they weren't going to chase her away. She may have even been part of their pod at some point, so I guess they were going to let her stay if she could stay.

BARBARA: It's an interesting thing that they do. I feel like they were totally detached. If she was there and she was swimming with them, that was fine, but they weren't going to run out a lifeline.

ELAINE: Well, there's a lot of reasons, biologically, why that would have been an important choice. They would have to be very, very attached to her. At first, we thought possibly that she delivered that calf. Because many times they'll have an aunty who will stay with them when they deliver. Maybe she was sick from that, and the baby went off with the healthier dolphin. But I think if it was her baby there would have been more interaction.

BARBARA: I don't feel that was her baby. I feel she ran across this pod or the pod passed by her, so she jumped on the opportunity instinctively knowing there is safety in numbers.

ELAINE: Right.

BARBARA: And I don't feel pregnancy nor do I feel a birth at all. It's interesting that there really wasn't any issue between them. She thinks she needed them. They didn't feel that she would jeopardize. If she could keep up, that would be fine. If she couldn't, then they were sorry. They didn't feel any emotion one way or another, and I know they do feel emotions among their own. But this didn't feel like her own pod. It didn't feel like that family was hers. It was the same species, but not the same family.

ELAINE: It's possible. This time of year there are so many dolphins. Even the offshore ones come inshore to have babies. There are lots and lots of dolphins around here.

BARBARA: Oh, okay. Still, I just don't feel pregnancy or a baby. I feel like it's the throat, the ingestion of something.

ELAINE: Yes, it could even be fish or fish bones, because people will throw them. They watch so many things on TV and think it's okay to feed them, or try and feed them. And they'll throw cut fish or the carcasses after they filet their fish, to try to attract the dolphins. It could be anything, really. I have a gut feeling about the fish hooks.

BARBARA: It could very well be. I get prickly and it felt like a fish going down the wrong way. So like you say, it might be a cut fish.

ELAINE: Or a carcass.

BARBARA: Yes. I can actually see little abscesses or that type of thing in the throat. Inflamed. Well, if you do bring her out, do give me an e-mail and let me know.

ELAINE: I will. I'll definitely let you know.

* * *

I received a email from Elaine about the dolphin:

We are still monitoring the dolphin. Several times she has been seen associating with a pod, and some days with just one other dolphin. We feel that the associations were mutual this time because the animals were definately communicating with her, and in one instance actually protecting her. She seems to not be getting any weaker, and for short periods seems stronger. I will let you know how it progresses.

Thanks again for your assistance.

Elaine

Epilogue

IN WORKING WITH THE READINGS AND LETTERS, the thing that touches me most is the love and dedication that so many people give to so many animals which might not have had fortunate lives without their care and devotion.

This is the best that I have ever seen of human compassion. Whatever is given to these pet owners in the readings, the unexpected gift is being someone who listens to and understands the feelings they express about their beloved animals—feelings that otherwise might never come to expression.

* * *

My feeling is that this book should end with a letter from Lisa about Arrow.

Hello Barbara,

What a nice surprise to find your e-mail about Arrow. I am still having a very hard time with the grief. I go in the barn and look in his stall and just cry. And I do feel him here very often. He has made his presence felt. I would love to honor him in your book. What a wonderful thing! I would like you to use our real names and say we lived both in the mountains and the prairie of Colorado.

Arrow is a very old soul, I think, and he transformed the idea of "horse" in everyone who knew him. The vets all said they'd never seen a thirty-three-year-old horse so magnificent, and people who are involved with horses daily have said he is more human then horse—which he was. It was my privilege to have him in my life and barn, and he'll remain in my heart until forever.

During the terrible forest fires we had here last month, I opened up my pasture and barn to five horses from the fire stricken area. They all got accustomed to the place and I walked the fence with them, ending up at Arrow's grave. They all crowded in around me. I was completely unable to move, held there by their huge bodies, but more—by their tenderness. They held me there for a very long time, I of course, sobbing all over their sweet selves. They all knew my dearest treasure was buried there, and during their stay that's the spot where they stood to doze and lie down to sleep. It touched me deeply.

The morning after I buried Arrow's body I was up at 5:30, as usual, standing out in the doorway of the barn sobbing. I asked him if he was all right—if he was near, and to please show me if he was, because this sorrow was crushing my heart. In the first light of day the sun lit up a few strands of his mane that he had left on a big fence post at the other end of the pasture. It was incredibly brilliant light—otherworldly. I walked out here and picked them up and tied them to the headboard of my bed. I know he is rejuvenating and resting after a huge life, and I hope he comes back to me soon. I have never grieved for any person as much as I have grieved for Arrow. Indeed, I have never loved anyone as much as I love him. This really has been a killer of my joy.

I have not done any drawings or anything, but there is a book in my heart about him—a children's book which I don't know how to get to a publisher. But I think it would be a great book about loving and healing after the passing of a beloved animal, and honoring them. It was very important that I tied roses and hawk feathers in Arrow's mane, to wash his hooves and brush his big body; it was important to lie him on a bed of red cedar the color he was, and cover with him with the huge star quilt I'd made for him. The honoring is very important and not very many people understand it or know how to do that. Maybe my book will come into print. The huge love behind it should draw the right publisher to it I think.

I sent you an e-mail picture of him, and if you send along your mailing address I'll send you a beautiful picture of him. Did the e-mail picture come through? It's the one I have as the wallpaper in my computer, and after he passed away I tried to change that picture to another one of him. My computer won't change it. I'm pretty computer literate and know how to do this simple task which I've done many times, but now the process won't work and there he is, as always, standing at the gate waiting for me, always there.

I hope the book flies out of your heart and the words come clearly. I know the intent behind it is strong and loving. I am so touched—humbled—that you want to include Arrow and me in it. I haven't had the courage to listen to your tape yet, because I know I'll just dissolve into tears and the heartbreak is complete, I don't think I could stand it yet. But one day when I'm further along from the emptiness and silence of the barn, and the deep sorrow of being apart from my beloved Arrow, I will. I know I'll know when the time is right, and it will give me peace and strength.

My great big Malamute, Neeko, and my black and white tuxedo marked cat, Mittens (who used to ride around on Arrow's back!), still go up there and sleep on Arrow's grave. Neeko did that for a week. He always slept in front of Arrow's stall or the barn door, which was always open. Now he sleeps on the grave and rests there during the day, still guarding his pasture. My cat goes with him, and lies down and purrs. When I'm sitting up there she climbs into my lap and purrs me and cries—which she never does any other time. Neeko guarded Arrow all during the night he passed away, and stayed there all the next day, until the backhoe man could come. He laid there and kept touching his nose to Arrow's and he was so sad, and so angry that the crows and the coyotes tried to get to Arrow. Oh God, what a terrible time we've had. I know day to day I will heal, but I don't know when that will really start manifesting.

Thank you for writing and remembering us.

Love to you, Barbara.

Lisa and the dogs, Neeko and Alli, and the Miss Mittens at the Red Arrow Ranch.

QUICK ORDER FORM

Name _____

Address _____

City _____ State _____ Zip _____

Telephone _____

E-mail address _____

Please send me ____ copies of *I Talk to the Animals* @$18.95 plus $4.00 shipping and handling. Please allow 2-4 weeks delivery time.

Sales tax: Please add 7.75% for products shipped to California addresses.

Shipping by air:
US: $4 for first book and $2 for each additional book. International: $9 for first book and $5 for each additional (estimate).

Payment: ☐ Check ☐ Credit card:
Visa   MasterCard   AMEX   Discover

Name on Card (Please print) _____

Card Number _____

Expiration Date _____

Signature _____

Fax orders: 760-324-5874
Telephone orders: Call 800-761-6416 toll free.
Email orders: *barbara@animalstalk.com*
Mail orders: Barbara Morrison
                Post Office Box 3326
                Palm Springs, CA 92263-3326 USA

Please send FREE information on:
☐ Consulting ☐ Speaking/Seminars ☐ Mailing lists

QUICK ORDER FORM

Name _____

Address _____

City _____ State _____ Zip _____

Telephone _____

E-mail address _____

Please send me _____ copies of *I Talk to the Animals* @$18.95 plus $4.00 shipping and handling. Please allow 2-4 weeks delivery time.

Sales tax: Please add 7.75% for products shipped to California addresses.

Shipping by air:
US: $4 for first book and $2 for each additional book. International: $9 for first book and $5 for each additional (estimate).

Payment: ☐ Check ☐ Credit card:
Visa   MasterCard   AMEX   Discover

Name on Card (Please print) _____

Card Number _____

Expiration Date _____

Signature _____

Fax orders: 760-324-5874
Telephone orders: Call 800-761-6416 toll free.
Email orders: *barbara@animalstalk.com*
Mail orders: Barbara Morrison
                Post Office Box 3326
                Palm Springs, CA 92263-3326 USA

Please send FREE information on:
☐ Consulting ☐ Speaking/Seminars ☐ Mailing lists

QUICK ORDER FORM

Name _____

Address _____

City _____ State _____ Zip _____

Telephone _____

E-mail address _____

Please send me ____ copies of *I Talk to the Animals* @$18.95 plus $4.00 shipping and handling. Please allow 2-4 weeks delivery time.

Sales tax: Please add 7.75% for products shipped to California addresses.

Shipping by air:
US: $4 for first book and $2 for each additional book.
International: $9 for first book and $5 for each additional (estimate).

Payment: ☐ Check ☐ Credit card:
Visa   MasterCard   AMEX   Discover

Name on Card (Please print) _____

Card Number _____

Expiration Date _____

Signature _____

Fax orders: 760-324-5874
Telephone orders: Call 800-761-6416 toll free.
Email orders: *barbara@animalstalk.com*
Mail orders: Barbara Morrison
                Post Office Box 3326
                Palm Springs, CA 92263-3326 USA

Please send FREE information on:
☐ Consulting ☐ Speaking/Seminars ☐ Mailing lists